FROM MALAISE TO MELTDOWN

The International Origins of Financial Folly, 1844–

From Malaise to Meltdown

The International Origins of Financial Folly, 1844–

MICHAEL LEE

UNIVERSITY OF TORONTO PRESS
Toronto Buffalo London

ISBN 978-1-4875-0689-6 (cloth)   ISBN 978-1-4875-3511-7 (EPUB)
                                   ISBN 978-1-4875-3510-0 (PDF)

Library and Archives Canada Cataloguing in Publication

Title: From malaise to meltdown : the international origins of financial folly,
    1844– / Michael Lee.
Names: Lee, Michael, 1983– author.
Description: Includes bibliographical references and index.
Identifiers: Canadiana (print) 2020023109X | Canadiana (ebook) 20200231332 |
    ISBN 9781487506896 (cloth) | ISBN 9781487535117 (EPUB) |
    ISBN 9781487535100 (PDF)
Subjects: LCSH: Financial crises – History. | LCSH: Deregulation – History.
Classification: LCC HB3722 .L44 2020 | DDC 338.5/4209–dc23

This book has been published with the help of a grant from the Federation
for the Humanities and Social Sciences, through the Awards to Scholarly
Publications Program, using funds provided by the Social Sciences and
Humanities Research Council of Canada.

University of Toronto Press acknowledges the financial assistance to its
publishing program of the Canada Council for the Arts and the Ontario Arts
Council, an agency of the Government of Ontario.

Contents

Figures and Tables

Figures

Tables

FROM MALAISE TO MELTDOWN

The International Origins of Financial Folly, 1844–

Chapter One

Introduction

Systems that reward extreme forms of success are often dominated by those willing to take on great amounts of risk. The international system is no exception. The most powerful countries reach great heights by testing out novel institutions, ideas, and military strategies. Great powers take great gambles. Dubious experiments undertaken by one state may often force rivals to embark on their own risky adventures. The sinews of state power are financial. As a result, financial regulation is frequently the site of risk-taking and experimentation. For the ordinary people whose livelihoods are being wagered, the results of these periods of competitive experimentation can be catastrophic. The story of John Law, and the stillborn financial revolution of the early eighteenth century, offers an illustration of the dynamics of economic rivalry in the global economy.

In 1694, John Law killed a well-connected dandy named Edward Wilson in a duel in London's Bloomsbury Square. Imprisoned at Southwark, he escaped prison with the help of well-placed benefactors and fled to the continent (Goetzmann 2016, 354–62). He ended up in Venice, where he made a fortune applying his understanding of the latest principles of probability to gambling. But Law was more than a gambler. Floating novel proposals for a bank backed by land instead of specie (i.e., metallic money), he established himself as an authority on monetary policy.

The 1710s were a golden age for gambler-economists. In 1713, the great powers of Europe emerged from the War of Spanish Succession, battered by decades of war. Years of intense fighting had established the importance of financial strength. As a more credible borrower than France, Britain could bankroll endless subsidy warfare while financing a powerful navy (O'Brien 1988; North and Weingast 1989). To manage debt, British policymakers had granted a charter to the South Sea

Company in 1711, giving it a monopoly on trade in much of South America. Investors could exchange government debt for shares, effectively swapping debt for equity. The scheme meant that Britain could service its debt more cheaply, while the South Sea Company would expand British influence in the New World. After the Treaty of Utrecht in 1713 granted Britain the right to participate in the Spanish *asiento* (licence) slave trade, the South Sea Company was effectively gaining privileged access to that trade in the Caribbean. In effect, South Sea shares were the securitization of human misery. At the same time, the venture had a good prospect of profit (Goetzmann 2016, 320–38).

Across the English Channel in France, John Law found a receptive audience for his theories. Following the War of Spanish Succession, France was desperate to manage its debt. After establishing a de facto French central bank in 1716, the Banque Générale, Law pushed an even bolder scheme: the Mississippi Company. This would be a publicly traded company, with monopoly rights to develop Louisiana. Investors could exchange government debt for a slice of the empire. When Law issued new shares at the Rue Quinquepoix, crowds formed to buy them. Even the regent, Philippe II, scooped up some shares. Between August 1719 and February 1720, prices surged more than twentyfold (Goetzmann 2016, 358–9).

British markets were engulfed in a similar orgy of speculation.[1] In 1719, the managers of the South Sea Company issued large numbers of new shares, which were snapped up by celebrity investors, including members of Parliament and the royal family. As share prices rose tenfold, otherwise intelligent people were seduced by dreams of easy wealth. Isaac Newton had purchased shares early and sold for a tidy profit. When the prices of South Sea stock rose higher, Newton was filled with deep regret at missing out on an even bigger payout. However, generous evaluations of South Sea's value were at odds with the underlying fundamentals. Indeed, war had broken out between Spain and the other European great powers, limiting the value of the *asiento* privileges. Rather than dampening speculation, however, South Sea's seeming defiance of economic gravity inspired imitators. Unscrupulous company promoters plied Parliament with bribes, as other companies sought to take advantage of the boom. Some new insurance companies, often using vague charters and the protection of limited liability to make risky investments, saw their share prices soar even more than those of the South Sea Company (Frehen, Goetzmann, and Rouwenhurst 2013; Goetzmann 2013).

But the age of unbridled prosperity envisioned by speculators would not come. Share prices in the Mississippi Company collapsed in 1720.

Capital flew from France to Britain, further inflating British markets. The British Parliament passed the Bubble Act, restricting the creation of new bubble companies. Enforcement of the Bubble Act sparked a free fall in the share prices of all the newly formed companies. After markets in London collapsed, Amsterdam followed soon after, in what became the first global financial crisis. The fallout of the South Sea Company crash was so severe that the Bubble Act remained in force for over a century. The rivalry between Britain and France had driven both to folly.

Financial folly transcends time and space. History is littered with instances of hopes poured into dubious enterprises: Dutch tulip bulbs, South Sea Company stock, developing-country sovereign bonds (fictional and real), new technologies, real estate, beanie babies, and bitcoins. Eventually, bubbles burst, destroying immense value in the process. When borrowers default and investors panic, credit freezes, driving real-world economies to a halt. In a world where capital is global, the fallout of crises is often global as well. Are recurrent bubbles and crises simply the product of unbridled human greed? Human nature is a constant, while financial crises are not. Between the 1940s and the 1970s, virtually no countries experienced financial crises. In contrast, the past few decades have seen many: the Latin American debt crisis of 1982, the collapse of savings and loan associations (S&Ls) in the United States, the Japanese bubble of 1989, the collapse of the exchange rate mechanism (ERM) in 1992, the collapse of the Mexican peso in 1995, the East Asian financial crisis of 1997, the Russian financial crisis of 1998, the dot-com crash of 2000, the Argentine Depression of the 2000s, the 2008 financial crisis, and the eurozone crisis of 2010.

The hard times of the recent past are neither exceptional nor par for the course. Figure 1.1 adapts and updates a graph from Reinhart and Rogoff (2009), depicting crisis severity over the span of the last two centuries. The index is constructed by taking a five-year moving average of the GDP-weighted share of all countries experiencing a crisis in a given year.[2] What we see are crisis waves – the Long Depression of 1873–96, the period from the crash of 1914 until the end of the Great Depression, and the period from 1980 to 2009 feature far more crises than the oases in between.

In light of our fluctuating fortunes, one question seems obvious: why do some periods of history experience frequent global financial crises, while others experience relative stability? Economists, increasingly armed with impressive macro-historical data sets, can tell us a great deal about the mechanisms underlying crises (Bordo et al. 2001; Reinhart and Rogoff 2009; Grossman 2010; Schularick and Taylor 2012; Turner 2014). Some economists emphasize global current account

Figure 1.1. An Index of Global Financial Crisis Severity, 1846–2009

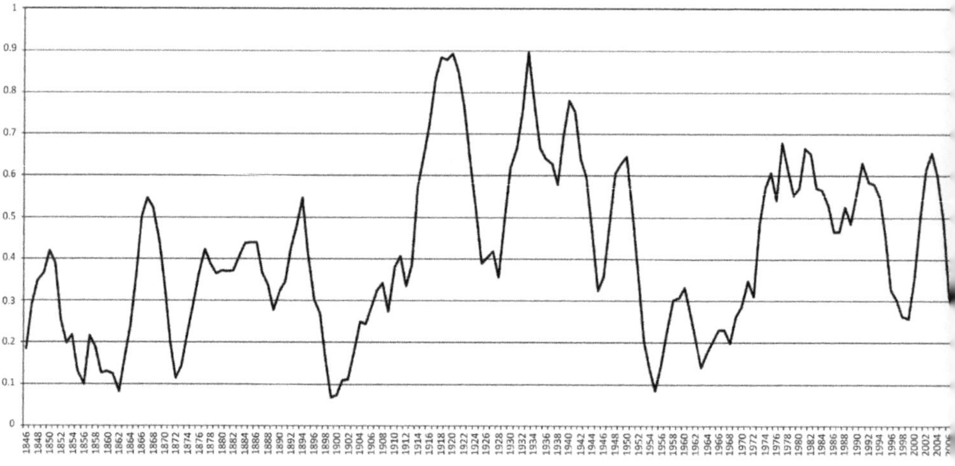

Sources: Crisis data: Reinhart and Rogoff (2009); GDP data: Maddison (2009).

imbalances (Kaminsky and Reinhart 1999; Reinhart and Rogoff 2009). Global imbalances exist where some countries run large current account deficits, effectively borrowing the savings of others, while others run large surpluses. Vast amounts of capital pouring into developing countries can create bubbles, which burst amid capital flight. Imbalances can create fundamental difficulties in managing economic systems, and adjustments to resolve them are difficult to negotiate. For instance, one explanation for the recent 2008 financial crisis highlights the role of Asian savers (Bernanke 2005). Eager to build up reserves after the 1997 East Asian financial crisis, many countries maintained high savings rates and big current account surpluses. Americans, in turn, were happy to do their patriotic duty by spending the windfall of cheap credit from Asia, fuelling a run-up in house prices. The bubble continued until American housing prices could go up no further, at which point the system fell apart.

Other works focus on how credit booms precipitate crises (Kindleberger 1978; Minsky 1992; Mendoza and Terrones 2008; Schularick and Taylor 2012). When governments and banks extend excess credit to the economy, bubbles proliferate. It is always easy to look like a genius when credit is abundant. However, scarce credit forces overleveraged actors to fail, leading to even tighter credit markets in an iterative and painful process. When bubbles burst, it is not always clear where the bottom of the market lies. For instance, to understand the 2008 financial crisis, it is important to consider the role of financial innovations like derivatives in extending the credit available to borrowers. Investment banks created securities by splicing together multiple mortgages of varying risk levels. Credit rating agencies rated these bundled assets more favourably, particularly if they were backed by other forms of derivatives, like credit default swaps (CDSs). Many ordinarily risk-averse investors, like pension funds, found themselves financing the mortgages of borrowers who had no jobs or incomes. Derivatives helped inflate the subprime bubble, and when real estate prices crashed, they helped spread the pain. Whereas a bank can repossess a house if a borrower fails to make their mortgage payments, financial institutions holding derivatives had no claim to a physical asset – only a piece of paper of extremely contingent value.

Economic theory can take us only so far. Whether we are discussing global imbalances or domestic credit booms, politicians enact policies producing those outcomes. Governments can liberalize or implement capital controls, create or repeal regulations, hire lawyerly regulators or embrace iron triangles, and instate or revoke implicit guarantees to financial firms. Politicians may not always listen to the best counsel of economists. Serving on the Board of Governors of the US Federal Reserve System, a prescient Benjamin Bernanke warned in 2005 that high savings rates in Asia were financing large current account deficits and surging house prices in the United States. True to the Fed's tradition of understatement, he warned that "the risk of a disorderly adjustment in financial markets always exists" (Bernanke 2005). Despite Bernanke's foresight, neither the Federal Reserve nor the Bush administration did much to prevent a financial crisis. The mere knowledge that a policy might cause a crisis is often insufficient to motivate change. The goal of managing systemic risk is often eclipsed by more pressing concerns like winning re-election, meeting the demands of critical interest groups, or competing internationally.

Many economists agree that the roots of financial instability are *political*.[3] For instance, Calomiris and Haber (2014, 4–12) contend that we know how to prevent banking crises – through regulation, governments can prevent banks from making high-risk loans, or they can ensure that banks possess adequate capital to absorb the losses from risky investments. However, only 6 out of 117 countries have banking systems that provide adequate credit without experiencing financial crises. Economists may be limited by their priors – the assumptions they make about the way the world works. Economists start from the perfect world that exists in their models, seeing politics as a constraint instead of an endogenous feature of every policy decision ever made. For instance, Calomiris and Haber (2014) do a wonderful job of describing the bargains made between different coalitions that have kept nearly every country either under-banked or unstable, but they cannot tell us why some bargains emerged over others. By their account, one of the few countries to escape a substandard banking system – Canada – did so only by virtue of an institutional accident that led to regular revisions of banking laws, mixed with path dependence (Calomiris and Haber 2014, 283–330). Admati and Hellwig (2013, 169–91) decry the Basel III capital ratios as inadequate[4] and easily gamed, but chalk the problem up to regulatory capture without going further (192–208). Very few economists, with the exception of Eichengreen (2012), address the role of international politics in crafting policy.

This book seeks to improve our understanding of financial crises by developing a political explanation of why governments adopt policies that aggravate the risk of financial crises, fusing international and domestic political forces. If we look around the world, we will see diverse policy environments in which regulatory policy is contested by a host of actors, including politicians, interest groups, and regulators. Some of these actors favour strict regulations, even at the cost of constraining growth and undermining international competitiveness. Others favour loose regulations, even when doing so increases the risk of financial crises. Through unending political struggle, policy environments will tend to converge on some political equilibrium, which probably diverges from the best advice of economists. Yet that is not the end of the story.

Every policy environment is nestled inside the global financial system, and global finance is more than the sum of its parts. Although financial regulation is hotly contested by domestic political actors inside a given policy environment, *global* power shifts can break long-standing domestic political equilibria, while prompting a search for new ideas. In a global financial system, the lead economy[5] enjoys considerable structural advantages, including control over the global reserve currency, dominance inside international institutions, the ability to borrow cheaply, control over the leading financial centre, and immense influence.[6] When the lead economy is relatively secure from external challengers, it can sustain stable regulatory regimes that reduce the risk of crises. But when global financial leadership is contested, leaders and their main challengers roll back regulatory safeguards to spur growth and make themselves more attractive to global capital markets. Initially cautious deregulation can be amplified as newly deregulated industries grow in economic and political clout, shifting the policy environment towards greater acceptance of risks.

Deregulation often diffuses to smaller economies as well, both as stronger countries pressure others to open their markets and, perhaps, due to the normative appeal of following the example of rich, powerful countries. Positional conflict at the heart of the global system weakens safeguards. Thus, we should expect to see riskier policies and an increased probability of crises during periods when the lead economy faces viable challenges to its leadership. But first, let us elaborate on the object of study: financial regulation.

Growth versus Stability in Financial Regulation

The best way to understand why policymakers repeatedly allow financial crises to happen is to look at financial regulation. States regulate their financial systems in myriad ways and for diverse reasons. However, the bulk of regulations address the delicate balance between the risk of systemic crises and the ability of firms to provide capital to the rest of the economy (Turner 2014). Once upon a time, financial firms were warehouses. Banks lent out money but maintained reserves equal to the funds lent out. Although warehouse banks rarely collapsed, they also provided little credit to industry. Intermediaries channel capital between savers and borrowers. For instance, today, banks[7] take in deposits from individuals and make investments in profitable enterprises. Intermediation is vital to innovation and growth – every Mark Zuckerberg needs a Sean Parker; every *Wirtschaftswunder* needs banks able to mobilize capital.[8]

Why don't depositors simply invest in profitable enterprises or lend money themselves? It would be prohibitively difficult for every single individual bank depositor to monitor potential borrowers. Specialized financial intermediaries play an important role by addressing the informational asymmetries between borrowers and lenders (Bhattacharya and Thakor 1993). However, there is a wrinkle: banks lend and invest more money than they hold in reserve, often investing in illiquid assets. Should every depositor withdraw their funds from a bank at once, the bank will be unable to redeem everybody and will collapse. Policymakers face a critical trade-off as they regulate financial firms: slowing down intermediation will cause economic stagnation as borrowers are deprived of capital, while speeding up intermediation risks a crisis.[9]

Figure 1.2 depicts a simple representation of a financial-regulatory-policy environment within some polity. Policymakers design rules subject to a real-world trade-off between intermediation and stability. Every policy environment contains actors with some ability to influence

Figure 1.2. The Trade-Off between Risk and Intermediation within Policy Environments

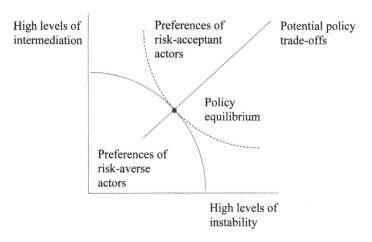

policy, whether as veto players or agenda setters. This might include important interest groups, policymakers, or regulators – the cast of characters will vary from one political system to the next.[10] Some actors are likely to favour more stability, even at the cost of less growth. Others might prefer to roll the dice, desiring a financial regulatory order capable of furnishing capital subject to few restrictions. These preferences are relative – few actors care only about stability or only about growth. Although states can potentially enact policies reflecting many combinations of stability and intermediation, policy will tend to converge upon some equilibrium between those political actors with the greatest influence over the regulatory process. For the purposes of this book, I view any movement towards the upper right of the growth–stability trade-off as a move towards *deregulation* and any movement towards the bottom right of the growth-stability trade-off as a move towards increased *regulation*.[11]

My definition of deregulation and regulation is idiosyncratic in some respects. Frequently, accounts of regulation and deregulation operate by counting the number and strength of formal rules.[12] However, such an approach misses important nuances as well as the reality that some government intervention is often necessary to *create* markets. In one seminal work, Vogel (1996, 3) distinguishes between liberalization, which he describes as the introduction of more competition into markets, and deregulation, which he defines as the elimination of government controls. He notes that, in some cases, such as Britain's 1986

"Big Bang" reforms to the London Stock Exchange (LSE), the Thatcher government opened up the market to greater competition, while simultaneously creating a more formal regulatory body. Freer markets sometimes entail more rules, not fewer.

Scholars often define terms in ways that make sense for the kind of enquiry they are undertaking.[13] Given the cross-country, macro-historical nature of this enquiry, an approach that is robust to the diversity of different policy environments is appropriate. Gauging the degree of regulation by seeing how similar nineteenth-century French banking laws were to the Dodd–Frank Act would have little scholarly merit. On the other hand, because this book is focused on the regulation of a single industry, it is possible to concentrate on the trade-offs that are most pertinent to that industry across time and space. In some policy environments and some time periods, the relationship between regulators and financial firms may be more important than formal rules in generating behaviour. Admittedly, I care very little about formal changes that do not alter the fundamental essence of why finance is interesting – that is, it is an industry capable of furnishing capital for economic expansion, and it is also an industry capable of exposing the economy to the risk of debilitating crises.

Informal does not mean incalculable. There are myriad techniques for understanding the relationships among key actors inside policy environments.[14] A better accounting for those relationships can shed important light on how regulation occurs in practice, often with surprising results. For instance, regulatory capture is often purported to be a catch-all explanation for lax regulation. However, Young, Marple, and Heilman (2017) examined employment networks between the US Securities and Exchange Commission (SEC) and financial firms and found that although movement of employees between finance and government is common, it does not lead to more lax enforcement. Indeed, as we contemplate the rising economic and geopolitical importance of China, a country where decisions occur not only through formal institutions like the Chinese state but also through informal ones (e.g., factional politics inside the Chinese Communist Party, *guanxi* networks), political economists would be wise to consider placing an emphasis on how things work in practice over how they operate *de jure* (Shih 2008; McNally 2011).

What rules count as *financial regulation*? Financial intermediation may happen through many channels. Some countries, including many late developers, rely on banks to intermediate capital, while others rely more on capital markets (Beck, Demirgüç-Kunt, and Levine 1999). As a result, it is useful to look holistically at many forms of intermediation.

Strict regulations on one type of intermediary that are not matched by rules governing another might encourage regulatory arbitrage rather than reduce risks (Rajan and Zingales 2004). To capture this possibility, I follow an approach similar to the one taken by Kaminsky and Schmukler (2008), who delineated among deregulation of banking, securities, and the capital market in a large data set of countries since 1973. Finally, regulatory regimes can become laxer by *commission* (e.g., a country eliminates some important safeguards) or by *omission* (Dewatripont, Rochet, and Tirole 2010, 3). For instance, in the 2000s, regulators failed to hold American International Group (AIG) to its obligation to hold collateral for the $441 billion in exposure implied by the large number of CDS contracts it had sold.[15] New financial innovations created new questions about whether and how to apply existing rules, and new opportunities for laxity. Regulators might have done well to heed the warnings of former American Finance Association president James Van Horne (1984), who cautioned that many things labelled as "financial innovations" contained little substance. Let us turn now to some more specific examples of the different dimensions of formal and informal regulatory mechanisms on banking and securities found in the real world.

Historically, governments managed systemic financial risk in a few ways, including micro-prudential and macro-prudential regulation.[16] *Micro-prudential regulation* involves measures aimed at supervising financial firms to make sure that they publish accurate financial information and are well capitalized relative to the riskiness of the activities they engage in. Yet the prudence of each individual firm may not always be enough. It is true that financial firms abhor financial crises and maintain risk-management divisions aimed at limiting the likelihood of collapse. When Winecoff (2017) examined leverage patterns among global financial firms, he found many firms clustered well *above* the regulatory minimum prescribed by the Basel Capital Accords. Unfortunately, some of the risks that financial firms take on pose risks for actors *other* than themselves (Selmier 2017). Financial firms lend to one another, act as counter-parties for insurance or hedging contracts, operate practices similar to one another, and may be tied to the same political allies or downstream industries.

All these activities represent channels whereby the risky activities of one firm can have implications for many others. Consider the case of systemically important financial firms, like JPMorgan Chase or Deutsche Bank. Some firms are so central to the global economy that their collapse would bring down many others with them. Such firms might take on excessive risks, knowing that they will profit during good times and be protected by policymakers in bad times. As a result, many governments have established macro-prudential regulations – that is, regulations that push firms to act as if they cared about risks to the financial system as a whole.

In addition to implementing prudential measures, some countries employ restrictions on the scale or scope of financial activity, at times justified on the basis that these rules limit risks. While many contemporary economists are critical of these *unit-banking* rules, the rules were frequently enacted with the aim of reducing the risk of crises. For instance, the Glass–Steagall Act of 1933 created a firewall between investment banks and commercial banks. The key rationale for the move was that it was a conflict of interest for the funds of ordinary depositors to be wagered in risky securities markets. Moreover, specialized institutions might be monitored more effectively because their activities were limited in nature. For instance, Bhidé (2009) argued that New Deal–era relationship banking was more stable than the arms-length system that emerged after the 1970s because it involved bankers with deep knowledge of the risks entailed in transactions – due diligence might outperform blind diversification. Rules favouring smaller financial institutions might also be justified on the grounds that smaller institutions can collapse without threatening the underlying payments system.[17]

In contrast, defenders of universal banks argue that big banks are more diversified, that unit banks suffer from moral hazard problems due to deposit insurance systems, and that securities activities may help in times of crisis. However, the biggest criticism of unit-banking rules is that they lead to undercapitalization. Despite these critiques, unit-banking rules also fit usefully into a growth–stability trade-off. This book is fundamentally about politics – examining why governments sometimes favour policies they perceive to be risky and sometimes favour policies they perceive to be less risky. Governments that implemented unit-banking rules did so, in part, because they believed that they reduced overall risks to the economy (although political bargains were also part of the story). Since unit-banking systems are worse at intermediating capital than universal ones, governments opting for them were sacrificing a lot of intermediation for small reductions in risks. The collapse of the American S&L industry in the 1980s certainly illustrates the fact that smallness by itself is not much of a virtue. However, the creation of more risk-averse subsections of the financial system may be a viable pathway for regulators to protect the savings of ordinary depositors. Moreover, restrictions on scope may be more politically robust than other forms of regulation because they create compliance constituencies likely to fight for regulation to protect their own turf.

Financial stability can also be influenced by the presence and nature of lender-of-last-resort institutions. During a financial panic, it helps to have some institutions capable of lending when other institutions are unable to do so. Minsky (1992) and Kindleberger (1978) propose the following scenario: imagine a mix of borrowers in which some are able to pay interest on debt, while paying down principal; some are able to pay interest, but not pay down principal; while other "Ponzi" borrowers can do neither and rely on asset appreciation to remain solvent. In a panic, credit markets tighten, pushing additional borrowers towards insolvency. As more borrowers go bankrupt, credit markets tighten even further. Lender-of-last-resort institutions are critical to stopping this cycle. In the United States, the Federal Reserve and the Federal Deposit Insurance Corporation (FDIC) act as lenders of last resort, while the International Monetary Fund (IMF) is a global lender of last resort.

Although lender-of-last-resort institutions can limit the severity of a crisis, poorly designed institutions might act procyclically, throwing credit at speculative bubbles and reducing it during crises. One problem is moral hazard – when people are insured against losses, they are more likely to engage in risky activities. The classic solution to the moral hazard problem faced by lender-of-last-resort institutions posed by Bagehot (1873) is the use of penalty rates: if rescued firms pay a steep price for their rescue, it is possible to limit crisis severity without encouraging moral hazard. A second potential complication can occur if countries blunt their lender-of-last-resort institutions with fixed exchange rates (assuming capital mobility). If countries with fixed exchange rates attempt to fight a recession by lowering interest rates, they will experience capital outflows as portfolio investors seek higher interest rates abroad. In the process, portfolio investors will sell the domestic currency to buy foreign money, weakening the currency and threatening the exchange rate. A lender-of-last-resort institution with appropriate penalty rates and the freedom to act counter-cyclically is a better safeguard against financial crises than one able to promote moral hazard or one weighed down by a fixed exchange rate.

Finally, states may opt for or against capital controls – regulations on the flow of capital in and out of the country. Ending capital controls can open up profitable new investment opportunities for financial firms, while also allowing domestic firms to receive capital from abroad. For states seeking to establish global financial centres, liberalization is critical – investors are far more likely to place their faith in centres from which they could withdraw in times of duress. On the other hand, capital-market liberalization exposes countries to the risk of crisis contagion and capital flight. Some countries – such as the most central economies in global financial networks – may be at less risk of contagion than others (Oatley et al. 2013). Nonetheless, the long-term historical pattern of crises tracks the level of global financial liberalization (Obstfeld and Taylor 2004, 24).

One of the downsides of capital-market liberalization is that it limits the ability of governments to respond to domestic conditions. In the face of a banking crisis, most governments would like to be able to enact expansionary monetary policy to prevent panics. Cutting interest rates in an environment of free-flowing capital, however, is likely to lead to capital outflows, thereby putting downward pressure on the currency. For countries with fixed exchange rates, this can undermine their fixed rates and prompt a currency crisis (Mundell 1963). As with unit-banking regulations, many economists have viewed capital controls as a form of financial repression that stymies growth. However, in recent years, voices have emerged positing the idea that capital controls might be part of a strategy that gives governments greater policy choices in a crisis (Bhagwati 1998; Rodrik 1998; Rey 2015). Indeed, even the ordinarily liberal IMF endorsed a heterodox rescue strategy following Iceland's 2008 financial crisis that included the use of capital controls.

My aim in this book is neither to explain every instance of deregulation nor to anticipate every crisis. Rather, I turn my attention to instances where the abandonment of prudence was deepest. Great deregulations and the global crises they proliferate warrant our attention. Financial regulation tends to follow a punctuated equilibrium pattern, with long periods of stability interspersed by brief periods of rapid reform (Freeman and Soete 1996; Perez 2002). For instance, the Glass–Steagall system[18] remained in place from 1933 to 1999. I am interested in those periods in which a given regulatory order gave way to another. Politics is economics with brickbats – organized interests vie to implement favourable policies. Because financial intermediaries fuel downstream industries with capital, they play a constitutive role in politics (Zysman 1983). Imagine if Charles Babbage's mechanical computer or Avro's flying car had received the funding necessary for its development. Either development would have transformed the economic and the political landscape of nineteenth-century Britain or twentieth-century North America, respectively. Financial regulation is not merely transactional; it is also constitutional. As a result, regulatory orders rarely change, and when they do, the implications are immense.

The Argument in Brief

Competition is likely to be fierce when (a) the stakes are high and (b) both sides have a plausible shot at winning. Imagine that you had to participate in a race for your life against a clone of yourself. You would wake up to train each morning to maximize your chance of winning against an equally matched opponent. Change the stakes to something worthless, or your competitor to a snail, and you would train much less. The global financial system is a vast network of transnational capital flows, with large benefits accruing to the lead economy. During periods where the capabilities of the lead economy are weak, states engage in intense regulatory competition, each aspiring to gain the structural benefits of leadership for themselves. Although regulatory rollbacks pose long-term risks to financial stability, they may be attractive as a means to enhance the financial prowess of a state.

All countries do not play equivalent roles in the global financial system. Since at least the Industrial Revolution, history has been characterized by successive waves of technological innovation as radical technologies spin off myriad new opportunities.[19] Across each wave of technological innovation, a single country has been able to monopolize global production of the leading sectors of the age (Modelski and Thompson 1996).[20] Great wealth and technological prowess facilitated the construction of powerful navies and air forces capable of exerting control over the vital arteries of world trade. In turn, with their ability to project force over long distances and their outsized wealth, technological leaders are well positioned to become the primary conduits of capital for the rest of the world.

A global economy necessitates the coordination of state activity in a number of areas. However, rather than posing a burden, the lead economy enjoys structural benefits because of its role in global governance. Global commerce benefits from the use of a shared medium of exchange. Which currency makes the most sense? Just as we might join Facebook because many other people are on it, there are positive network externalities to using a currency that others are also likely to employ. Although most countries maintain their own independent currencies, the currency of the leading economy is an obvious choice as global reserve currency. The use of the lead economy currency in reserves is, in effect, a large, interest-free loan to the lead economy. In addition to enjoying seigniorage benefits, lead economies can finance budget deficits more easily, can deflect adverse exchange rate movements, and can earn high returns by effectively acting as the world's venture capitalist (Gourinchas and Rey 2007; Eichengreen 2012; Oatley

2015; Cohen 2015). These advantages help ensure that financial markets cluster in the leading cities of the lead economy (Cassis 2006). Both as an essential actor in global governance and as a country able to print the world's money, a lead economy also exercises an outsized role in international institutions (Copelovitch 2010). This influence can be parlayed into insistence on the diffusion of global standards that are compatible with its interests. Not only are the advantages of global financial leadership great, they are also heavily top-loaded.

Lead economies inevitably decline, allowing others to challenge them for leadership. Existing technologies may diffuse abroad, diminishing the lead economy's edge. Other states may enact ambitious reforms that allow them to mobilize capital and spur innovation. Although the technical capabilities of the lead economy weaken, other states may actually be able to intensify their *structural* advantages in the early stages of decline by opening up global capital markets. The rise of the rest of the world provides lead-economy investors with great opportunities. Should global markets open up further, the structural benefits of global leadership might actually increase. For instance, the opening of capital markets in the 1970s and 1980s increased global economic volatility, requiring countries to hold more dollars in reserve (Helleiner 1996).

All good things must come to an end, and global leadership is no exception. As competitors build up vast stores of wealth, they may begin to supplant the lead economy as a major source of investment capital. Although the incumbent lead economy benefits from a degree of path dependence, it faces increasingly viable contenders from abroad. Interest groups in the lead economy, whether cognizant of the impending loss of structural advantages or simply reacting to hard times, will push for decisive action to shore up the position of the leader. Long-standing ideas will appear increasingly passé, amid worsening outcomes. Financial deregulation, employing the broad definition of this book, will emerge as an attractive option. Freeing up international capital flows can enhance profits and squeeze greater structural benefits out of the system. Slashing leverage and reporting requirements or offering implicit guarantees to financial institutions will allow for the mobilization of much more capital.

Broadening the range of activities that financial institutions engage in can also encourage both financial and technological innovation. Sectors once thought too risky by major financial institutions may find themselves showered with capital (Freeman and Soete 1996; Perez 2002). The promise of deregulation is an attractive one: renaissance. Although removing safeguards is risky, systemic risks materialize slowly, whereas financial-power transitions can occur quickly. While financial reform is typically difficult to enact, the impending loss of financial leadership represents a serious threat to many key actors inside the lead-economy policy environment, prompting shifts in long-standing political equilibria.

The trouble with deregulation is knowing where to stop. Finance is not like other industries. Like a snowball rolling down a snowy hill, political coalitions favouring deregulation may gain momentum and grow (Hammond and Knott 1988). Even small regulatory changes can disrupt long-standing political equilibria, leading to second-order effects. More risk-acceptant financial institutions fuel more risk-acceptant downstream industries, expanding the constituency favouring less regulation. Strong contenders for global financial leadership, too, are unlikely to acquiesce. Often, they may enact reforms of their own, attempting to win the structural advantages of leadership. The impact of first-order competitive shocks and second-order snowball effects on the lead-economy policy environment is depicted in figure 1.3. The threat of foreign competition is likely to shift the policy equilibrium towards greater intermediation and more acceptance of financial instability. Lax regulations, in turn, are likely to expand the power and influence of the risk-acceptant coalition over time, leading to a second-order shock, pushing the policy equilibrium even further to the top right.

Competition for global financial leadership does not preclude cooperation in other domains. For instance, all contenders for global leadership share an interest in maintaining free capital flows, even if they would rather that those flows were centred on themselves. Through processes of imitation, coordination, and competition for capital, smaller states may, similarly, adopt the laxer standards employed by the world's most vital economies (Simmons and Elkins 2004). Why not adopt similar rules to those that work in the world's leading economies? States all over the world shift to weaker standards. As more and more countries expand credit to fuel booms, as lax oversight allows companies to take big risks without maintaining correspondingly large reserves, and as economies grow more exposed to one another, the conditions for major financial crises – credit booms and global imbalances – intensify.

Figure 1.4 summarizes a hypothetical financial power transition at the systemic level. At first, in the plateau stage, Country A is clearly dominant, although its relative power is gradually ebbing. In this phase, Country A is likely to be fairly secure in its position, while it would be difficult for Country B to envision itself overtaking A. Towards the end of the plateau phase, Country A might attempt to compensate for some of its material decline by intensifying the structural benefits of leadership, and B might begin to envision new strategies, setting the

Figure 1.3. The Impact of Global Competition on a Lead-Economy Policy
Environment

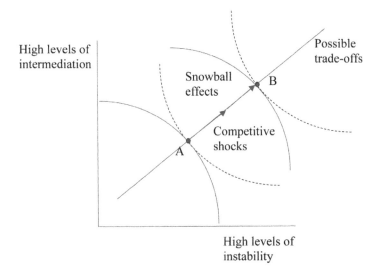

stage for the next phase: competition. In the competition phase, the relative position of the incumbent leader, A, collapses rapidly. Both A and
B are likely to remove regulatory safeguards in this phase, as global
financial leadership is increasingly in question. Second-order snowball
effects and third-order effects from policy diffusion will lead to even
greater deregulation, further increasing the risk of crises. Finally, in
the reconstitution, a new order establishes itself, either as a challenger
decisively overtakes the incumbent leader or as the incumbent staves
off challenges (figure 1.4 depicts the former). Crises will continue due
to the policies enacted in the previous era. However, as competitive
pressure recedes, states will have greater room to increase regulatory
safeguards.

Scope

There are limitations to the scope of analysis undertaken here. My
argument is premised on the potential existence of an interlinked
global financial system. After all, structural benefits form a key part
of my causal mechanism – no structural benefits, no reason for competition. Conventional economic historians have tended to situate the
emergence of global finance in the late seventeenth century (Neal 1993),
and certainly the French and British financial revolutions of the 1720s

Figure 1.4. A Hypothetical Financial Power Transition

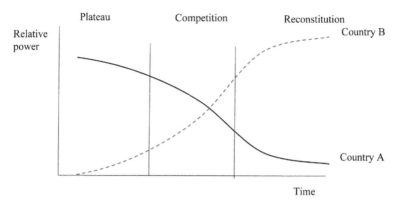

suggest that regulatory competition existed as well as the potential for global financial crises. Frank (1998, 108–17) pushes for an earlier start date, arguing that there was a Chinese-centric global financial system between 1400 and 1800. China ran consistent trade surpluses, received tribute from other states, and accrued large shares of the world's bullion. On the other hand, if one compares the value of total foreign-investment assets to the GDP of the primary "core" countries, foreign investment never exceeded 3 per cent of core GDP until the 1840s, as Britain abolished the Corn Laws.[21] By comparison, foreign-investment assets represented 26 per cent of core GDP in 1914. If I were to divide historical periods, I would say that my argument does not apply before 1714, that it applies less systematically from 1714 to the 1840s, and that it applies most strongly after the middle of the nineteenth century.[22]

I do not mean to suggest that all "great deregulations" are equivalent. Although competitive challenges are a strong inducement towards deregulation in any system, different policy environments possess distinct features that influence the sensitivity to such challenges. For instance, in Japan in the 1980s, each set of actors – regulators, incumbent interest groups, and factions inside the governing Liberal Democratic Party – possessed a great deal of power and, hence, reasons to favour inertia (Rosenbluth 1989a; Calder 2017). In contrast, the power of a British prime minister in command of a majority government is quite strong indeed (McGillivray 2004). One skit from *Spitting Image* (the satirical British television puppet show), which was so believable that it has become an apocryphal anecdote, depicted Prime Minister Margaret Thatcher in a restaurant with her Cabinet members. After Thatcher orders a raw steak, the waitress enquires, "And what about the vegetables?" Thatcher, looking at her Cabinet, responds, "They'll have the same as me."

Alternative Explanations

Interstate financial competition is not the only factor driving the likelihood of great deregulations or great crises. Domestic political shifts and changing economic ideas exert influence on regulatory patterns as well. However, the role of these factors is less systematic than global competition, and many popular stories implicating unscrupulous bankers or ill-conceived economic ideas miss complex realities. Let us imagine what the next financial crisis will be. Perhaps a Chinese effort to loosen capital controls will prompt massive capital flight and a panic in the world's second-largest (or largest) economy. Perhaps an investment mania in artificial intelligence will go bust, filling the streets of Palo Alto with unemployed robots exchanging services for WD-40. Perhaps a series of populist leaders will sweep into power, escalating a series of trade wars and shattering global financial stability. Although I am not much of a futurist, I can predict how your friends and acquaintances will likely attribute the crisis: "It was the *&^%ing bankers!"

After a financial crisis, it is unsurprising that many blame the bankers. A crisis often involves bailouts for the very banks whose inordinate risk-taking caused the crisis.[23] Everybody loves bank-bashing, from left-wingers in Che Guevara T-shirts to your conservative uncle who read about the evils of fractional reserve banking on Internet comment boards. It is with good reason that many are quick to blame deregulation on bankers. Financial crises often expose financial firms engaged in risky or even fraudulent activities. It is true that financial firms think about risks differently than ordinary citizens. Investment banks maintain excellent risk-management divisions; however, they are concerned primarily with limiting risk to the firm, not risk to the entire financial system.

One might expect financial firms to prefer laxer rules on finance than the average citizen. By increasing leverage – lending out more capital without increasing reserves – financial firms can increase their returns, taking in the bulk of the upside of greater leverage. The downside of leverage is that it increases the risk that a financial institution will become insolvent during times of duress – a cost that implicates not only the financial institution but also its counter-parties, depositors, and often taxpayers. Indeed, precisely by making the financial system vulnerable, financial institutions may gain *political* leverage. Johnson and Kwak's (2010) account of the 2008 subprime crisis offers a powerful example of this story. In their telling, firms designed risky new derivatives, allowing them to circumvent limits on leverage. Large financial institutions used political influence to cow regulators. With lax regulation and new financial instruments, the biggest financial institutions in the United States became so big and central that their failure meant catastrophe. Knowing this, they took yet more risks, correctly assuming that they would be bailed out by the government in the event of collapse.

Although financial firms are doubtlessly powerful, let me present an unpopular proposition: not all bankers are at fault. Consider the Rothschilds – an august banking dynasty that is frequently alleged to possess unlimited power and malign intent.[24] In France during the Second Empire, James de Rothschild fought against the profligate institutions that had helped drive a Europe-wide crisis in the 1870s (Ferguson 2000, 167–88). When the United States faced a severe banking panic in 1907, it was the New York Clearing House, led by John Pierpont Morgan, not the government, that staved off collapse. More recently, one of the greatest defenders of the Glass–Steagall system was the Security Industry Association (SIA). Even in the 2008 financial crisis, mergers between major financial institutions and ailing firms, such as JPMorgan Chase's acquisition of Bear Stearns, averted an even worse crisis.

Finance is not monolithic – history is replete with examples of different kinds of financial institutions wanting different things. In American history, bankers in the interior were at odds with those in the northeast (White 1983; Sanders 1999); S&Ls had different preferences about interstate branching than other institutions (Kroszner and Strahan 1998); commercial banks wanted to abolish Glass–Steagall against the initial objections of insurance companies and investment banks (Suarez and Kolodny 2011). Similar distinctions can be found in accounts of British banking, with historical divisions among joint-stock banks, merchant banks, and country banks (Harris 1997; Taylor 2006) or between international investors and domestic industry (Kennedy 1987). Studies of financial liberalization in countries where business–government relationships are common find differences between insider firms and those without access to the corridors of power (Haggard 2000). Insofar as regulation has implications for exposure to global capital markets or exchange rate policy, there is also a rich international political economy (IPE) literature emphasizing the implications of financial openness across different sectors of the economy (Frieden 1991, 2015; Haggard and Maxfield 1996). Even where financial firms possess common goals, and the means (whether campaign donations, revolving doors, or privileged information) to influence political outcomes, they may not always favour deregulation (Hendrickson 2001; Young 2012; Young, Marple, and Heilman 2017).

Moreover, as the financial assets held by firms and individuals grow more complex, even these preferences may be hedged into oblivion (Walter 2013). Let us consider an example outside the realm of financial regulation. It is not hard to imagine Charles Koch, CEO of the manufacturing firm Koch Industries and devout libertarian, waking up in the middle of the night after having had a nightmare about the Environmental Protection Agency. If Charles Koch wanted to sleep better at night, he could diversify his portfolio. With a large enough position in environmentally friendly exchange-traded funds,[25] he might even benefit from stronger environmental regulations. Returning to financial regulation, it might be more useful to think of financial firms as diverse actors, some preferring a habitat that allows for greater risk-taking, some opposing such an outcome (Winecoff 2017). Doubtless, some bankers favour deregulation, but the financial sector is not the sole source of pressure for change. Financial reform requires broad political coalitions that often cut across different sectors. Capital-starved regions, new industries, borrowers with poor credit, and risk-acceptant financial firms may favour deregulation just as established regions, old-growth sectors, well-heeled borrowers, and risk-averse financial firms favour stringency.

The point is not that domestic interest groups are irrelevant to regulatory change – quite the contrary. It is *because* domestic interest groups are powerful and deeply interested in financial regulation that financial reform is typically difficult to enact. Why would key players seek to disrupt the conditions that made them key players? External competition is important not only because it motivates policymakers concerned with the national interest but also because there are domestic interest groups that reap disproportionate benefits from global financial leadership. For instance, the early twentieth century saw the United States overcome its long-standing suspicion of central banking. The coalition to reform the banking system included many figures in the American financial establishment seeking to internationalize the US dollar so that they could compete with Britain in the profitable market for trade acceptances (Broz 1997b). Once external competitive challenges open the door to reform, there may often be second-order effects as new policies alter the relative strength of domestic actors, as mentioned above. For instance, the United States continued down the path of financial deregulation through the late 1990s, even as some initial precipitants for reform, such as the threat of Japan, receded. Rather than thinking about ideas versus domestic politics, it is useful to think about how each interacts with the other.

Others argue that hegemonic ideas drive deregulation and financial crises. After the last crisis, one could find no shortage of symposia on the evils of neoliberalism, with Milton Friedman taking centre stage as a villain. As a political economist myself, I am flattered to think that my ideas could shape entire historical epochs. If we had a time machine, we could test this idea properly. What if we sent a great art teacher back in time to inspire a young Milton Friedman to become a painter instead of an economist? Perhaps we might end up with surrealist paintings of free lunches and the continued reign of Keynesian economics. Somehow, I am sceptical.

Many believe that ideas matter to economic policy, although their arguments vary. At one extreme, there are the "great man" arguments, which posit that economists are endowed with prolific powers of influence. Skidelsky (2010) imagines John Maynard Keynes as such a figure – armed with his (1935) *General Theory*, politicians could confidently stimulate demand to avert recessions. Other scholars avoid the great man frame, but still posit that ideas can take on a pseudo-religious character. They might see the Great Depression, for instance, as the product of an unquestioned faith in the gold standard. Adhering to the rules of the game for the gold standard meant that each country had to maintain the relative value of its currency, even at the risk of ignoring a domestic crisis. It is certainly true that many governments doggedly defended their currency even as unemployment spiked and their banking systems collapsed (Eichengreen 1995).

The ideas that shape policy decisions are enormously important. However, it is not clear to me that individual economists, or even particular epochs of economic thought, shape policy in the way some might imagine. My scepticism comes from reading archived discussions by actual policymakers. Broadly speaking, leaders consult widely when making policy decisions – they look at what other countries have done and consider alternative options.

For instance, let us briefly consider Britain's decision to implement limited liability banking in the 1850s – supposedly the height of the era of laissez-faire. The prime minister, Lord Aberdeen, held a royal commission, which received dozens of responses and a mix of ideological, economic, and pragmatic arguments, while considering how limited liability had worked in France, the United States, and elsewhere. More recently, in the neoliberal 1990s, the deputy secretary of the Treasury in the Clinton administration, Larry Summers, considered the merits of abolishing the Glass–Steagall system. Memos show that he, too, considered the risks of such a move in the wake of the 1997 East Asian financial crisis and the collapse of hedge fund management firm Long-Term Capital Management (LTCM).[26] Policymakers rarely take decisions about financial regulation lightly. Although epistemic communities – groups of policy entrepreneurs that come together and forge common ideas – can penetrate the corridors of power, their rise is not incidental to the prerogatives of the leaders that appoint advisers. Moreover, the broadest sets of ideas (e.g., "the Age of Keynes," neoliberalism) are often so vague as to defy useful categorization. Was the securitization of mortgages in the 2000s a socialist scheme to force banks to house the poor? Or was it yet another case of free markets run amok? Is allowing individuals to form limited liability partnerships an extension of free trade ideas? Or does the socialization of risk implied by such a scheme invalidate such comparisons? Intelligent people, sharing the same ideology, have disagreed about such questions, suggesting that even if hegemonic ideas frame policy choices, they contain room for intellectual pluralism.

The ideas that drive policy are granular ideas that spread inside existing political structures. Some of the most useful works on the ideational roots of economic change explore the idea of epistemic communities. For instance, Hall's (1989) seminal work posits that national contexts shaped the reception of Keynesian ideas by different bureaucracies in the 1930s. Different initial interpretations exerted long-lasting, path-dependent effects. Many ideational explanations of economic policy employ the concept of *Knightian* uncertainty (Knight 1921; Blyth 2002; Nelson and Katzenstein 2014; Widmaier 2016). Knight (1921, 197–233) distinguishes between types of probability that we can know with some certainty (e.g., that the likelihood of rolling a one on a six-sided die is one in six) and those things about which we can make only empirical generalizations in reference to a group (e.g., the likelihood of a particular building burning).

Let us apply the concept to the economy: in a given year, it might be unclear whether the economy will experience a recession. However, you could calculate the *probability* of a recession with a reasonable level of accuracy. Knightian uncertainty exists where the underlying probability distribution of some quantity of interest is unknown. Financial crises challenge many of the assumptions that people have made about the way the world works, and they could be thought of as moments of Knightian uncertainty. Think of the uncertainty emerging from the 2008 financial crisis: was the crisis caused by low interest rates? Global current account imbalances? Moral hazard related to too-big-to-fail financial firms? Government pressure on banks to make risky subprime loans? Given that uncertainty, it may be difficult for even key actors to comprehend their own material interests.

Actors can overcome Knightian uncertainty through trial and error, eventually constructing an estimation of reality. For instance, Blyth

(2002) examines how the United States experimented with different policies during the Great Depression, Nelson and Katzenstein (2014) explore how investors developed beliefs about the economy in the 2000s, Widmaier (2016) looks at how presidential rhetoric shapes broad regulatory orders, while Blyth (2013) examines the evolution of myths surrounding austerity over time. After a passage of time, particularly as these ideational structures are elaborated upon, regulatory orders drift away from reality. For instance, in the early 2000s, many investors came to believe that "housing prices always go up," even though that assumption was provably false. Alternatively, Chwieroth (2010) reports on how IMF conditionality packages came to recommend that countries liberalize short-term portfolio investment despite a dearth of supportive evidence. Yet it is important to remember that ideational and material forces interact in complex ways. We would see a lot more class analysis if the estate of Karl Marx had provided a large grant to support anti-capitalism studies. While Widmaier, Blyth, and Seabrooke (2007) have a point that crises *can* be constructed, many of the moments of great policy adaptation correspond with very real shocks to the economy.

Ideas are important to regulatory change, but they do not exist in a vacuum. Ideas about economic policy have currency, in large part, because they are tied to successful cases or because they can plausibly solve fundamental problems. Even many leaders of states whose very existence is tied to some ideational cause – like Pope Alexander VI or Josef Stalin – often end up practising something akin to realpolitik. Shifts in the global power structure tend to discredit the prevailing policies of declining powers, while attracting positive attention to those of rising ones. For instance, former Alibaba CEO Jack Ma can evangelize about the China model today precisely because of China's economic success. As declining powers seek out ways to avert their own demise, riskier ideas become more attractive. Just as dislodging long-standing political equilibria can create a kind of momentum of its own, so too can ideational shifts. Drawing on new ideas rooted in tolerance of long-term risks to boost growth always seems like a good bet – until risks begin to materialize.

Decline, Deregulation, and Crises through History

How can we test a theory of great deregulations? Although it can be useful to investigate particular cases of deregulation, disjointed case studies have some deficiencies. Often, scholars end up studying the same few cases to the exclusion of others. We race to prove that the latest crisis, or the Great Depression, fits into our favourite theory, while neglecting other examples. Sometimes the view from 20,000 feet can be useful for divining historical patterns that more granular modes of enquiry can miss.

This book takes a macro-historical approach – by examining broad sweeps of history, we expose our argument to more rigorous tests. Earlier, I argued that history exhibits a systematic pattern: decline by the lead economy leads to the relaxation of regulatory safeguards against financial crises by challengers and leaders alike. Which periods in history were most strongly characterized by decline in the relative financial prowess of the lead economy? Looking at the relative share of foreign-investment assets in a given year gives us a direct measure of the degree of control that each major economy has over the world's capital.[27]

Figure 1.5 depicts the global battle for financial leadership. While Britain was the leading capital exporter from 1846 to 1936, the United States took over in 1937.[28] There are three cases in which the leading exporter was challenged by others: In the 1850s and 1860s, France rapidly converged on Britain, only to fall back after the Franco-Prussian War. In the 1920s, the United States rapidly converged upon, and then passed, Britain. In the 1980s and 1990s, Japan and Britain came close to surpassing the United States. If my argument is correct, we should expect those periods to exhibit intense competition for economic leadership. Industry groups impacted by declining competitiveness should voice their concerns loudly. Policymakers in the lead economy may face tighter constraints, making them more willing to take policy gambles. Most importantly, we should see the repeal of financial safeguards as well. We might first see tentative steps inside the countries contesting global financial leadership. Later, as political coalitions favouring regulatory rollback gain greater strength, the pace of policy change may intensify. Smaller economies, too, may begin to adopt similar policies as the ideas of the core diffuse abroad.

The evolution of financial regulation is interwoven with the struggle for mastery over the global economy. Although I will examine the history in greater depth in three empirical chapters of this book, it is useful to summarize it here. Let us begin at the period in which large-scale transnational movements of capital first materialized. At the dawn of the nineteenth-century wave of globalization, Britain possessed a stringent regulatory order: banks were required to maintain capital reserves and submit company reports. In addition, banks and corporations were subject to unlimited liability – if they went bankrupt, shareholders were on the hook for the entirety of the obligations of the company (Turner 2014).

The primary financial rival to Britain, France, actually possessed more dynamic banking and corporate rules, including limited liability

Figure 1.5. Relative Shares of Global Foreign-Investment Assets, 1846–2007

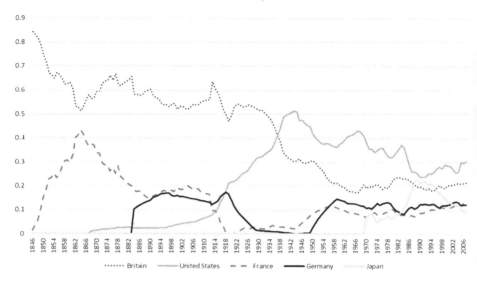

Source: Lee (2016).

incorporation. However, the French Conseil d'État restricted access to dynamic corporate forms, and the banking system was dominated by the conservative *haute banque*, like the house of Rothschild, which lent from their own fortunes (Plessis 1994).[29] Following his 1851 coup, Emperor Napoléon III sought to revitalize the French economy with a bold set of reforms (Davies 2016). Desiring to spark the industrialization he had seen during his exile in Britain, the emperor surrounded himself with advisers inspired by a Saint-Simonian vision of massive financial institutions that would mobilize capital and finance sprawling transportation networks centred on France – a new Mediterranean system. The Crédit Mobilier, a limited liability banking company authorized just after the coup, went on a massive building spree, bankrolling railroads and industrial enterprises across Europe (Cameron 1953). France used its new-found centrality in networks of trade and finance to form the Latin Monetary Union, a franc-led currency bloc. The Second Empire also ramped up naval construction. The rise of France inspired fear in Britain, prompting policymakers to drop their long-standing antipathy to limited liability, while simultaneously abandoning many other regulatory safeguards.

Imitators of France sprung up across Europe – there was even a Credit Mobilier of America. These new institutions lent heavily, often overleveraging themselves – in part because their dense relationships with figures in government made them confident that they were "too big to fail." Eventually, though, the new behemoths fell, wreaking havoc on the larger financial systems around them. Severe financial crises followed, including the Overend Gurney crisis of 1866, the French crisis of the 1860s, the global panic of 1873, the City of Glasgow Bank crisis of 1878, and the continuing misery of the Long Depression of 1873–96.[30]

Even though Britain was impacted by the crises of the Long Depression, it maintained its leadership position. With France in disarray following its defeat in the Franco-Prussian War, Britain stood alone as the world's banker. Many countries adopted the gold standard, long the basis of Britain's currency. A vast market in trade acceptances developed in London, providing credit to merchants and earning the City substantial profits (Gallarotti 1995). With London's position secure, British policymakers implemented modest increases in regulation after major crises. For instance, the 1878 City of Glasgow Bank crisis saw the advent of double liability banking – limited liability for shareholders but unlimited liability for the directors, with the agency to take big risks. As Britain declined technologically relative to Germany and the United States, it was able to make up for these deficiencies with substantial "invisible earnings" from overseas investment and the profits of the City.

Competitive pressures resumed during the First World War. In 1913, the United States passed the Federal Reserve Act. The Federal Reserve could serve two important functions – acting as a lender of last resort in the face of banking panics and serving as a means to standardize and internationalize the US dollar. The latter function was particularly attractive to the American financiers who hungered for a slice of the trade acceptances market. The problem was that these two objectives were at odds with one another. States can have only two of the following three "goods" – monetary autonomy, fixed exchange rates (like the gold standard), and free flows of capital (Mundell 1963). Although the Fed might have acted to regulate business cycles, internationalists won the internal battles in its early years. As war broke out in Europe in 1914, belligerent states – including Britain – were forced off the gold standard, implementing capital controls. As the sole country to retain gold convertibility, the United States experienced vast inflows of gold (Sibler 2008). Following the war, Britain and the United States engaged in an awkward mix of cooperation and competition (Cleveland and Costigliola 1977). The United States needed others to restore free flows of capital so that it could take advantage of its new-found position, while British policymakers thirsted to restore the City to its "rightful" place.

Disastrous decisions followed, creating a global monetary order characterized by massive imbalances. British policymakers pushed for a gold-exchange standard in which sterling, dollars, and francs might serve as reserves, though each remained tied to gold. Britain reopened its capital markets and returned to the gold standard at its pre-war parity in an attempt to signal credibility.[31] However, at the pre-war rate of $4.86, the pound was overvalued and at risk since many countries had reserves of sterling, which could be traded for gold. France returned to the gold standard at an undervalued exchange rate, aiming to build up its gold reserves (Mouré 2002). As Britain's position grew weaker, the United States was forced to accommodate the rest of the world with monetary easement lest the system fall apart. Cheap credit fuelled a massive bubble on Wall Street (Ahamed 2014, 291–306). When American policymakers moved to burst the bubble in 1928, they exported high interest rates to the rest of the world, triggering a global crash, complete with rolling bank failures. The constraints of the gold standard limited the ability of the Federal Reserve to inject adequate liquidity into the banking system, particularly as banking collapses eviscerated the supply of credit (Eichengreen 1995). The result was the worst financial crisis in world history: the Great Depression.

The pain of the Great Depression saw many countries implement new measures to prevent another crisis. In the 1930s, the United States passed the Glass–Steagall Act, separating investment and commercial banks, and created the SEC. Globally, the Bretton Woods system saw many countries implement capital controls, thereby limiting the scope of financial globalization. While American predominance made it easy for the United States to implement stringent rules in 1945, this position eroded over time. In the 1960s and 1970s, the United States allowed for the creation of the Euromarket, then abandoned fixed exchange rates in 1971, allowing the dollar to float. Shortly thereafter, it also took advantage of this new-found freedom by ending capital controls. In the face of mounting volatility, demand for the American dollar as a currency reserve grew (Helleiner 1996).

As in previous eras, exorbitant privileges inspired jealousy abroad. Japan and Britain abolished their own capital controls, while also deregulating their own financial firms. Japan, in particular, roared ahead, with the market capitalization of the Tokyo Stock Exchange approaching that of New York and Japanese banks dominating the list of top global banks (Terrell 1990).[32] In the early 1980s, similar efforts to reform American finance dragged as the securities and banking sectors were stymied by turf wars (Reinicke 1995). By the late 1980s, however, interest groups had begun to coalesce behind a reform agenda. Although Congress was initially unable to pass a bill, the Federal Reserve reinterpreted the

Glass–Steagall Act, allowing banks to engage in some securities activity. Commercial and investment banks grew more similar, larger, and more willing to lobby for further deregulation (Suarez and Kolodny 2011).

By the year 2000, the United States had abolished interstate branching rules, repealed the Glass–Steagall Act, and liberalized derivatives trading. Meanwhile, foreign investment surged as many other countries abandoned capital controls. The results should be familiar to the contemporary reader: the Mexican peso crisis, the East Asian financial crisis, the Russian and LTCM crises, the dot-com bust, the Argentine Depression, the crash of 2008, and the eurozone crisis all took place in narrow proximity. It is possible to debate the importance of particular components of deregulation in this series of crashes or the relative importance of credit booms versus global imbalances. Yet it is difficult to contest that the great deregulations of the 1980s and 1990s undermined global financial stability.[33]

Table 1.1 summarizes this story of competition, regulation, and crises over time, using dates derived from the relative foreign-investment asset data. A few historical regularities stand out. Plateau phases tend to see lead economies make few changes to limit their domestic financial regulatory regimes or to increase regulation. However, global regimes may grow more liberal, consistent with the idea that lead economies desire to increase the structural benefits of leadership as they plateau. Significant crises may then occur, though they usually involve debt crises in developing countries (Suter 1992; Perez 2002). During competition phases, regulatory scrutiny progressively decreases in all major contenders for global financial leadership, although policymakers in some states may realize the emergence of a competitive environment before others. While political resistance to deregulation may be strong at the start of a competition phase, it tends to wear down over time. Competition phases also see the frequency of financial crises begin to increase, although the worst crises often occur later as the outcome of global competition has been realized. Regulatory rollbacks may continue, even as competitive challenges subside, due to the snowball effects induced by the rise of risk-acceptant political coalitions and the currency of risk-acceptant economic ideas. On the other hand, reconstitution phases tend to see the strongest tendencies towards increased regulation in the lead economy often, though not always, after crises.

Other factors than just structural ones have doubtless played a role in regulatory upheavals. Domestic political actors care a great deal about financial regulation, after all. However, shifts in the balance of power among domestic political actors have tended to follow, rather than lead, major regulatory reforms. Let us consider a simple, plausible, domestic political explanation for great deregulations: perhaps financial firms

Table 1.1. Competition, Regulation, and Crises, 1844–2018

Era	Phase (contenders)	Leader/challenger reforms*	Major global crises
1844–51	Plateau (Britain)	**Joint-stock companies/ banking reforms of 1844 (Britain)**; *abolition of Corn Laws (Britain/global)*	
1852–70	Competition (Britain, France)	*Limited liability (Britain); Crédit Mobilier (France)*	Crédit Mobilier crash; Overend Gurney crash
1871–8	Reconstitution (Britain)	**Double liability banking (Britain)**	Panic of 1873; Long Depression of 1873–96
1879–1918	Plateau (Britain)	*Spread of gold standard (global);* **Defence of the Realm Act; gold embargo (Britain)**	Long Depression (cont.); Panic of 1914
1919–30	Competition (Britain, United States)	*Procyclical monetary policy (United States); gold standard restoration (Britain)*	Great Depression
1931–59	Reconstitution (United States)	**Glass–Steagall system (United States); Bretton Woods (global)**	Great Depression (cont.)
1960–85	Plateau (United States)	*End of Bretton Woods, creation of Euromarket (global); abolition of exchange controls (Britain/ Japan)*	Latin American debt crisis
1986–2000	Competition (United States, Britain, Japan)	*Glass–Steagall repeal, commodity futures modernization (United States); Big Bang (Britain); various reforms (Japan)*	East Asian financial crisis
2001–?	Reconstitution (United States)	**Dodd–Frank (United States)**	Dot-com crash; 2008 financial crisis; eurozone crisis

* Reforms decreasing regulation are denoted with *italics*, while reforms increasing regulation are denoted in **bold**. This formatting is used in later tables as well. More detailed descriptions of reforms are provided in subsequent chapters.

favour less regulation than the general public. As a result, during periods of financialization, when finance outpaces the rest of the economy, financial-sector actors will use their growing influence to overthrow regulation. If we examine financial wealth as a percentage of GDP in the lead economies during our period of enquiry, we see evidence of an interesting pattern. In Britain, financialization intensified rapidly in both the long nineteenth century and the period following the election of Margaret Thatcher (see figure 1.6).

Figure 1.6. Financial Assets as a Percentage of GDP, Britain and United States, 1846–2007

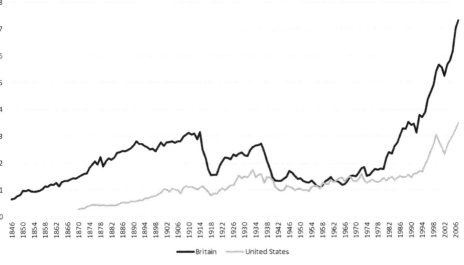

Source: Lee (2016).

In the United States, the overall patterns are similar, although they are less pronounced than in Britain. The core problem with the financialization thesis is one of timing. Britain's financial wealth surged *after* the liberalization of capital controls in 1979 and the Big Bang. The degree of financialization in the United States surged *after* the Fed reinterpreted Glass–Steagall in 1987. At other points in time, such as in late nineteenth-century Britain, financialization rose alongside stricter regulations. In other words, while each financial regulatory rollback featured domestic political fights, shifts in the power of key interest groups alone cannot explain the long-run variation in financial regulation.[34] As Oatley (2011) notes, the dominant "Open Economy Politics" model of IPE rests heavily on the idea that domestic politics drives decision-making. Such a conclusion might appear true to anybody observing the substance of politics at any given time – politicians surely sought donations, interest groups surely lobbied, and so on. However, relying on domestic politics alone misses the forest for the trees. Many of the key regulatory changes initiating waves of financialization occurred during periods when the financial sector was relatively weak and would have had to rely on other actors to press for change. Competitiveness challenges provide the vital trigger to build those new coalitions. However, initially modest reforms can trigger major shifts in the relative power of domestic actors, as illustrated by the surges in financialization through history. Often the result of those shifts can be to amplify the pace of reform.

It is undeniable that ideas shape the interests and preferences of policymakers. Yet an obsessive focus on the role of governments versus markets may not capture the ideational changes that drive shifts in regulatory policy. We can test whether eras in which the leading economies were dominated by laissez-faire ideas systematically exhibited deregulation. Since the nineteenth century, debates over the relative importance of markets and the state have played a central role in policy debates. Liberal economists from David Ricardo to Irving Fisher to Milton Friedman can be thought of as participating in a grand, continuing tradition. There are ways of measuring how ideas have fluctuated over time, at least in the leading economies. Lee (2016) examines the relative mentions of economists favouring free market solutions, and those more questionable of markets, in Google Books over time. If ideas drive policy, we might expect greater deregulation during periods in which pro-market ideas were *en vogue*. Alternatively, perhaps elite ideas matter more than those held by authors in general. To capture these possibilities, Lee (2016) applies the same technique to policy discussions in the British Parliament and US congressional committees over time.

The data accord well with our intuitions – free-market economists dominated references in the pre–First World War period, with market-critical economists such as John Maynard Keynes gaining currency in the interwar period (see figure 1.7). After 1970, the neoliberal age dawned, and references to market-friendly economists like Milton Friedman surged. Thus, if free market ideas systematically drive policymakers to support deregulation, we should expect very little regulation in the nineteenth century, increased regulation in the interwar period and early Cold War, followed by a regulatory rollback following the 1970s. However, when we look at the prevalence of markets across the broad sweep of history, from the liberal age to the neoliberal age, some holes emerge. Changing economic ideas cannot account for the considerable variation in British financial regulation through the nineteenth century. The restoration of the gold standard in the 1920s, likewise, occurred even as market ideas fell out of fashion. Philip Snowden, chancellor of the exchequer in Ramsay MacDonald's Labour government, may not have been an erstwhile capitalist, but he did believe in the gold standard.

If we drill down into particular historical cases, we do find some instances of free market ideologues, such as Margaret Thatcher, instituting great deregulations. However, it is not clear that figures like

Figure 1.7. The Prevalence of Pro-market Ideas, 1846–2007, Five-Year Moving Average

Source: Lee (2016).

Napoléon III, Bill Clinton, or Lord Palmerston can be tarred with the same brush. Ideas are not irrelevant, but they are also inseparable from material circumstances. Ideas promising expansion and renaissance – some of them market-heavy and some of them more statist – have tended to crop up during periods of intense interstate competition for financial leadership. Such ideas may also remain influential longer than is justified by the data. Just as reforms create new political equilibria, so policies that involve greater long-term risks to spark short-term growth tend to be self-confirming in the short run.

The Plan of This Book

There is an uncanny relationship between periods of lead-economy decline and shifts towards riskier regulatory regimes. However, this book aims to illustrate evidence not only of correlation but also of causality. How do we know that deregulation occurs for the reasons specified by this book? The rest of this book develops the argument presented here and elaborates on the evidence that lead-economy decline sets off great deregulations. Chapter 2 fleshes out the concept of financial leadership. Integrating recent work on financial and monetary power, I present a basis for understanding why some countries enjoy the lion's share of the structural benefits of the global financial system. Next, I explore the implications of decline for lead economies and discuss why they may (a) intensify globalization to wring greater structural benefits out of their position and (b) deregulate their financial systems to stave off external challenges. Finally, I examine the counterargument that international regulation affords states a reliable means to increase regulation while skirting competitiveness concerns.

Next, I introduce three empirical chapters (3 through 5), supplementing the macro-history of this chapter with a more detailed historical analysis. Each empirical chapter covers instances where the lead economy shifted from the plateau phase to the competition phase. To assess the impact of competition, it is necessary to examine the system before *and* during periods in which global financial leadership was hotly contested. After describing how competition led to deregulation and crisis, at the end of each chapter, I examine the emergence of a new power structure. In addition to describing systemic variables (e.g., the relative position of different states), I investigate the motivations of the key actors, such as politicians, regulators, and interest groups, in regulatory debates in the policy environments of the most prominent states in the global financial system.

Chapter 3 examines the period from the end of the Napoleonic Wars until the Long Depression of 1873–96. The chapter begins by describing British regulatory debates in the 1830s and 1840s. In particular, it looks at the success of those favouring prudential regulation and the degree to which they were buoyed by rosy assessments of Britain's relative position. I then turn to the rise of Napoléon III and the financial revolution he launched in France, with the creation of the Crédit Mobilier as its centrepiece. Returning to the British case, I examine how French successes altered debates on financial reform in Britain, resulting in the successful implementation of limited liability. Next, I look at how reforms snowballed in France, Britain, and around the world, culminating in a series of painful crashes and the Long Depression, beginning in 1873. Finally, I look at how the global financial order reconstituted itself in the face of these crises and how Britain began to implement a new regulatory regime following the French decline.

In chapter 4, I turn to the causes of the Great Depression. I begin the chapter by describing the operation of the global financial system during the Pax Britannica, stressing how the gold standard system granted immense structural advantages to Britain. Next, I look at the campaign to create the Federal Reserve and internationalize the dollar. Although the Fed could serve valuable prudential purposes, the goal of an internationalized dollar blunted the institution's ability to serve such a role. Next, I examine the impact of the First World War on the global financial system and the British response to its diminished circumstances. Although British policymakers had viable policy alternatives, they promoted a risky gold-exchange system to maintain the reserve role of sterling. Britain also returned to the gold standard at a heavily overvalued pre-war parity of $4.86, believing that doing so would restore London to its former role as the world's financial centre. Returning to the United States, I also look at the decisions taken by the Federal Reserve to use monetary easement to expand the gold standard club, thereby creating conditions for a massive bubble on Wall Street. I examine French efforts to attain monetary leadership by returning to gold at a devalued rate and then running large current account surpluses. Collectively, the desire of each state for financial primacy led to policy decisions that produced the worst financial crisis in history.

In chapter 5, I turn to the origins of the most recent wave of crises. I begin with an examination of the Bretton Woods/Glass–Steagall era and its subsequent breakdown in the 1970s and 1980s. I show, too, that although free-market ideals were increasingly *en vogue* among policymakers, efforts to reform the American financial system were stymied by turf wars among different components of the financial sector during the early years of the Reagan administration. I then look to Japan and Britain, exploring the role of aspirations for financial leadership in driving efforts at reform in the 1970s and 1980s. Returning to the United States, I describe the degree to which external competitive channels dislodged old obstacles to financial reform, culminating in the abolition of interstate branching rules, the abolition of the Glass–Steagall Act, and the liberalization of derivatives trading as well as regulatory repeal by others. I also discuss the linkages between deregulation and the series of financial crises that occurred in the 2000s.

Finally, in chapter 6, I present the conclusion to this book. After summarizing the book's findings, I look at emerging challenges to American financial leadership, from the rise of China to a more integrated EU. Although neither is a near-term challenge, I suggest that the position of the United States is less secure than it may seem.

Chapter Two

A Theory of Great Deregulations

Why do states at the apex of global financial power embark on great deregulations? It seems strange that successful states would gamble by transforming the financial foundations of that success. Yet, in the 1850s, financial reforms by Napoléon III in France spurred Britain to abolish its own regulatory safeguards, adopting policies such as limited liability banking, which had been decried as unwise but a few decades before. Again, in the 1920s, despite warnings that such a move would generate unsustainable global imbalances and massive unemployment, Britain reopened the sluice gates of global capital markets by returning to the gold standard. The United States accommodated Britain with a substantial expansion of credit, unleashing a bubble of legendary proportions in the process. In the 1970s, Britain, Japan, and the United States dismantled regulatory orders that had prevented banking crises for decades. Reforms were implemented despite the initial resistance of many entrenched bureaucratic, industrial, and financial-sector interests. In many instances, leaders advocating reform were not laissez-faire ideologues but rather pragmatists, sensitive to the risks of reform.

Power plays a more important role in financial regulation than is commonly acknowledged. Global finance is not just another industry. There is a global financial system in which different states play distinct roles. Global financial flows cluster around the state with the greatest financial fitness (e.g., the most efficient financial firms and the greatest capital exports) (Oatley et al. 2013). Even a small advantage in financial fitness can yield substantial and lasting structural benefits to the lead economy. When the relative fitness of the lead economy begins to decline, however, those structural benefits become threatened. As a result, broad domestic coalitions will press the governments of leading economies to take actions to preserve the status quo. Two types of action are particularly common: governments try to increase structural benefits by intensifying global flows (e.g., removing capital controls) or try to increase the viability of their own financial sector by freeing up financial firms to take bigger risks.[35] Absent strict rules, reformers hope that capital will flow to profitable enterprises, as new financial innovations restore the vitality of the financial system. Deregulation is a gamble paid for by future generations and foreigners – it is not difficult to see why it is attractive to politicians.

Why do great deregulations produce financial crises? Although they spur growth in the short and medium term, they also generate risks for the global economy. Seemingly minor reforms disrupt long-standing political equilibria, all the while sowing the seeds for additional deregulation. For instance, the collapse of the American S&L sector in the 1980s removed the most powerful defenders of the Glass–Steagall system. Deregulation by the lead economy often prompts competitive responses by contenders for global leadership. Imitation and the promotion of lax regulatory standards by international institutions further amplify policy diffusion from the core of the global financial system to the rest of the world.

As more countries repeal safeguards, systemic dangers intensify. Although financial institutions can seek more profitable investments absent constraints, they may also take on more risks. While financial firms are good at managing risk to themselves, actions by investors may pose risks for other actors (Cerny 2014; Selmier 2017). Consider the actions of the insurance company AIG during the early 2000s. AIG offered investors large amounts of CDSs, effectively insurance contracts against defaults on loans (particularly collateralized debt obligations – securities whose value depended on pools of loans from different tranches of risk). AIG's exposure was massive, relative to the assets of the company, posing immense risks if many loans failed simultaneously. The collapse of AIG did not merely have ramifications for the company itself; it also had implications for investors on the other side of the CDS contracts. With AIG unable to pay out on CDSs, loans that had formerly seemed safe (mostly because they were secured by an A-rated firm like AIG) experienced waves of default. Overexposure had implications for AIG *and* every firm relying on CDSs. Without safeguards, systemic risks proliferate.

Although many works have stressed a link between competitiveness concerns and deregulation, few explore how the structure of global finance shapes competition. Let us turn now to some key questions, such as "What is financial power?" and "Why do leading economies reap the lion's share of structural benefits from the system?" and "What are the consequences of losing global leadership?"

What Is Financial Leadership?

Today, vast amounts of investment capital and money flow across international borders. At first glance, capital flows seem to be driven mostly by market forces. In the unit on exchange rates in most introductory economics classes, students grapple with questions like "How will a decline in global demand for bananas impact the Philippine peso?" But many aspects of the flow of capital and money are difficult to square with market forces. For instance, why is the dollar such a popular reserve currency? Why do American investors earn such high returns compared to others? Is that *just* a function of the financial rectitude and economic size of the United States, or is something else at play?

A smooth-functioning global economy requires governance. At a minimum, free trade and investment require the protection of goods in transit and the protection of global property rights (North 1990). It can also help if states have a shared medium (or media) of exchange. In times of crisis, the system benefits from the existence of a lender of last resort as well as a market for distress goods (Kindleberger 1973). We also benefit from shared standards, rules, or forums for cooperation and coordination. Market decisions may drive the world economy, but those decisions hinge on the presence of the US navy, the reserve power of the US dollar, the existence of the IMF, and coordination within organizations like the Group of Seven (G7) and Group of Twenty. Global finance is a system, and it is a governed system.

Decisions must be made about which currencies become reserve currencies, whose sea lanes are open, what terms should drive lender-of-last-resort operations, and what rules should govern international institutions. To understand power within those systems, it is useful to distinguish between relational and structural power. *Relational power* is the ability to use direct coercion to encourage people to do things that they would not otherwise want to do (Dahl 1957). *Structural power* is the ability to influence others by altering the structure of incentives and payoffs (Strange 1988; Cohen 2015, 38–41). In a sense, relational power is that within a system, whereas structural power is the power to alter the nature of the system itself. The leading economy is frequently the state with the greatest *relational power* capabilities – an edge in high-tech production, a preponderance of global-reach capabilities, and the most vibrant domestic financial system. By offering privileged positions to other states – for example, the Group of Five (G5) today – however, the lead economy gains the contributions of others to global governance. By controlling membership in the "winner's circle," and the rules of decision-making, the lead economy also exercises *structural power* over others. Often this leads to a system centred on the lead economy, with others using its currency as a reserve, capital markets clustering in its biggest cities, and global financial networks sprawling out from a lead-economy hub. Let us expand on each of these elements of the system.

Many actors, including countries, firms, and non-governmental organizations, would love to have influence over the rules of the global financial system because, with apologies to American bank robber Willie Sutton, "That's where the money is." How, exactly, is the global financial system governed? Hegemonic stability theory posits that the prerequisites (e.g., open seas, a shared medium of exchange, etc.) of a stable global economy are public goods (Kindleberger 1973). Public goods are *non-rival* in consumption (my consumption does not take away from your ability to consume a good) and non-excludable (it is difficult to exclude others from enjoying their benefits) (Ostrom 2005, 24). Because actors can enjoy the benefits of public goods without footing the bill, free-riding is rampant. Drawing on Mancur Olson's ([1965] 1993) idea that the free-rider problem could be overcome by privileged groups, Kindleberger argued that a hegemonic state was the ultimate privileged group. A hegemon is a state so powerful, and able to reap so much of the benefits of a smooth-functioning global economy, that it will foot the bill of global leadership. Periods of history dominated by hegemonic actors, then, would tend to be more stable, while those without hegemony tend to be less stable.

Other works, though agreeing with the idea that global financial governance is shaped by the rise and decline of hegemons or system leaders, describe power structures in more precise ways than Kindleberger. Power over the global financial system, rather than being a singular capacity, exists as a series of complementary attributes. For the leadership long cycle (Modelski and Thompson 1996), technological innovation leads to naval preponderance. Command over the vital arteries of world trade grants states immense power to build global orders. The World-Systems school (Wallerstein 1974; Arrighi 1994) puts a Marxist spin on the story, but, similarly, looks at how powerful states in the industrialized core parlayed economic advantages into military strength, in turn facilitating greater exploitation of those on the less developed periphery. Technological diffusion and overexpansion variously act as limiting factors, giving power a cyclical nature (Gilpin 1981).

Are leader-hegemons really lonely Atlases holding up the world on their shoulders? Some scholars question whether a single hegemon is necessary to provide global public goods (Snidal 1985; Bailin 2005). Why can a cabal of powerful states not cooperate to provide public goods? Arguably, many of the public goods described by Kindleberger are not public goods but rather *club goods*. Club goods are those that are non-rival in consumption but excludable (Ostrom 2005, 24).[36] Can we exclude some countries from enjoying the freedom of the seas? Cubans might agree, in light of their long-standing embargo. Can a global lender of last resort choose to bail out some countries and not others? The degree of latitude that the IMF has over the countries seeking bailouts, and the great differences between the size and nature of IMF programs, suggest that rescues are far from automatic (Copelovitch 2010). Even the existence of a universal medium of exchange grants immense powers of exclusion to the holder of such capabilities. When the United States imposed a transaction ban on Russian banks in retaliation for Russia's invasion of the Crimea, Russian bank earnings fell 50 per cent (Rapoza 2016). The question of who gets to be inside the winner's circle is hotly contested by states and others seeking to advance their own narrow interests.

In addition to the fact that global governance is excludable, actors can earn structural benefits from their position within the global economy (Norloff 2010). Trade and finance benefit from a shared medium of exchange, which can lower transactions costs. At the same time, the country that controls the global supply of the reserve currency gains a great deal of leverage in the process.[37] In 1965, French Finance Minister Valéry Giscard d'Estaing complained bitterly about the "exorbitant privilege" of the American dollar. Even today, the United States runs current account deficits with limited adverse pressure on the dollar because of the desire of other countries to hold dollars in reserve (Eichengreen 2012).[38] Due to the dollar advantage, the interest paid by Americans on their overseas debt is lower than the returns achievable on long-term investment. By some estimates, the United States earns excess returns on investments of about 3 per cent by "borrowing short and investing long" (Gourinchas and Rey 2007). Schwartz (2009) argues that the United States enjoyed a growth premium over others for an extended period due to these advantages. In other words, American financial leadership did not just make Americans richer; it made Americans richer in ways that no other country could replicate, thereby reinforcing American power in a relative sense.

What factors enable states to dominate the global monetary system? Many works discuss the presence of regularized interstate competition for dominance (Cohen 2004; Katada 2008; McNamara 2008; Chinn and Frankel 2008). Some, such as Kirschner (1997), focus more narrowly on how states might employ reserves as a weapon vis-à-vis one another. For instance, in the interwar period, British policymakers feared that the French central bank would exchange its holdings of sterling for gold, thereby draining British reserves and causing the collapse of the pound. However, monetary power is about more than just reserves. Others have developed broader indices of state capabilities in the financial arena. Norloff (2010) emphasizes GDP, trade volume, capital-market openness, and defence expenditures. Armijo, Mülich, and Tirone (2014) include shares of global output, population, measures of technology, military spending, and reserves in their own index of financial power. Roberts, Elliott Armijo, and Katada (2017) develop this line of analysis further, examining the range of strategies that the BRICS countries (Brazil, Russia, India, China, and South Africa) are using to turn their new-found material capabilities into influence over global economic policy.

The nature of monetary power may not always be easily understood as bilateral or unidirectional. The existence of a monetary system requires the participation of many actors – competitive tensions exist alongside complex, interdependent relationships. Does the reserve currency status of the dollar give the United States power over China, or does China's possession of vast dollar reserves give China influence over the United States? For Cohen (2015, 48–76), the latter is clearly true. The United States runs large current account deficits because it can. Cohen sees monetary power as the ability to delay and deflect adjustments. Although some countries possess extensive reserves or a great capacity to borrow, the power to deflect owes to deeper, structural variables. Similarly, Oatley et al. (2013) argue that structural power in global finance can be captured by centrality in global networks of financial flows. Relatively small advantages in financial fitness might lead to global financial networks clustering around a few key economies. Once financial networks are established, change may be difficult due to the strong network externalities enjoyed by the most central state. For instance, despite the rise of China, Britain is still the second-most central power in global networks of capital flows. Those emphasizing structural power tend to be more bullish on continued American financial leadership, while those looking at material capabilities are more inclined to see possibilities for the rise of the BRICS.

Sometimes the practice of financial realpolitik undermines global financial stability. For instance, Helleiner (1996) argues that the United States pushed for a world of free-flowing capital after the collapse of the Bretton Woods system, in part, so that other countries would have to maintain dollar reserves in the face of major fluctuations. Alternatively, Oatley (2015) offers a compelling story of how financial power can be abused by states. Defining *financial power* as the ability to borrow cheaply, Oatley examines how successive American governments used that power to foster booms with deficit-financed tax cuts and military spending. Financial crises have frequently occurred in the wake of such actions. To paraphrase Robert Mundell (1993, 10), with great powers come great currencies, but not necessarily great responsibility.

States may not always have the upper hand against firms, however. In his masterful history of sovereign debt, Tomz (2007) emphasizes the powerful disciplining influence of global capital. Yet it is not only indebted states that face the wrath of capital markets. Sobel (2012) describes the role of capital in facilitating hegemonic transitions between the powerful liberal hegemons through history (e.g., the Dutch Republic, Britain, and the United States).

IPE scholars of many stripes agree on a number of points. Decisions about global financial governance are dominated by relatively few states. States at the top (and possibly some interest groups in those states) gain structural benefits as a result of their position in the system. However, IPE theorists differ about the degree to which different types of power are connected to others. For some, financial, economic, and military power are interconnected. For others, financial power can be broken up into smaller categories. For some, relational capabilities can be transformed into structural power quickly; for others, not so much. Although there are minor disagreements among scholars, these are not fundamental disputes.

I propose an integrated understanding of financial power, one that encapsulates most of the sub-definitions of financial or monetary power, addresses the distinctions between relational and structural power, and accounts for the interactions among types of power across different subsystems (e.g., military versus financial). If we look at past history, some forms of power are more fungible than others. For instance, although the Soviet Union possessed nuclear weapons and the world's strongest land army for much of the period from 1949 to 1989, it was a minor player in global finance. Similarly, in 1820, China possessed a GDP twice the size of western Europe, and yet it exerted limited influence outside Asia (Maddison 2009).[39]

Some capabilities are clearly both complementary and fungible. The most economically influential states have followed a fairly consistent progression: domination of the production and export of high-technology goods,[40] then the development of powerful navies and air forces to patrol trade routes, and, finally, the investment of accrued wealth abroad (Modelski and Thompson 1996). Technology, power projection, and financial power are highly complementary capabilities. An advanced high-tech sector helps countries develop the most technically intensive forms of military power – namely, navies, air forces, and space power. Even if a state lacks the largest economy or army, by monopolizing global power projection capabilities, it can exert influence over long distances, while denying access to the global commons to others (Posen 2003).

Because few states are capable of producing high-tech goods, high-tech producers earn high margins on their goods. Profits generated by high-margin exports facilitate the accrual of vast reserves of capital. Technology diffuses over time, and, eventually, the advantages accrued by the initial innovators fade. However, by investing in rising economies, the technological leader can extend its lifespan. On the other hand, the countries offering investors the highest returns are often fraught with political risks (Lucas 1990). Expropriation, debt default, war, civil war, and contract violations remain serious risks for investors. Navies and air forces developed to protect trade routes can also be used to protect property internationally.[41] Technological prowess, naval and air power, and financial flows are the *capabilities* undergirding global financial leadership.

Yet the lead economy is more than just a state with great capabilities. As it becomes more and more central in global financial networks, structural benefits flow to it. Lead economies exercise power through the exercise of structural advantages, rather than through overt coercion. Wielding the threat of exclusion, they craft privileged groups – showering some states with advantages in exchange for patronage and cooperation. Today, for instance, the G7 occupies the winner's circle, although the United States may sometimes play it off against the BRICS countries (Stuenkel 2013). Indeed, American exclusion power is institutionally enshrined – when the IMF was created, the United States was granted enough votes to veto structural changes to the distribution of votes. At times, the leading economy may shirk its presumed duties, forcing costs on others. When an American balance-of-payments deficit threatened the Bretton Woods system in 1971, did Richard Nixon accept the tough medicine of deflationary policies to save the dollar? No, he closed the gold window and slapped tariffs on America's trading partners, forcing others to pay the cost of adjustment. American policymakers acted in a similar fashion a decade later, offloading the adjustment costs of an overvalued dollar onto Japan (Funabashi 1989). Global governance does not flow from the benign decrees of benevolent hegemons, but rather from the jockeying inside a cartel of powerful states. However, the lead economy – possessing the power of exclusion – exercises an outsized role inside that cartel.

Lead economies also offer useful points for convergence. Global economic governance involves many coordination games. The value of a global reserve currency depends largely on network externalities – a currency is useful when it will be accepted by many states.[42] When international conferences or organizations select a language of operation, it makes sense to select a language spoken by many of the powerful states whose attendance is desired. When states meet to agree on standards or conventions, and when organizations promote them, those standards proliferate. Capital seeks a capital. Global financial markets cluster in a small number of cities – and where better to cluster than inside the state with the currency used by the global financial system, control over membership of the most influential global cartels, and an unparalleled ability to exert force over distance (Cassis 2006).

Lead economies nudge the global system into coordinating around the standards and rules they prefer. Other states are likely to adopt policies that are compatible to the lead economy because they desire investment capital. Global institutions, disproportionately staffed by economists from the lead economy and governed by lead economy interests, amplify the coordinating effects. The use of conditionality by the IMF is perhaps the most obvious instance of institutions prompting policy convergence, though it is hardly alone. Capital-importing countries may also adopt similar institutions to the leader to benefit from network externalities. Consider, for instance, the emphasis of many institutions on "anti-corruption" measures that often entail adoption of American common-law legal traditions (Kelemen and Sibbit 2004).

Other states often adopt policies that are complementary to those of the lead economy. Since the lead economy is the producer of desirable high-tech goods and a ubiquitous investor, its currency is likely to be widely accepted. Because the reach capabilities of lead economies are strong, they can exert influence over distant regions. Consider Saudi Arabia's denomination of sales of oil in dollars – a decision that vastly increases the desirability of the dollar as a reserve currency. In exchange, American foreign policy in the Middle East frequently supports Saudi objectives – most notably, the organization of a coalition to defeat Saddam Hussein in 1991 (Spiro 1999). Other states cannot similarly woo client states because they lack the necessary power projection capabilities. Certainly, states can form monetary blocs that enhance the desirability of their own currencies – the French-led Latin Monetary Union in the nineteenth century and the contemporary eurozone are historical examples. In neither case, however, did the rival currency bloc supplant the lead economy's currency from its place in the global order (Gallarotti 1995; Einaudi 2001; Cohen 2012).

Realists depict international relations as a knife fight, with victory going to the person with the biggest *gun*. John Law and Alexander Hamilton notwithstanding, the battle for global financial leadership is

Table 2.1. Lead Economies and Major Challengers, 1846–2016

Lead economy	Significant challengers
Britain, 1846–1938	France, 1852–70
	United States, 1913–38
United States, 1939–	Japan, 1981–94
	Britain, 1986–2000

not a duel. Rather, global financial competition is more like a prom in an American high school.[43] Aspiring prom kings and queens need great capabilities to crush their opponents. However, they also need to occupy strategic locations in social networks. Moreover, they need the competition to show up so they get something out of their victory. Global finance is similar – aspirants might cooperate in the construction of an open financial order even as they compete vigorously to ensure that they get the most out of that order. The states with the strongest capabilities, and particularly the greatest centrality to the financial system, gain significant structural advantages. However, should their capabilities wane, others may prove able to usurp their position. I will refer to the economies that most successfully innovate, export capital, and command the global commons as *lead economies*. Other economies that, while not at the apex of the system, could conceivably have supplanted the leader I will refer to as *challengers*. Table 2.1 summarizes the list of lead economies and their principal challengers[44] through history, drawing on the data on foreign-investment assets in the previous chapter.

The Causes and Consequences of Decline

How does the international system respond to fluctuations in the distribution of financial power? The lead economy's structural advantages can be lost if another state becomes a more obvious focal point for global economic flows. Innovations tend to diffuse over time. Other states can reverse-engineer or license advanced technology and may even exceed the productivity of the lead economy. Alternatively, new technological paradigms might emerge that disfavour the incumbent lead economy. In time, technological diffusion allows others to challenge the incumbent lead economy.

   Initial innovators do not always gain the most from their inventions. Consider the synthetic dye industry – a precursor to the chemical industry. Before the middle of the nineteenth century, dyes for textiles were produced from natural sources. For instance, indigo plantations grew crops from which blue dyes might be derived. Although synthetic dyes were invented in Britain, a lack of industry–academic ties, strict patent laws, and considerable investment in natural dyes prevented Britain from becoming the leading producer (Murmann 2003). Rather, Germany had superior institutions for the development of the synthetic dye industry. Similarly, the United States excelled in implementing Fordist mass-production techniques in the first half of the twentieth century. However, it was difficult for it to compete with a country like Japan, which could employ assembly-line workers trained in calculus, thereby enabling the use of techniques like just-in-time inventory management. By the 1980s, Japan and Germany had overtaken the United States in many industries like steel, automobiles, and electronics, aided in part by institutional features better suited to those industries (Moe 2007; Hart 1992).

Even as lead economies are challenged by others in high-tech production, they can transform themselves from the workshop of the world to the world's banker. Lead economies accumulate substantial wealth during their ascendancies. By investing that wealth abroad, they can profit from the rise of others. By constructing dense networks of global finance, lead economies can enhance their structural power. For instance, even as British industry fell behind Germany and the United States in the late nineteenth century, British investors gained from the rise of industrial America (Kennedy 1987). The centrality of London to global financial markets enabled the City to earn massive profits by managing the trade acceptances market.

The lead economy cannot live on its "inheritance" forever. As other states catch up economically, they too grow wealthy and less dependent on foreign finance. As other states accumulate capital, they too may become capital-exporting states. France made such a transition in the 1850s, the United States in the 1910s, and Japan in the 1980s. Challengers face down the incumbent lead economy at an initial disadvantage. However, they may be able to carve out blocs of dependent states (e.g., the French-led Latin Monetary Union) or clusters of institutions (e.g., the BRICS-led New Development Bank) by offering greater benefits or more compatible policies for participants.

The consequences of relative economic decline are dire. Even if the lead economy is prosperous in an absolute sense, the expectations of lead-economy electorates are difficult for politicians to satisfy. Voters may wax nostalgic about a past golden age that politicians will never be able to reproduce. Businesses exposed to international competition and financial firms will complain about waning competitiveness. Military leaders may find it ever harder to match the military strength of rivals. Leaders may find it ever more difficult to exercise influence over institutions that were once pliable. Many of the innate advantages of lead-economy financial institutions (e.g., experience in the types of transaction that cluster in the lead economy, like trade acceptances in the early twentieth century) may diffuse, as other financial centres grow larger. Weakening material conditions threaten the structural advantages of financial leadership. For the lead economy, the loss of the top-loaded structural benefits of global leadership is a terrifying prospect.

The costs of lost global leadership are not merely political; they are also existential. The loss of economic leadership to geopolitical rivals has often presaged military action (Copeland 2000). Yet even the loss of leadership to a friend is risky. Allies may prove unreliable in times of need (Leeds 2003), and every state is potentially vulnerable to regime change. For instance, the efforts of French diplomats to build an alliance with Russia before the First World War were rendered obsolete overnight by the Russian Revolution of 1917. Moreover, even an ally may have starkly different preferences about how to run the world. While in many respects the Anglo-American leadership transition was a soft landing for Britain, a world led by the United States entailed the explicit rejection of British imperialism. Lead economies are likely to exert heroic efforts to avoid decline.

How Do Lead Economies (and Challengers) Respond to Decline?

Imagine that you are a leader struggling to keep pace with rivals in naval construction in the face of strict budget constraints. Perhaps you were elected on a pledge to make your country great again. Captains of industry and CEOs of major banks – critical donors all – are breathing down your neck, demanding that you take national competitiveness seriously. What if I told you that it was possible to solve all these problems at once? What if I told you that such results could be accomplished without additional sacrifices by constituents? Like a fund manager desperately seeking to increase returns, or a hockey coach down by two goals in the third period, you can win greater returns at the cost of greater risks. Fund managers can increase returns by making riskier investments, hockey coaches can pull the goalie, and governments can increase growth and innovation by reforming financial regulation and accepting greater risks. In this section, I discuss why financial reform is difficult in ordinary times, but common as a response to decline. Moreover, I explain why deregulation often goes further than intended.

Debates about financial deregulation are typically dominated by the trade-off between growth and stability. In ordinary times, it makes sense to favour stability because incumbent firms prefer the status quo. Regulatory orders – the clusters of complementary rules, institutions, and domestic actors that work together to uphold a set of financial regulations – are politically robust because they develop political ecosystems around them. In many respects, financial reform is akin to constitutional reform. The rules governing finance determine which firms receive capital and, in turn, are able to jockey governments into action. Because financial regulation determines the shape of the domestic economy, regulatory decisions *also* influence the balance of power among different economic interest groups within a polity. For instance, a country with tight financial regulations may tend to funnel capital to established industries, while a country with lax regulations may finance high-risk, high-return enterprises. Whichever group receives the lion's share of financing will also be in the best position to influence government decisions. However, firms are unlikely to lobby against the rules that enabled them to be successful in the first place.

What is true of the downstream recipients of capital is even truer for financial firms themselves – regulations shape their interests. *Ceteris paribus*, financial firms prefer laxer regulation than the general public. However, financial firms also dislike competition from other financial firms. As a result, financial regulations that determine the degree of specialization and scope among financial firms can also influence the preferences of financial firms. In a specialized system, it is difficult to get the financial industry as a whole to agree to reforms. For instance, it took two decades to repeal the Glass–Steagall Act, despite consistent administrative support, because banking, securities, and insurance firms wanted deregulation on their own terms (Suarez and Kolodny 2011).

Regulators, too, have an interest in maintaining the status quo. The primary source of power for regulators is expertise, and expertise is intrinsically related to the status quo (Barnett and Finnemore 2004). Radical shifts in the nature of an economy could result in the redistribution of responsibilities among different regulatory agencies and resultant turf wars. For instance, the Reagan administration avoided creating supportive legal infrastructure for over-the-counter (OTC) derivatives in the 1980s out of fears of a turf war between the SEC and the Commodity Futures Trading Commission (CFTC) (more on this in chapter 5).

Lead-economy decline imposes costs on some domestic political actors, prompting them to support efforts to avert the decline. The structural benefits of global financial leadership are distributed unequally across constituencies inside a country. Sometimes the beneficiaries are direct – for instance, the London financial firms that dominated the nineteenth-century trade acceptances market were obvious beneficiaries of British financial leadership. Some constituencies are indirect beneficiaries of the structural benefits of global leadership. For instance, during the 1980s, the SIA swung towards support of a repeal of Glass–Steagall, emphasizing that although it was concerned about increased competition from American commercial banks, it was more important to preserve American economic leadership (Reinicke 1995).

Oatley and Petrova (2016) find evidence that the financialization of the American economy tracks closely with the expanded use of American dollars as reserves, suggesting that the American financial sector disproportionately benefits from American leadership. There may also be bureaucratic interests tied to the pursuit and maintenance of financial leadership. For instance, much has been written about the idea of a City–Treasury compact in Britain, wherein Whitehall bureaucrats came to see the priorities of the financial sector synonymously with the national interest. Goldman Sachs, similarly, has earned the nickname "Government Sachs" for its ability to employ former executives in government. Decline can galvanize divergent actors behind a common agenda: revitalization. It is often easier to sell a revitalization agenda as serving the broader national interests than to advocate for financial reform on other grounds.

Deregulation can be a useful component of revitalization strategies. Financial deregulation is rarely a salient issue among ordinary voters. The benefits (e.g., stock market booms, expansions of credit) tend to occur up front, while the costs (greater risks of financial crises) occur later. What is more, deregulation may actually work. Entrepreneurs seeking capital for innovative, paradigm-challenging ideas that drive productivity improvements often experience difficulties in a restricted financial system (Perez 2002; Rajan and Zingales 2004; Beck et al. 2008). Established financial firms rarely finance emergent industries because it is difficult to know whether a paradigm-shifting innovation will play out as expected. Incumbent financial firms will have evolved alongside the last technological revolution, not the next one. For instance, consider the emergence of Silicon Valley as the hub of the information revolution. At first, few established financial actors were willing to invest in companies like Apple or Microsoft. Over time, however, venture capital markets developed, capable of finding and financing such enterprises. Every great technological paradigm shift has been accompanied by the development of financial innovations that are able to infuse new-industry firms with capital (Freeman and Soete 1996).

Even if deregulation fails to spark a renaissance of innovation, lax regulations can restore the vitality of the lead economy's financial markets. Unlike other industries, capital is highly mobile, and firms can easily move to avoid regulatory costs. Deregulation can also expand the pool of capital available for investment. For instance, the introduction of limited liability banking laws in Britain encouraged companies to take on smaller investors to purchase shares in companies (Alborn 1998). Financial institutions themselves, freed from restrictions on leverage (or requirements to disclose their leverage) can also lend and invest at higher rates. In addition, the elimination of restrictions on international capital flows can enhance the centrality of the lead economy in global markets, amplifying structural benefits and potentially compensating for low growth rates.

But financial deregulation can be a slippery slope. When states remove regulatory safeguards, they disrupt a *political* equilibrium. Absent regulation, more capital is able to flow towards risky enterprises, which can grow and expand their influence. Other firms may see their interests evolve in the new environment, further expanding the constituency favourable to deregulation. For instance, France overhauled its regulatory system in the 1850s, creating large limited liability investment banks like the Crédit Mobilier, which put pressure on traditional banking houses like the Rothschilds. Unable to earn the same returns as the Crédit Mobilier, the Rothschilds adopted similar strategies themselves, forming a new investment bank in Austria (Cameron 1953, 468). Similarly, in the United States, deregulation transformed S&Ls from one of the most risk-averse actors to one of the most risk-acceptant. Unscrupulous or fraudulent firms, operating at the edge of what is allowable, may set the pace of the market as a whole. Frustrated board members may ask their CEO why their firm is not doing as well as the City of Glasgow Bank, AIG, or Bernie Madoff. Long-term risks may eventually manifest as bank runs, but until they do, financial-sector actors face pressure to emulate rather poor role models. When more domestic actors become risk-acceptant, the coalition favouring deregulation will expand. In other words, deregulation creates a new political equilibrium, setting the stage for further deregulation (Hammond and Knott 1988).

Processes of emulation and competition play out internationally as well as domestically. When lead economies loosen capital controls to expand the structural benefits of global leadership, they are painting a target on themselves. Other states envy the benefits of the lead economy and may foment financial revolutions of their own. Is it a coincidence that the United States overcame decades of suspicion of central banking at the very peak of the London acceptances market?[45] Due to the centrality of the lead economy, deregulation tends to diffuse as other states compete for capital (Simmons and Elkin 2004). Other states may simply imitate those policies prevailing in the core of the global economy, perhaps abetted by international institutions promoting "governance standards" (Henisz, Zelner, and Guillén 2005). Not only does the diffusion of deregulation open up new channels for crises to spread, but convergence around a narrower set of policies also undermines the robustness of the overall financial system. Just as monoculture increases the vulnerability of crops to disease, the diffusion of regulatory standards can spread designs rife with serious flaws. As much of the world rolls back safeguards simultaneously, crises become more probable, more severe, and more viral.

States are most likely to engage in competitive deregulation when they have a shot at winning the structural benefits of leadership for themselves. Imagine a race with an extremely top-loaded reward structure: ten million dollars for first place, while all others win nothing. If a runner was in contention for first place, they might do anything to give themselves an edge – including taking risky gambits like using steroids. Even if they were personally disinclined to use steroids, the knowledge that their competitors faced similar pressures might prove convincing. A flatter reward structure would weaken the pressure to take risks. For example, in professional golf tournaments, all contestants receive prizes, so the marginal gain of moving from fourth to third place is not especially large. Doping scandals in the Professional Golfers' Association, as far as I know, are less common than in sports like Olympic running, where medallists receive the lion's share of the glory. Steroid use might be disincentivized by the presence of a dominant competitor – one so dominant that even steroid use would not put others in striking distance of first place. I believe that this is where perceptions of "hegemonic stability" come from. Hegemons do not stabilize the system through overt actions (e.g., investment in public goods); rather, they promote stability by making risky competition fruitless for challengers. This is why, historically, we can see evidence of races to the bottom in the 1850s–60s, the 1910s–20s, and the 1980s–90s, but not during intervening decades.

When the leading economies engage in regulatory competition, the rest of the world is caught in the downward spiral. Newly deregulated firms may use their expanded freedom to invest abroad. As firms invest abroad, they gain clout, with which they can encourage host countries to implement policies that are compatible with their interests. Global institutions – dominated by the lead economy and its major challengers – may be retooled to make the world safe for speculative capital. Consider, for instance, the role of the IMF – not only can it help ensure that debts are repaid to international lenders amid a crisis, but it can also demand investor-friendly conditions (e.g., the elimination of capital controls) by borrower states (Gould 2006). Additionally, as global institutions develop expertise to accomplish specialized missions, they, too, influence the perceptions of best practices. Even without action by international institutions, lead economies and challengers themselves are powerful examples of successful economies. Other states will emulate their practices, seeking similar results. In short, there are economic, political, and ideational channels by which competitive deregulation by the most powerful states diffuses to the rest of the world.

International Regulation

International regulation has been floated as a potential solution to the twin dilemmas of sagging competitiveness and a rising risk of crises. States can come together to propose *global* regulatory standards rather than national ones. Lead economies may be able to use their structural power to insist on global standards favouring their institutional mixes. For instance, with the 1987 Basel Capital Accords, British and American policymakers coerced Japan into adopting a scheme whereby states agreed to limit the risk-weighted leverage ratios of their financial firms (Oatley and Nabors 1998; Singer 2007). The scheme undermined Japan's more heavily leveraged financial institutions, while not imposing burdens on the United States or Britain.

International regulation is not a magic bullet, however. International cooperation is often a fair-weather friend to stability. The lead economy's ability to coerce others is likely to be weakest precisely when the need for negotiated alternatives to regulatory competition is greatest. The competitiveness concerns of lead economies and their major challengers may also result in an insistence on inadequate or even deficient global solutions.

Notably, the Basel capital rules failed to prevent the 1997 East Asian crisis or the 2008 financial crisis. Enforcement of the agreement is weak, and many states did not take much action to reduce leverage ratios despite being party to the Accords (Quillin 2008). Faced with a simple number, such as the capital adequacy ratio, firms will find ways to game the system (Turner 2014). They may even lobby their home governments to insist on exceptions that create loopholes. For instance, Admati and Hellwig (2013, 169–91) argue that the practice of risk-weighting gives financial institutions a substantial informational advantage over regulators because it is their experience that informs understandings of which activities are risky and which are not. In a sense, the simple declaration that an activity is "low risk" may open up opportunities for that distinction to be gamed. At any rate, the kinds of restrictions that states have been able to agree upon internationally are not very stringent. Basel III, formulated in the wake of the 2008 financial crisis, requires only that firms set aside 3 per cent of their equity – one-tenth of the amount recommended by Admati and Hellwig. Indeed, if one looks at the behaviour of financial institutions, most cluster well above the regulatory minimum, suggesting that global standards lag even the preferences of the firms they are meant to rein in (Winecoff 2017).

Conclusion

Putting the ideas of this chapter together, we can see why some eras experienced the widespread abandonment of regulatory safeguards and severe financial crises. The global economy is more than a big flea market – it is bound together by a political structure. Historically, lead economies have arisen and led that structure, first by leading in technology and industrial output. Later, they served as the world's banker, while also developing powerful navies capable of commanding the arteries of global commerce and finance. Lead economies can thus use their central position to structure the global economy in their favour, although they may share the spoils with others.

When lead economies experience declining technological and financial competitiveness, they frequently turn to risky policy options. Freeing up international capital flows allows them to wring more out of their structural position. Other forms of financial deregulation increase the attractiveness of financial centres inside the lead economy. New financial instruments may also revitalize techno-industrial competitiveness by financing innovative enterprises. Decline creates opportunities for challengers, who may adopt deregulatory policies in a quest to take economic leadership for themselves. Competitive deregulation among the world's largest and most central economies diffuses further through a mix of competitive and imitative processes, aided by institutions dominated by lead-economy interests. In short, lead-economy decline pushes the global economy towards deregulation. Like a snowball falling down a snowy hill, deregulation grows larger through a host of diffusive mechanisms.

As many countries remove safeguards, the vulnerability of the global system to bubbles, manias, panics, and crashes intensifies. Credit booms encourage firms to take large, and often levered, risks (Kindleberger 1978; Schularick and Taylor 2012). Feedback mechanisms strengthen the bona fides of the biggest risk-takers, perhaps shoring up some new-era paradigm (Shiller 2005; Nelson and Katzenstein 2014). As expectations of returns increase, even Ponzi schemes can seem credible. Credit expands internationally as well as domestically. Growth in international capital flows offers countries the prospect of rapid growth. Temptations abound for policymakers. As countries liberalize their financial markets, they may also peg their currencies at rates, inflated by hot money, that will prove difficult to defend later (Stein and Streb 2004). In the lead economy, politicians may be tempted to take advantage of their exorbitant privilege and run big deficits to pay for bread and circuses ... or bombs and tax cuts, as the case may be (Eichengreen 2012; Oatley 2015). Under these conditions, global imbalances will proliferate.

Eventually, the music stops. When highly leveraged firms collapse, chaos ensues among their creditors. Collapses diminish the risk appetite of lenders, who become more reluctant to lend out funds (Minsky 1992). Some firms that were able to borrow to keep operations going in good times fold. Others that could service debt in good times find themselves unable to do so in tighter credit markets – they have become Ponzi schemes. As more firms collapse, credit markets tighten further. In a globally interlinked market, the shock waves are not simply domestic either. Like a virus, financial crises can spread, engulfing the entire international system. Capital flight from one country can spark flight from others. In a dark twist, capital often flies to safe harbours – and nowhere is safer than the lead economy.

Chapter Three

The Great Deregulation of the 1850s

Today, one could run multiple companies into the ground while remaining a billionaire thanks to *limited liability*. When companies go bankrupt, creditors carve up the assets of the company itself, but not the private fortunes of company directors or shareholders. Before 1855, *unlimited liability* was the rule of the day in Britain – the lead economy of the nineteenth century. All shareholders were responsible for the liabilities of bankrupt corporations, even if they had no hand in running the company. An inability to pay debt came with steep punishments as well, including debtor's prison. In effect, unlimited liability represented a powerful regulatory tool, aimed at preventing firms from gambling with investor capital. Even where limited liability corporate forms were available, such as in France, regulations often restricted firms from having access to riskier corporate forms.

This chapter tells the tale of how new, often highly leveraged, limited liability corporations and banks proliferated in France and Britain during the 1850s and 1860s. In the middle of the nineteenth century, major financial reforms shook up the global pecking order, challenging British leadership. In France, Louis-Napoléon[46] dreamed of achieving by peaceful means what his uncle had won by arms: a European order centred around a dominant France. Guided by a Saint-Simonian dream of massive banks mobilizing capital to build a network of infrastructure, he would later, as Napoléon III, spark a financial revolution with the creation of the Crédit Mobilier.

Shocked by a resurgent France, British policymakers launched reforms of their own, repealing stringent financial regulations and liberalizing limited liability. British regulatory rollbacks triggered similar actions by France, while other countries adopted similar, limited liability firms. While the business cycle was friendly, big speculative bets seemed to pay off. Yet as the business cycle became ugly, highly

Table 3.1. British and French Financial Reforms, 1844–70

	Britain	France
Plateau (1844–50)	**1844: Joint Stock Bank Act and Joint Stock Companies Registration and Regulation Act strictly regulate financial sector** *1846: Repeal of Corn Laws launches nineteenth-century era of globalization*	**1844–50: Existence of diverse corporate forms (including limited liability), but strictly regulated by *Conseil d'Etat*; banking dominated by merchant banks**
Competition (1851–70)	*1855: Limited Liability Act allows formation of joint-stock companies 1856: More expansive Joint Stock Companies Act grants limited liability and repeals older safeguards 1858: Limited liability extended to banks, with minimum share denominations of £100 1862: Minimum-share rules repealed, limited liability extended to insurance companies*	*1851: Crédit Mobilier created Ongoing: Rothschilds and others (e.g., Crédit Lyonnais) emulate Crédit Mobilier 1863: French government creates société à responsabilité limitée: limited liability corporation with capitalization ceiling 1867: Companies freely able to form limited liability société anonyme (with no capitalization ceiling)*

leveraged firms began to collapse like flies, triggering a series of severe financial crises, and protracted economic pain, culminating in the crash of the Crédit Mobilier in France and Overend Gurney in Britain as well as the series of global crises of the 1873–96 Long Depression. Table 3.1 summarizes the major regulatory reforms in Britain and France during this period.

The Origins of the Joint Stock Bank Act

In the nineteenth century, Britain underwent both an industrial revolution and a *financial* revolution. As the "dark satanic mills" of Blake's ([1804] 2008, 95) prose filled the lungs of workers with coal dust and the railroad transformed long-standing communities, financial innovations also created new challenges. The way that speculation might instantaneously create and break fortunes is well chronicled in the popular writing of the day. In Dickens's *Martin Chuzzlewit*, one can follow the rise and fall of the Anglo-Bengalee Disinterested Loan and Life Assurance Company, a Ponzi scheme luring in many with the promise of riches. In Trollope's (1858) *The Three Clerks*, one can read the cautionary tale of Alaric Tudor, an ambitious civil servant corrupted by speculation in the shares of a mining company under his regulatory purview.

Although speculation retained a grubby reputation, it was a prominent feature of British life nonetheless.

Britain emerged victorious from the Napoleonic Wars. However, twenty-five years of warfare against the greatest military mind in history had not come cheap. Heavy debt coupled with deflationary policies at the Bank of England produced hard times – real per capita incomes fell 12 per cent from 1815 to 1819 (Neal 1998; Maddison 2013). In 1822, the Bank of England reversed its deflationary course, stirring the speculative appetites of British financial markets. As numerous Latin American states won independence from Spain, London traders hawked sovereign bonds (Chancellor 1999, 96–121). Many of these bonds were of dubious quality – one audacious swindler even floated a bond issue for the fictional Republic of Poyais. Investors – many with allies in Parliament – sought to stoke the frenzy even further (Harris 1997). The Bubble Act, passed a century before to stop the formation of speculative joint-stock companies,[47] was repealed. As many of the underlying assets being traded were revealed as fraudulent or dubious, British markets were beset by panic in 1825. In the next few years, the resultant crash spread to the United States, the Netherlands, Italy, Germany, and Austria – perhaps the first instance of a coordinated global financial crisis unrelated to a war (Neal 1998).[48]

Despite the crash of 1825, the powers afforded joint-stock banks were expanded when the Bank of England Charter was renewed in 1833. Looser rules produced a boom in bank formation, with the number of joint-stock banks jumping from 57 to 113 by 1836 (Cottrell and Newton 1999, 84). The epicentre of the boom was Lancashire, Yorkshire, and other towns where the Industrial Revolution was taking off (Chapman 1979). Many of the new banks collapsed soon after, having lied to depositors about their financial conditions. By 1843, 24 banks had disappeared, and many others were under great duress (Cottrell and Newton 1999, 84).

A third wave of speculative frenzy took place in the rail industry. Much like the "new era" mentality that drove the dot-com bubble in 1999–2000 (or the Canal Mania of the 1790s), the steam engine offered myriad prospects for economic transformation (Perez 2002). Railroads, steamships, and the telegraph promised to conquer distance. Speculative technologies, such as the horseless carriage or Charles Babbage's "difference engine" (a mechanical computer), might achieve even more. For an empire on which "the sun never set," a revolution in communications and transportation technology was an immense boon. Cheaper transport costs enabled intensified economic specialization inside the empire, increasing output. Investors were dazzled by the possibilities of the steam age. By 1849, railroad stocks comprised 73 per cent of the market capitalization of the LSE (Acheson et al. 2009). While the economic promise of the railroad was great, investors overbuilt, and many rail lines were unprofitable due to excess competition. As railroads began to collapse, the British economy swung once again into a deep recession (Odlyzko 2010).

As British policymakers considered how to underwrite the Industrial Revolution without provoking financial crises, deep divisions crystallized over financial reform. Some favoured loosening the rules on the financial system. Radical MPs and some Whigs supported the expansion of joint-stock banking and the extension of limited liability privileges. Politically, such representatives were closer to the interests of the rising industrialists and newly industrializing areas. Joint-stock banks were critical to financing new mills, while also providing access to banking services for working-class individuals. Some advocates drew intellectual succour from the well of laissez-faire ideas. Others, including John Stuart Mill, favoured limited liability as a means of democratizing the capital markets (Alborn 1998; Loftus 2002). Companies were often reluctant to take on working- or middle-class subscribers, whose personal assets would be insufficient to pay off company debt in the event of bankruptcy.

Following the joint-stock company bust of the 1830s, the debate over financial reform measures intensified. In 1837, a parliamentary committee investigated the desirability of limited liability rules. The committee consulted thirteen individuals, including lawyers, bankers, and academics. Those advocating for limited liability argued that the country needed more capital. They included some illustrious figures, such as Lord Ashburton and George Warde Norman. Before receiving his peerage, Lord Ashburton had been Alexander Baring of the British banking house later nicknamed "the sixth great power" (Ziegler 1988). A former president of the Board of Trade, and one of the practitioners of finance who also guided British banking policy, Ashburton was widely respected (Gordon 1979, 5–7). Commenting on his experience with limited liability *commandite* partnerships in France, he supported similar policies in Britain because "it would bring additional capital into commerce; it would favour the enterprise of men of talents with insufficient capital; and, generally speaking, under proper regulations, it would furnish sufficiently substantial and secure commercial establishments" (Britain. Parliament. House of Commons 1837, 46). Norman, a director of the Bank of England, also hailed from the upper echelon of the banking world. He defended against the idea that limited liability would lead to overtrading and also argued that there was a shortage of capital outside London. He noted, "In my immediate neighbourhood,

I could point out many tradesmen, honest, respectable men, with good connexions, who suffer greatly from want of capital, which they would probably obtain under an altered system; and farther from the metropolis the evil must be much greater" (36).

Limited liability advocates were outgunned by their opponents, however, because most respondents believed that British primacy was secure. The most common objection to limited liability was that it would lead to runaway speculation and overtrading. Kirkman Finlay, a prominent Scottish merchant, warned that "the greatest possible mischief might be expected to arise from its introduction now ... there is too much excitement and too much desire to embark in speculative adventures in the country." However, Finlay also qualified his statement, noting that it might have done some good in Scotland, fifty to one hundred years earlier, when capital was insufficient (Britain. Parliament. House of Commons 1837, 49). Thomas Tooke, an economist and businessman frequently consulted by Parliament on such matters, took a similar tack. He suggested that limited liability might make sense in France due to "the spirit of commercial enterprise being comparably languid" (33). However, in Britain, such encouragements were unnecessary – if anything, there was greater risk of overtrading and speculation. Indeed, the idea that Britain already had sufficient capital was widely cited by the bulk of the opponents of limited liability. Apart from fears of speculation and confidence in the superiority of the British financial system, the only other argument widely stressed was a normative one: that individuals had no right to claim profits without taking responsibility for the risks that an enterprise might fail.

The positions of the speakers on the parliamentary committee departed considerably from their parochial interests. The Barings and Normans were merchant bankers without depositors or shareholders, unlikely to take advantage of limited liability themselves. Indeed, the Barings Bank remained an unlimited liability concern until late in the nineteenth century. If anything, Finlay stood to gain the most as a business figure in a relatively capital-poor region. The absence of grand economic ideas from the debate, such as the principle of laissez-faire, is also striking. Rather, most speakers engaged in pragmatic assessment of the advantages and disadvantages of the policy. Implicitly, the thinking of the critics owed a great deal to Britain's comparative position in the world. In 1837, it was impossible to find peer competitors to the British economy. The risk of encouraging further speculation was simply not worth the upside. Indeed, with policymakers relatively confident of Britain's relative position, the regulatory pendulum was about to swing in a more prudential direction under Prime Minister Robert Peel.

Robert Peel is probably best known for overturning Britain's Corn Laws, a series of tariffs on imported wheat (Kindleberger 1975; Irwin 1989; Schonhardt-Bailey 2006). Although elected as a member of the Conservative Party, traditionally the protectionist party, he and a rump of "Peelites" broke from the Tories on trade, forming a free trade coalition with the Whigs (Schonhardt-Bailey 2006). As the world's most technologically advanced economy, Britain could gain by specializing in manufacturing while importing grain. Such an economic transition, however, was anathema to the economic interests of the landowning class, a mainstay of the party. The new policy of unilateral free trade is often accepted as the dawn of a nineteenth-century wave of globalization. Trade, foreign investment, and immigration all accelerated, eventually hitting a peak in 1913.

Despite his opposition to protectionism, Robert Peel was not a laissez-faire ideologue. Just as his "bobbies" imposed order in London, Peel reined in British financial markets. Surveying the wreckage after the 1836–7 joint-stock-banking crash, he brought in stringent rules to prevent another such event. Through the Joint Stock Companies Regulation and Registration Act of 1844, Peel created a process by which companies could register and form without parliamentary approval. However, this seemingly liberal offering was paired with a requirement that all partnerships with more than twenty-five people submit company reports and remain subject to audits – bringing large numbers of unincorporated companies into a regulatory structure (Harris 2000, 284). A separate piece of legislation was passed for banks in the same year. Under the Joint Stock Bank Act of 1844, banks had to obtain a charter every twenty years, maintain minimum levels of capital, and charge share prices that limited subscription by working-class investors. This was in addition to the Bank Charter Act of 1844, which removed the ability of banks to create private notes – shifting that power to the Bank of England (Turner 2014, 39–40; Grossman and Imai 2013). In short, in a Britain free from serious external challenges to its economic leadership, stringent regulations were politically viable (Harris 2000, 285–6).

Napoléon III and the French Financial Revolution

British confidence in its empire's military and economic security was about to face a serious challenge. The 1848 election victory and subsequent coup by Emperor Napoléon III frightened Britons fearful of the return of Britain's greatest nemesis. Yet Louis-Napoléon was not the same as his uncle – where Napoléon I had sought military hegemony, Napoléon III challenged British global leadership peacefully. During his exile and imprisonment, Louis-Napoléon was influenced by a set of thinkers following the ideas of the Count of Saint-Simon, including Michel Chevalier, Isaac Pereire, and Émile Pereire. The Saint-Simonians proposed an economic path to primacy. Specifically, this entailed building a massive investment bank capable of mobilizing capital to develop networks of railways, shipping lanes, and finance through the arteries of a Mediterranean system centred on Paris. Firmly ensconced, France could build global institutions that would enable it to achieve its own objectives.

The idea of the Mediterranean system is an exemplary case study on how states might seize the structural benefits of global leadership in an interconnected, networked world. However, French global ambitions posed two problems for global financial stability. First, the mobilization of capital on such a large scale involved overleveraged, risk-acceptant financial institutions like the Crédit Mobilier. Second, success breeds imitators, whether through adaptation or competitive pressure. If many other countries mirror the risky policies of the leading economic powers, the risk for systemic financial crises will be greatly enhanced.

In this section, I will discuss the emergence of a Saint-Simonian grand strategy of using large banks to mobilize capital, constructing transportation networks, and linking them together in the Mediterranean system. In effect, the Saint-Simonians were proposing ways to seize for themselves some of the structural benefits enjoyed by Britain. Following his coup of 1851, Napoléon III turned to a set of elites and thinkers distinct from those who had dominated the July Monarchy and the short-lived Second Republic. In part because of his own interest in the Saint-Simonian strategy and his desire to reduce the influence of the Paris *haute banque* over his government, he approved the Crédit Mobilier. The new limited liability firm revolutionized French finance, both domestically and internationally. Domestically, the new firm stimulated rapid, highly visible successes, although economic growth was not particularly rapid. In Europe, France became a major outward investor, while massive investments in transportation financed rail networks and shipping lanes centring on France. To defend this network, France increased naval spending as steamships rendered Britain's massive sailing fleet obsolete. In short, the launch of the French Second Empire represented a massive economic and geopolitical challenge to British power. Let us now turn to the first part of the story – why did Napoléon III turn to the Saint-Simonians?

"Complexion: pale. Head: sunken in his shoulders ... Back: bent" (Séguin 1990, 81) was how the 1840 prisoner manifest at the Château de Ham prison described Louis-Napoléon Bonaparte, their newest inmate. The nephew of Emperor Napoléon I, Louis-Napoléon had spent a great deal of time plotting to take power in France, with little success. Failed attempts to foment revolution had resulted in exile and, finally, to imprisonment in 1840. Both in exile and during his incarceration, Louis-Napoléon sought to develop a set of ideas that could define Bonapartism. One pamphlet written during his exile in England, *Des idées napoléoniennes*, cast Bonapartism as a cogent ideology, declaring that "the Napoleonic idea is not one of war, but a social, industrial, commercial idea, and one that concerns all of mankind" (Bonaparte 1839, 136). Much of the pamphlet was an *ex post* defence of Napoleonic policies. What had Napoléon ever done for the French? Dams, roads, canals, and schools featured prominently. Louis-Napoléon ended on a hopeful note, declaring that although France had been beaten on the battlefield, Napoleonic policies had left the French economy intact, while Britain was saddled with immense debt – Britain was vulnerable (133).

Despite the pamphlet's inadequacies, Louis-Napoléon sold 500,000 copies amid widespread dissatisfaction with the July Monarchy (Price 2001, 16). It was during his imprisonment in Ham, however, that Louis-Napoléon developed the ideas that would shape his economic policy into something more than nostalgia. In prison, the would-be usurper met with frequent visitors. His 1844 pamphlet, *Extinction du paupérisme*, focused on alleviating the lot of the poorer French through ambitious schemes, including the provision of cheap credit. The pamphlet bore the distinct mark of Saint-Simon.[49] Soon Louis-Napoléon would literally don the mantle of the working class – he disguised himself as a workman and escaped prison in 1846.

What was Saint-Simonism? Claude-Henri de Rouvroy, the Count of Saint-Simon, was an eclectic thinker with a motley group of followers. The alleviation of the suffering of the poor was one of his central goals. He also admired the ideas of Adam Smith and sought to create a "new Christianity" – all in a day's work. When he died in 1825, his followers continued writing in Saint-Simonian journals, developing his ideas further. One faction, led by Prosper Enfantin, emphasized the need for free love and equality between the sexes. The other – which influenced Louis-Napoléon – focused on economics. Two brothers, Émile and Isaac Pereire, participated frequently in these debates, with Émile writing for Saint-Simonian journals like *Organisateur* and *Le Globe*. Sephardic Jews from Bordeaux, the Pereire brothers were initially drawn to Saint-Simonism because of its tolerance for Jews. Born into a family bankrupted by a financial panic, the brothers understood the effects of credit shortages. In his writings, Émile advocated for the creation of a massive bank capable of mobilizing French capital.

In particular, the new bank could finance the construction of large-scale projects such as railroads (Davies 2016, 33–60). These arguments were complemented by the ideas of a second Saint-Simonian, Michel Chevalier. Chevalier envisioned the creation of railway networks and canals linking the port cities of the Mediterranean. He believed that the networked nature of transportation and communication could unite Europe (as well as the Middle East), forming the basis for perpetual peace. Naturally, the Mediterranean system would centre on France (Drolet 2015).

The July Monarchy clamped down on Saint-Simonism in 1832, leading to the imprisonment of some members, including Chevalier. Despite these setbacks, many followers gained influence in subsequent years. Fellow Saint-Simonian Gustave d'Eichthal put the Pereires in touch with James de Rothschild, head of a powerful banking dynasty and dominant figure in the *haute banque* (Davies 2016, 61–86). Cautious by nature, Rothschild was sceptical of railroad investment. However, the promise of the new industry was so great that, in the 1840s, he set aside his reservations. Chevalier continued writing and became a respected adviser to the July Monarchy. After visiting Mexico, the United States, and Canada, he wrote a book envisioning France as the protector of a Latin civilization. Fearing the encroachment of Protestantism in Latin America, he proposed a French-led reconstruction of Mexico. Some of Chevalier's other writings were more conventional. For instance, in *Des intérêts matériels en France: Travaux publics, routes, canaux, chemins de fer*, Chevalier lamented France's lack of development vis-à-vis Britain and advocated for the creation of new public works to address that deficit. On questions of regulation, he favoured a lax approach, writing in his political economy textbook that although regulations might prevent some abuses, the benefits of abolition were usually greater (Chevalier 1844, 436). In short, Saint-Simonism had evolved into both a pro-growth (and high-risk) economic program and a potentially viable strategy for French global pre-eminence.

In 1848, amid a continent-wide wave of discontent in Europe, revolution broke out in France. King Louis-Philippe abdicated the throne in favour of his grandson, but, instead, the National Assembly proclaimed a Second Republic. Like other French revolutions before it, fear of revolutionary violence saw conservative elements take power rather than radical ones. Louis-Napoléon ran in the 1848 presidential election, appealing to diverse constituencies – to Catholics, he promised to improve the temporal power of the papacy; to the poor, he promised ambitious projects of industrial expansion; and to a fearful bourgeoisie, he promised law and order. Bonapartism proved an immensely appealing program – Louis-Napoléon won 74 per cent of the vote, making him president of France (Price 2001, 18). The new regime, however, retained much of the power structure of the July Monarchy. Louis-Napoléon's plans ran counter to the interests of many elements of that regime.

In 1851, on the 2 December anniversary of Napoléon I's victory at Austerlitz, Louis-Napoléon staged a coup d'état, declaring himself Napoléon III, emperor of the French. Opposition was quickly suppressed, and the new regime was endorsed in a referendum held on 20 and 21 December. With Napoléon III firmly entrenched, what did the French policy environment look like? Napoléon III brought together a mix of powerful figures in banking and industry, with many drawn from supporters of the former conservative prime minister, François Guizot, and many linked to the Saint-Simonians (Plessis 1985). For instance, Michel Chevalier served as an economic adviser, while the Pereire brothers possessed numerous points of access to the regime.

On the other hand, those suspected of Orleanist sympathies, such as James de Rothschild, were largely excluded from the corridors of power, as was the intelligentsia (Plessis 1985, 8). The Conseil d'État and the legislature exerted less influence over policy during this period. Reforms passed in 1860 – launching the so-called liberal empire – changed that balance of power somewhat, increasing the influence of the legislature. Nonetheless, imperial prerogative remained substantial, particularly in the realm of finance (Plessis 1985).

The structure of the French financial system before the coup had involved some seeming paradoxes. On the one hand, French businesses had access to many more corporate forms than British ones: the *société en nom collectif*, the *société en commandite*, and the *société anonyme*. Respectively, these were unlimited liability, double liability,[50] and limited liability corporate forms (Sherman 1974). However, company formation was heavily regulated by the Conseil d'État. Indeed, it might even reject applications to form a *société anonyme* for firms that met the burdensome legal requirements (Freedeman 1965). At times, the rationale of the Conseil might be to combat speculation, though protection for incumbent firms was another motivation.

In the realm of banking, the Paris *haute banque* had been dominant. It consisted of a set of wealthy banking families, including the Rothschilds, the Gallieris, the Foulds, the d'Anvers, and the d'Eichthals, who used their family fortunes to finance trade, industrial activity, and sovereign debt. Collectively, *haute banque* families had close access to policymakers and extensive influence over the French central bank (Plessis 1994). Being neither publicly traded entities nor deposit-taking institutions, the *haute banque* was a closed network. Even marrying one's way into an *haute banque* family could be difficult – for instance, the Rothschilds frequently married cousins to avoid dispersion of the family's capital (Ferguson 2000, 33).

The new regime believed that it had to alter this structure of financial power to have freedom of action. At the same time, plenty of members of the *ancien régime* participated in the new order. Achille Fould, an important coup planner and later finance minister, expressed this view directly to the emperor: "It is absolutely essential that you free yourself from the tutelage of Rothschild who reigns in spite of you" (Davies 2016, 115–16). In addition, the regime was full of Saint-Simonians, who believed that new institutions could facilitate rapid development. Prefiguring Alexander Gerschenkron (1962) by over a century, they aimed to create large investment banks capable of mobilizing capital.

Saint-Simonians were not the only advocates of a new approach. Achille Fould suggested that mobilizing middle- and working-class savings could hasten economic expansion. Belgium, which was seen as an economic success, represented an important example for Second Empire planners. Achille Fould's brother, Benoît, saw a prospective model in Jules Mirès's *Caisse des actions réunies*, a French investment bank formed along lines similar to the Belgian banks. Impressed by the firm's success with only five million francs in capital, he believed that a larger institution might be able to accomplish even more. Certainly, it was also true that Saint-Simonian ideas played an important role. Another of Napoléon III's ministers, Victor de Persigny, had been contacted by the Pereire brothers, who proposed the creation of a public-works bank capable of mobilizing capital on a large scale to create a network of railways, canals, and shipping lanes: the Mediterranean system (Davies 2016, 112–38). Ideas matter, but they matter most when they can weave together grand strategic objectives with factional politics.

Plans were drawn up to create the Crédit Mobilier, a massive, publicly traded investment bank with limited liability.[51] Benoît Fould became president of the new institution, while Isaac Pereire served as deputy president.[52] The firm went public in November 1852, finding great interest among traders on the Paris Bourse. Collectively, the Fould bank and the Pereire brothers owned 30 per cent of the shares of the new institution, and they were joined by some other prominent members of the *haute banque* (Davies 2016, 117–18). One member remained decidedly unimpressed, however. James de Rothschild wrote a letter warning that the new firm would be a vehicle for monopoly and unbridled speculation, eventually becoming so powerful that it might challenge the regime. The Conseil d'État also took a dim view of the scheme, avoiding a recommendation.

Although de Rothschild had self-interested reasons to oppose the Crédit Mobilier, he had a point. If a single investment bank successfully mobilized capital to the scale promised by the Crédit Mobilier's promoters and managed the dense rail networks of a Mediterranean system, the economic vitality of France would be tied up in the affairs of a single firm. In other words, the Crédit Mobilier was "too big to fail," 1850s-style. The dense relationships between public and private actors implied by the scheme added a further layer of risk. Many of the stakeholders and directors of the Crédit Mobilier had explicit ties to the regime. Benoît Fould was the brother of the finance minister, and the Pereires had close relationships with members of the court of the Second Empire. In many instances, the Pereires lent large amounts of money to political figures, including the emperor himself, without insisting on repayment, while at other times they bribed officials outright (Davies 2016, 196–8). In turn, the Crédit Mobilier invested in many firms directed by regime insiders, including the Pereires themselves. By 1864, the Pereires directed at least fourteen companies, the Foulds seven, and the d'Eichthals six (Vitu 1864).

It would be inappropriate to apply twenty-first-century Anglo-American norms about government–business relations to Second Empire France – the age of the *haute banque* had been characterized by similar linkages. However, the banking families of the July Monarchy had been investing their own family fortunes and had every incentive to engage in careful oversight. The directors of the Crédit Mobilier, on the other hand, were playing with shareholder money and were shielded by limited liability.

Insulated against collapse and armed with large amounts of investment capital, the Crédit Mobilier lent heavily. The bank financed the ambitious reconstruction of Paris, managed by Prefect of Seine Baron Georges-Eugène Haussmann. The scheme involved building a beautiful, gas-lit Paris, redesigned to minimize problems like the spread of disease. The reconstruction served the political purposes of the regime as well. Parisians had a nasty habit of barricading the streets and overthrowing the incumbent regime. As a result, the wide-open boulevards of the Second Empire served the needs of a closed political system – they were difficult to barricade, while allowing easy access for police on horseback.[53] The scheme depended greatly on a certain lack of accountability – Haussmann spent extravagantly, going well over budget.

The creation of a rail network integrating Paris and the Mediterranean was critical to the ambitions of the Crédit Mobilier. In the Second Republic, many railway concessions had been authorized; however, most lacked funding and were not organized on the scale required by grand visions of the Mediterranean system. In its first three years, the Crédit Mobilier completed the Midi railway in the southwest of France; bankrolled the Grand Central, Est, and Ouest railways; and established the Compagnie Générale Maritime (CGM), a shipping company. The rapid pace of expansion encouraged others to mobilize their capital as well. The Rothschilds organized a competing institution, the Réunion Financière, bringing together some of the leading *haute banque* dynasties (Galliera, Talabot, and Bartholony) as well as some prominent foreign bankers (Davies 2016, 132). Other investment banks formed along the Crédit Mobilier model, such as the Crédit Lyonnais. The abundance of capital, combined with the competitive pressure to develop railway lines, prompted a rapid expansion in France. Between the coup of 1851 and 1860, the length of French rail track tripled (Mitchell 2013, 4423), while the weight of rail freight in France *sextupled* (4438).

Nor were the activities of the Crédit Mobilier confined to France. By one estimate, during the Second Empire, between one-third and one-half of French savings were invested internationally (Cameron 1953). The Crédit Mobilier was critical in abetting such a transformation, with massive railway investments in Spain, Austria, Switzerland, and the German Confederation. Frequently, when the firm invested abroad, it would establish banking institutions along similar lines, such as the Darmstädter Bank in Germany, the Kreditanstalt in Austria, and the Spanish Crédit Mobilier.[54] This aggressive international expansion pushed the Rothschilds to intensify the pace of their international activities as well (Landes 1956). For instance, in Austria, they formed the Kreditanstalt für Handel und Gewerbe, organized along the same lines as the Pereire bank, to defend their turf. As a result, France became an increasingly important source of capital abroad, moving from negligible outward investment in 1844 to nearly matching Britain by the early 1860s (see figure 3.1). Thus, many countries in continental Europe found their transportation networks linked to that of France, with their enterprises increasingly reliant on French capital. At the same time, French banking structures diffused internationally (Cameron 1953; Ferguson 2000, 233–44).

Because of its international orientation, the Crédit Mobilier was a useful tool of French foreign policy. For example, when Napoléon III sought to strengthen ties with Austria-Hungary, he pushed the Crédit Mobilier to increase lending to that empire. The French government also aimed to enhance French maritime presence, offering a generous subsidy to the Crédit Mobilier–financed CGM to build steamships (Davies 2016, 200). The firm's dependence on Napoléon III entailed risks as well. It would, at times, lend to the emperor and other prominent

Figure 3.1. Relative Shares of External Investment Assets, Britain and France, 1844–70

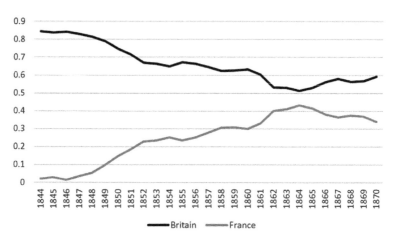

Source: Lee (2016).

figures. Such well-placed borrowers did not always repay according to a set schedule. Indeed, such unremunerated loans might be construed as bribes – down payments on the social network undergirding the physical network of rail lines and shipping lanes (196–8).

All these developments bear a close resemblance to Chevalier's vision of a Mediterranean system. Although French GDP growth did not outpace its competitors,[55] French success was highly visible. Visitors to France could easily see the successes of the new regime, such as the rapid transformation of Paris. In 1855, France showcased its industrial advances in the Exposition Universelle, a direct attempt to compete with Britain's 1851 Crystal Palace exhibition. One can imagine visitors evoking similar sentiments to those often expressed about Italian dictator Benito Mussolini: "Say what you will about Napoléon the little, at least the trains run on time." Moreover, by increasing the centrality of France in global financial networks, shipping networks, and European transportation networks, its ability to influence others was greatly enhanced – French *structural power* was growing. The realization of the Mediterranean system is a good illustration of Oatley et al.'s (2013) depiction of network power.

The early success of the Crédit Mobilier is difficult to understate. In 1855, the firm earned thirty-one million francs on a capital base of sixty million – an incredible rate of return (Cameron 1953). This success attracted even greater numbers of investors, allowing for yet more

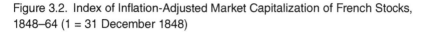

Figure 3.2. Index of Inflation-Adjusted Market Capitalization of French Stocks, 1848–64 (1 = 31 December 1848)

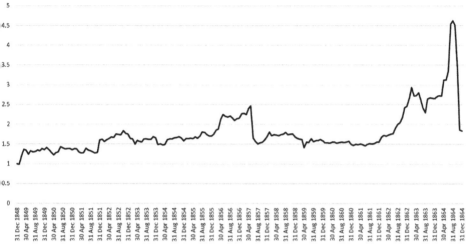

Source: Global Financial Data (2018).

large-scale projects to be built in France and abroad. However, the problem with the expansion driven by the Crédit Mobilier and its imitators was that it relied on unsustainable risk-taking. The Crédit Mobilier was overleveraged – it had invested and lent out far more than the capital of the firm itself. In years of expansion, the firm performed incredibly. However, once the business cycle turned negative, it would experience problems. If the profitability of its many investments waned, broader market panics could ensue. A look at French stock market capitalization during the early Second Empire illustrates this point well. Overall, the capitalization of French markets doubled in a short period of time, yet within this impressive rise were periods of even greater booms and dramatic busts, such as in 1857 and 1864 (see figure 3.2).

Enhanced French financial and industrial capabilities facilitated growing French naval power. Steamships enabled the creation of much faster, more powerful vessels. By 1859, steamships powerful enough to be clad in armoured plating were technically feasible. This revolution in naval technology rendered wooden ships obsolete, erasing the massive lead in naval power held by the British Empire. Figure 3.3 illustrates this point – France matched Britain in its relative share of naval power for a brief moment in the 1860s. British policymakers were disinclined to take such matters lightly.

Figure 3.3. Relative Share of Capital Ships and Naval Spending, Britain, Russia, and France, 1848–70

Sources: Lee and Thompson (2017); Modelski and Thompson (1988).

The Turn to Limited Liability in Britain

When we think of mid-nineteenth-century Britain today, we tend to imagine "the workshop of the world" at the heart of an empire where "the sun never sets," defended by a peerless navy. This view, reinforced by hindsight, misses the uncertainty of Britain's relative position during the era. As described in the previous section, France challenged Britain as a centre of finance, innovation, and naval power. The potential threat to Britain's structural position was felt in numerous quarters: British commercial interests were terrified by the Crédit Mobilier, while supporters of a strong British fleet, like Prime Minister Palmerston, saw a threat to Britain's long-standing naval pre-eminence. The French challenge could be addressed, but it required a new approach to policy. Despite the alliance forged between the two countries during the Crimean War and the Cobden-Chevalier free trade agreement of 1860, suspicions remained deep in Britain, and invasion scares were frequent.

To compete with France, Britain needed to enhance its economic vitality. The character of Pip in Charles Dickens's 1861 novel *Great Expectations* embodies a larger British dilemma. Pip is an apprentice blacksmith working with his uncle (and guardian), Joe, when he learns that an anonymous benefactor has designated him the heir of a large fortune. Driven by his infatuation with the wealthy and unattainable Estella Havisham, Pip abandons the honest life of a blacksmith, becoming a gentleman in London while racking up large debts against his expectations. Across Britain, millions of Pips faced the choice to either continue as their parents had or make a play for an uncertain fortune. A revolution in finance might stoke the speculative appetites of the British people, encouraging many to choose the latter. At the national level, such risk-taking might spark growth by mobilizing capital and entrepreneurial activities and, in turn, shore up British economic primacy. Of course, reality does not always match expectations, and such a course risked large-scale financial ruination.

Ultimately, Parliament repealed the Joint Stock Bank Act – allowing for the creation of limited liability corporations (and later banks) and removing many of the reporting and capital requirements required by the 1844 law. From the Royal Commission on Limited Liability of 1854, it is clear that a key part of the shift towards limited liability involved a collapse in confidence in the superiority of Britain's position and increased discussion of commercial challenges abroad. Although competitiveness concerns were not universally held, the coalition favouring limited liability grew from a few MPs concerned with increasing access to the working class and some radical, laissez-faire MPs to the majority in Parliament. Critical to that transformation was the faction of Whigs affiliated with Lord Palmerston, who became prime minister in 1855. Although Palmerston was not particularly interested in economic policy, he was obsessed with the threat of a French invasion and waning British naval power. A commercial boom could help finance his military ambitions without crossing those in his government fearful of deficits.

Reformers were also aided by newspapers trumpeting fears of French commercial competition. Ironically, the very newspapers publishing excoriations of speculation by Dickens and Trollope profited from the new advertisements that would accompany a company subscription boom (Taylor 2006, 168–9). The abolition of unlimited liability has also been explained as an example of a shift towards laissez-faire ideology or a reaction to corporate scandals, but neither of these explanations holds water (Hunt 1936). Many observers were resistant to the idea that limited liability was analogous to the free trade debate, while few would have seen the move as one likely to *lower* the incidence of financial scandals.

In the decade following the enactment of the Joint Stock Bank Act, British politics underwent radical changes. Let us briefly discuss those changes and how they influenced the political equilibrium in British financial regulatory policy. In 1846, Parliament debated the divisive question of whether to abolish the Corn Laws – a series of protective tariffs on imported grain. Supporters of abolition possessed a powerful political machine, the Anti–Corn Law League, founded by John Bright and Richard Cobden. They were opposed by Tories representing aristocratic, rural constituencies (Schonhardt-Bailey 2006). The abolition of tariffs would result in an influx of imported wheat, decimating the ability of aristocrats to profit by leasing to tenant farmers. On the other hand, industrialists stood to gain considerably from free trade. Whig MPs broadly represented the concerns of the industrialists.

The free trade debate disrupted the British party system until 1859, in a manner that amplified factionalism. Prime Minister Robert Peel, though a Tory, split from his own party and formed a free trade coalition government between the Whigs and "Peelite" Tories. The Peelites maintained the balance of power in Parliament for much of the 1850s. From 1846 to 1852, they backed Lord John Russell, a Whig, as prime minister; led their own administration under Lord Aberdeen from 1852 to 1855; and, finally, were important backers of the government of Lord Palmerston after 1855.

While the Peelite–Whig coalition was united in its support for free trade, conflicts over policy and personality provoked differences about almost everything else. Let us consider the constituencies that made up the coalition behind Lord Aberdeen during his tenure as prime minister. Peelites favoured free trade, tight-fisted fiscal policy, and sober scrutiny of financial institutions. In some matters, such as the role of the Church of England, they differed from other Whigs. Although small in number, they won strong representation in Cabinet. Future prime minister William Gladstone and Vice-President of the Board of Trade Edward Cardwell were two influential members of the faction (Conacher 1968).

Former prime minister Lord John Russell was also a necessary partner for the coalition. He had reformist instincts despite his own aristocratic background (Scherer 1999). Although he was a reliable free trader, he often differed from his coalition partners on other issues. He was a consistent supporter of political reform (in part because he thought it could defer revolution), a priority that put him at odds with more cautious Whigs. Peelites, in turn, chided his propensity for extravagant spending (Hawkins 1998). In addition to having supporters in Parliament, Russell frequently used the threat of resignation from Cabinet to exert leverage over the government.

Absent durable policy coalitions or party allegiances, Lord Palmerston and his allies occupied the "catbird seat" of British politics. On issues such as electoral reform, Palmerston was on the opposite end of the spectrum from Russell, opposing the expansion of the franchise. A long-serving foreign minister in Whig administrations, his appeal, at its core, lay in his foreign policy bona fides. His liberal, nationalist foreign policy was important in holding the rickety coalition together.[56] His penchant for leaking information to the press in exchange for favourable coverage also greatly enhanced his profile (Jenkins 1994, 80). The 1850 Don Pacifico affair is a good example of Palmerston's appeal (Brown 2002, 101–32). A British subject – David Don Pacifico – sought reimbursement from the Greek government after an anti-Semitic mob damaged his property. When the Greek government refused Pacifico's demands for considerable compensation, Palmerston, who was foreign secretary at the time, ordered the British fleet to Greece, risking a war with France and Russia, both of whom had sworn to protect that country. In Parliament, Palmerston defended his actions in a passionate speech, declaring, "As the Roman, in days of old, held himself free from indignity, when he could say *Civis Romanus sum*; so also a British subject, in whatever land he may be, shall feel confident that the watchful eye and the strong arm of England, will protect him against injustice and wrong" (Britain. Parliament 25 June 1850). Both the public and the press responded with overwhelming support for the move, although many elites thought differently.

Palmerston's knee-jerk policymaking created problems for some administrations, however. For instance, when he congratulated Napoléon III after his successful coup in 1851, Queen Victoria demanded his dismissal: he had failed to consult the Queen over the move. Although he resigned, he soon took revenge – joining the Tories in a successful vote of no confidence against Lord John Russell. The Queen then turned to the Tory leader, the Earl of Derby, to lead the government, which lasted less than a year. Palmerston and the rump of MPs around him could play the role of kingmaker.

At times, the Whig–Peelite coalition also worked with the rump of laissez-faire "radicals," including Richard Cobden and John Bright. Although the number of radical MPs was small, they could be decisive in close votes. Cobden was doggedly laissez-faire in his outlook, supporting free trade while opposing naval expenditures. These stances owed, in part, to a belief that free trade could prove to be the basis for perpetual peace. Cobden was not without a sense of realpolitik – he feared the repercussions of long-term economic competition with the United States.[57]

The apparent success of limited liability in France strengthened the case of British advocates for financial reform, while injecting a new sense of urgency into the debate. Pressure grew on Lord Aberdeen to address the limited liability question, until by 1854 he could delay no longer. Hoping to resolve the question without taking an explicit position, and thus threatening his rickety coalition, Aberdeen approved a royal commission on Britain's mercantile laws. He opposed limited liability, but believed that most respondents would share his opposition, thereby limiting momentum for reform (Taylor 2006, 149–50; Djelic 2013).

The 1854 royal commission sent out 152 detailed questionnaires to lawyers, academics, bankers, and chambers of commerce, receiving 74 responses (Bryer 1997, 42–3). The commission found a great deal more support for limited liability than had existed in 1837. Moreover, the arguments for and against limited liability also exhibited marked changes. Table 3.2 reports the proportion of all respondents making one of six common arguments for or against limited liability in 1837 and 1854. The most striking change, by far, is the decline in those emphasizing the superiority of the British financial system as a reason to implement the new policy.

A number of respondents argued directly that limited liability could aid economic progress and shore up Britain's relative position vis-à-vis France. In other words, these were domestic actors responding directly to the spectre of British decline. John Howell, a merchant, argued that French company law had facilitated rapid recovery after the 1848 revolution: "In 1848 the governor of the Bank of England observed to me, that in her industrial pursuits France could not recover from the effects of the shock of that day, in twenty years. He was mistaken; we see her again busy and prosperous ..." (Britain. Parliament. House of Commons 1854, 174–9). James Kennedy, another merchant, lamented that British investors neglected development in Britain and, instead, spend their capital abroad (135–42). Thomas Baker, a lawyer, reported a similar belief that many British companies constituted themselves in the United States or France, where they could take advantage of limited liability (239–42).

Many others, though lacking a comparative perspective, believed that limited liability could stoke a boom in British industry. A key idea was that wealthy investors were sitting on their fortunes because unlimited liability meant that a bad investment might swallow up the whole of their wealth. For instance, Leonne Levi, a lecturer at King's College, argued that "owing to this unlimited responsibility, men of capital are prevented from assisting individuals of industrious habits, or possessing special knowledge, or promoters of useful inventions" (Britain. Parliament. House of Commons 1854, 77).

Robert Lowe, an MP from Sheffield, and former editorial writer of the *Times*, believed that limited liability would foster a boom. Although

Table 3.2. Percentage of Respondents Making Arguments for or against Limited Liability

Year	1837 (%)	1854 (%)
Against limited liability		
Leads to speculation	23.1	26.8
We have enough capital	46.2	18.3
No right to profits without losses	15.4	8.5
For limited liability		
Will provide more capital	23.1	31.0
Foreign competition	0.0	8.5
Restricts free contract	0.0	15.5

Source: Author's calculations.

he acknowledged some risks, he disclaimed any public responsibility, declaring, "It is no part of a legislator's business to take care of persons too ignorant and reckless to take care of themselves" (Britain. Parliament. House of Commons 1854, 83–6). Lowe twinned predictions of a boom with ideological arguments for limited liability. For him, barring firms from forming on a limited liability basis was a restriction on their right to free contract. He asserted that the burden of proof lay on limited liability opponents to explain why such an exception should hold. In taking this position, Lowe was joined by others, in a departure from the situation with the 1837 parliamentary committee, where no such effort to twin laissez-faire principles with limited liability had taken place.

Many respondents opposed limited liability, emphasizing different reasons for scepticism. The most common objection was that limited liability would lead to dangerous speculation. For instance, John Kinnear of the Glasgow Chamber of Commerce agreed that limited liability might produce new enterprises, but believed that "many of them would be deplorably unsuccessful, and result in loss to the creditors and ruin to the partners" (Britain. Parliament. House of Commons 1854, 87). In contrast with the belief that limited liability would benefit the working class, Kinnear offered a common position among opponents that "persons in humble life are not likely to consider the risks of trade and speculation; but they are very likely to believe that in a law passed for their special benefit, the legislature had taken care to protect them against all risks" (87). Lord Overstone, a wealthy investor, respected economic theorist, and peer in the House of Lords, also responded. He believed that it was wise to correct "the hope of unlimited profit" with "the sense of unlimited responsibility." The core problem was that "a man will often leap before he looks where the penalty on failure is comparatively slight" (93). In other words, precisely because limited liability restricted the cost of making reckless actions, the economy was bound to see more of them.

The responses to the questionnaire were mixed. Indeed, simply count-ing the numbers in relative support or opposition to limited liability is difficult because respondents gave long answers full of caveats. Viscount Goderich, heading the Mercantile Laws Commission, scored the slant of respondents 43–31 in favour of limited liability (Bryer 1997, 43), though others disagree. Taylor (2006, 151) found the number to be closer to even. Having read the reports myself, I was able to draw clear conclusions about 71 respondents, 39 of whom appeared to support limited liability. One striking aspect of their responses was the lack of a sectoral divide. Although academics and lawyers tended to support limited liability, the world of banking and commerce was decidedly split (see table 3.3). Indeed, many chambers of commerce underwent acrimonious debates before taking positions on limited liability (Taylor 2006). Insofar as the commission aimed to present Lord Aberdeen with a clear endorsement or rejection of limited liability, it was a failure.

Parliament began discussion of legislation soon after the royal com-mission had submitted its report, with limited liability advocates point-ing to the policy's success in France. John Collier, the MP for Plymouth, introduced a resolution supporting limited liability. Following a reci-tation of the history of countries employing *commandite* partnerships, Collier turned to the critical question: if limited liability was such a wise policy, how had Britain come so far without it? To this, he argued that Britain's greatest achievements – including railroads, canals, docks, fleets of steamers, and the Crystal Palace – had been accom-plished through exceptions to unlimited liability. He continued, "All our noblest monuments, which would attest our national greatness when our race has passed away, attested the working of the principle of limited, and not of unlimited, liability" (Britain. Parliament 27 June 1854). Collier went on to echo the point that Britain's policies under-mined its competitive position: "I could mention whole trades which, thirty years ago, were entirely carried on by English houses, in which at the present moment scarcely one is to be found; their places have been entirely supplied by foreigners" (ibid.). The debate to reform the financial system had been launched on terms that were overt about the relationship between financial regulation and interstate competition.

Some vigorously applauded Collier's motion. Viscount Goderich, a Tory MP and former prime minister, echoed Collier's call to unleash British firms from the regulation. He rejected the notion that "the greater credit that was afforded to them [Britain] in the market of the world, than was afforded to those of France" owed to limited liability (Britain.

Table 3.3. Sectoral Distribution of Royal Commission Report, 1854

Respondents	For	Against
Merchants, manufacturers, chambers of commerce	17	20
Bank of England governors, directors, bankers, bill brokers	6	7
Lawyers	13	3
Academics	5	1
MPs	2	0
Totals	43	31

Source: Bryer (1997, 43).

Parliament 27 June 1854). Rather, he argued, France had been held back by the fact of it having had six revolutions in the previous seventy years. Free of revolution, it might be able to outcompete Britain. Cobden, too, voiced his support, arguing that the current law was overly burdensome and prevented capitalists from assisting promising young men in launching business enterprises. However, not every supporter of limited liability was talking about the same thing. One MP, J.G. Phillimore, extolled the merits of a partnership *en commandite*, which entailed limited liability for shareholders but unlimited liability for the directors. Other speakers favoured a much broader application of the policy.

Among those opposed to the resolution, Edward Cardwell represented a particularly influential voice. As the Peelite vice-president of the Board of Trade – the institution regulating the creation of new joint-stock companies – he was the Aberdeen government's point man on limited liability. Cardwell challenged the idea that limited liability was analogous to free trade and warned of speculation. He painted the picture of a person of small capital embarking on some ruinous enterprise, with massive losses falling upon creditors. He also recited the long list of eminent persons opposed to limited liability, including Thomas Baring and Lord Overstone.

Lord Palmerston, then serving as home secretary, interceded in the debate in a curious way. Though intimating a degree of sympathy for the resolution, he urged against a vote on the matter at that time, to which Collier agreed. But why might a minister sympathetic to limited liability avoid a vote? Circumstances would soon provide Palmerston with the ability to push much further. In January 1855, MP John Roebuck criticized the conduct of the Aberdeen government in the Crimean War, proposing a vote of no confidence. Lord John Russell had resigned from the government in advance of the vote, further undermining Aberdeen's position. Aberdeen was defeated decisively (Hawkins 1998, 50–5; Conacher 1968).

Queen Victoria sought to form a government headed by anybody but Lord Palmerston. According to the diary of Edward Cardwell, she first turned to the Tory Earl of Derby, who failed to command the support of the House of Commons (Viscount Edward Cardwell: Papers, PRO 30/48/54, The National Archives [TNA], Kew). Next, Lord John Russell flopped. His earlier resignation from the Aberdeen administration over the conduct of the Crimean War had hurt his standing among the Peelites. As other Whigs failed to muster sufficient votes, the Queen was forced to bow to the power of the median legislator, selecting the only man who could form a government: Lord Palmerston.

Multiple figures can claim to be the "father of limited liability." Although Robert Lowe authored the most important legislation, Lord Palmerston's support was critical because he and his allies represented pivotal votes on most legislation in mid-nineteenth-century Britain. Palmerston is remembered more for his views on foreign policy than those on domestic policy, and there is no "smoking gun" memo in which he explained his support for limited liability. However, that support was consistent with his mortal fear of France and corresponding desire to stoke economic growth (Hilton 1988).

In 1854, Britain and France formed an alliance, intervening against Russia in the Crimean War. However, British motivations for joining the war had little to do with fondness for Napoléon III. The war had begun as a conflict between the Ottoman Empire and Russia. Britain feared that Ottoman Empire defeat might result in Russian control over the Dardanelles strait, the only channel connecting the Black Sea with the Mediterranean (Lambert 2011). Despite the alliance with France, panics about a French invasion broke out among the British public in 1851 and 1858.

Palmerston's private papers reveal that he too was terrified of a French attack. For instance, he regularly monitored reports of French naval fortification. To an 1851 report of French naval construction activity in Cherbourg, he wrote that the construction "proves that however peaceable the inclinations and policy of that country may be, its statements are at least determined to be prepared for war, and for a condition that must give them great weight in negotiations with Great Britain." Palmerston also expressed worry that the new fort could be integrated with railways, thus enabling a quicker invasion (Palmerston to Unidentified, 1851, MM/FR/22/3, Palmerston Papers, Special Collections, University of Southampton).

Although Lord Palmerston was primarily worried about military challenges, limited liability could ease the financial constraints on military mobilization. Many had argued for limited liability as a means to revitalize the British economy vis-à-vis France. Not only would revitalization enhance British competitiveness, it would also produce a boom in new company formation. Palmerston's plans for coastal fortification and naval construction were prohibitively expensive – a fact that frequently put him in conflict with other members of Cabinet (Brown 2006). A boom would increase government revenues, helping Palmerston fund his cherished navy without running large deficits.

Additionally, the move could count on a positive response from the press (Taylor 2006, 168). New companies advertised for investors in the newspapers, contributing a large proportion of their revenue. Moreover, the Palmerstons had cultivated a personal relationship with a number of critical media outlets, like the London *Times* (Fenton 2013). Lady Palmerston was noted for her relationship with John Delane, its long-time editor. Robert Lowe,[58] now a Whig MP, was a former editorial writer for that newspaper and a strong advocate for limited liability. He continued in that capacity, even as an MP.

Although the *Times* usually emphasized theoretical rationales for limited liability, it also linked regulatory policy to international competitiveness. One editorial asked, "Why are foreign houses to increase every day in this metropolis, and get possession of our trade, all of them supported by capital advanced upon conditions forbidden in this country?" (*Times* [London], 28 June 1854). Alternatively, another article about the Exposition Universelle linked the exhibition's glittering success with superior French company law, saying, "One can scarcely fail to observe how extensively the rising manufactures of France are worked by companies *en commandite*" (22 September 1855). Coverage of the Crédit Mobilier trumpeted the challenge it represented to Britain. Another article asked, "What chance has the private speculator, with his half million of money and his unlimited responsibility, against the Crédit Mobilier, which wields six millions under the shield of limited liability, and has the power of creating twenty-four millions more by the issue of obligations?" (12 January 1857).

Many other newspapers joined the call for limited liability, emphasizing the apparent success of the Crédit Mobilier as a reason for action. The rapid reconstruction of Paris was testament to the banking company's power as a vehicle for transformation. Further, the sheer amount of capital mobilized by the firm threatened the financial primacy of London. The *Economist* declared of the Crédit Mobilier, "We doubt whether anything so grand has been seen in France since the days of Law and the Mississippi Scheme" (15 September 1855). The *London Illustrated News* declared that "a mighty race of competition is going on between ourselves, America, France, and other nations – all bidding for the markets of the world," cautioning that "we shall not win this mighty race if we be unduly weighted; and our peculiar Law of Partnership, which subjects every man who enters into trade to responsibility to the extent of his whole substance" (22 September 1855). Thus, even if the British press had doubts about the long-term viability of the Crédit Mobilier, it clearly represented a tangible threat to British commercial enterprises.

As prime minister, Lord Palmerston sought to enact limited liability legislation. He appointed Edward Pleydell-Bouverie as vice-president of the Board of Trade. On 29 June 1855, Bouverie introduced a bill enacting limited liability. He argued that the measure would spark innovation, noting that many of the great innovators had been poor men with little ability to raise capital. He also continued the earlier reference to British companies forming in France to take advantage of limited liability there (Britain. Parliament 29 June 1855). Palmerston supported the bill, expressing the belief that it would expand the capital of the nation. He also tried to link the issue to free trade, but this point was met with cries of "No!" from many MPs (Taylor 2014, 165). Some objected to aspects of the bill as not going far enough – for instance, John Collier wondered why the bill excluded banks and insurance companies. He went on to object to the publication of the names of shareholders and the stipulation that firms making errors in registration would incur the penalty of unlimited liability. Robert Lowe also offered principled opposition to the bill for not going far enough. Others, such as Edward Cardwell, continued to express opposition to the bill, arguing that it would lead to speculation. Despite these objections, the bill passed.

Although the Bouverie bill passed, many considered it deficient. Supporters and opponents alike moved to enshrine their preferred position in legislation the following year. In August 1855, Palmerston appointed Robert Lowe as vice-president of the Board of Trade. Lowe proceeded to write a new limited liability bill that went much further than its predecessor. Lowe's Joint Stock Companies Act of 1856 allowed any group of seven people to form a limited liability corporation without any safeguards. Further, Lowe used his other hat as editorial writer of the *Times* to advocate forcefully in the press for the principle of limited liability (Taylor 2006, 168).

Opponents of limited liability mustered resistance to the Lowe bill, stressing fears of speculative excess. As consideration of the bill reached the House of Lords, Lord Overstone pushed against reforms. He delivered a speech decrying limited liability, although the text is lost to time. Complaining that he spoke "without preparation and under the impulse of a nervous temperament," Overstone requested that Lord Monteagle revise the record of his speech in Hansard, then a common practice (Lord Overstone Papers, MS804/348, Senate House Library Archives, University of London). Simultaneously, he appealed to Lord Granville, a fellow peer, seeking to swing him against limited liability. Overstone lamented that, because the limited liability bill had been passed "*without safeguards of any kind*," one might see "Joint Stock Companies taken up without even knowing what they mean or what they propose to do." Calling upon his own memory of the 1825 financial crisis, Overstone was convinced that limited liability would summon "the Demon of Speculation." Of Palmerston's efforts to link limited liability with free trade, Overstone derided these as "the most flimsy sophistry" (MS 804/349, ibid.). He feared that Robert Lowe was manufacturing the appearance of public support for limited liability with his position in the press. In Overstone's estimation, Lowe was dangerous because he had "no practical experience nor any respect for it" (MS 804/350, ibid.).

Lord Overstone was not alone in his opposition to limited liability. For instance, Lord Grey wrote to Lord Granville, expressing his opposition: "Overstone is a man whose judgment on commercial questions has great weight with me, while Palmerston's has none at all, partly because I know him to be personally ignorant of them, and his opinions so far as he has any show him to be generally wrong" (Lord Grey to Lord Granville, PRO 30/29/23/5, TNA). Grey was content that higher levels of "commercial morality" in Britain precluded the need for limited liability and explicitly rejected the idea that limited liability principles related to free trade. Lord John Russell, too, solicited the economist J.R. McCullough, expressing his opposition to limited liability. McCullough responded that he agreed but added, sombrely, "tho' the current at present, runs all the other way" (McCullough to Russell, MS 804/351, Lord Overstone Papers).

Events soon confirmed McCullough's sentiments. In 1844, the stringent banking reforms ushered in by Robert Peel had passed by a vote of 167–16 (Schonhardt-Bailey 2006). Then, in 1856, the majority of its provisions were wiped out by the Joint Stock Companies Act in a 94–14 vote (Britain. Parliament 1856, 5). This sea-change in opinion was not a victory of laissez-faire attitudes. Many of the same MPs who had voted for the Joint Stock Bank Act were still in Parliament to vote for its repeal. Among the most radically laissez-faire, there was actually some disagreement over whether limited liability was a form of government intervention (Jefferys 1938). At any rate, the radicals represented a small share of MPs in both 1844 and the 1850s, by the estimate of Lord John Russell (Conacher 1968).

The shift towards limited liability can be best understood through the lens of international competition. The launch of the Crédit Mobilier inspired fears of French commercial and financial power. With British companies listing themselves in Paris to obtain the benefits of limited liability, the status quo was a direct threat to British primacy. The Crédit Mobilier also shifted attitudes about ideal policy. Comparing the 1837 and 1854 investigations into limited liability, the most pronounced change was declining confidence in the superiority of British institutions over French ones. For an administration trying to appeal to nationalists with a steamship navy and coastal fortifications, while appeasing "skinflints" in Cabinet, the move was an appealing one. Not *all* legislators supporting limited liability were motivated by competitive challenges, but enough MPs shifted, breaking the legislative status quo.

While competitiveness opened the door to a modest reform, regulatory rollback gained further momentum through the following decade. The 1856 Joint Stock Companies Act extended limited liability to joint-stock companies but excluded banks and insurance companies. The response by firms was initially restrained. In 1857, calls arose in Parliament for the extension of limited liability to joint-stock banks. Proponents argued that it did not make sense to allow one type of company to obtain limited liability while restricting it among others. Opponents warned of the risks of speculation. By 1858, limited liability had been extended to banks, albeit with minimum share denominations of £100. The restriction considerably limited the ability of poorer individuals to purchase shares of a hypothetical limited liability bank (Alborn 1998; Taylor 2006). Once minimum share prices were eliminated in 1862, company formation rates skyrocketed: the sought-after boom had arrived. Competitiveness concerns drove Britain to abandon long-standing apprehensions about limited liability, while reforms themselves shifted the political equilibrium in a direction favourable to even greater acceptance of risk-taking.

The Spiral

The creation of the Crédit Mobilier and the dawn of limited liability in Britain produced booms. Those booms reinforced the political coalitions that had spawned them and wedded governments to new policies. Newly empowered constituencies pushed for greater leeway from regulators in Britain and France. Internationally, competition between Britain and France intensified, as growing financial markets proffered even larger rewards for the country able to lead the system. Imitators in the United States and Western Europe, in turn, adopted the financial structures that seemed to be successful in Britain and France, amplifying the orgy of speculation. Let us describe how risk-taking spiralled in the 1860s.

In Britain, limited liability produced a boom in company promotion. The sense of prosperity this created encouraged new sectors of the economy to adopt limited liability. Equity markets benefited from the reform, with bank stocks, in particular, surging from 12 per cent of market capitalization on the LSE in 1854 to 21 per cent by 1865 (Acheson et al. 2009, 1118–19). On the other hand, the real economy was tepid, growing at a modest 1.3 per cent per annum during the same period (Maddison 2013).

Many banks were reluctant to employ limited liability. However, there are notable exceptions, whose conduct would lead to disaster in 1866. Overend Gurney & Company was a highly successful discounting house: its business model was built around bills of exchange and lending to other banks. In 1865, the firm became a limited liability corporation, using the added security to greatly expand its leverage. By 1866, however, markets had experienced a downturn, putting immense pressure on Overend Gurney, which had four times as much in liabilities as liquid assets (Turner 2014, 79–83). When it collapsed that year, it brought down hundreds of other companies with it.

In France, the overexpansion wrought by the Crédit Mobilier initially brought about efforts to contain speculative pressures. Even some ministers with family ties to the enterprise, such as Achille Fould, expressed concern. In 1856, the Law of July 17th limited the transferability of shares of the *société en commandite* type (Sherman 1974, 164). The move was intended to prevent unscrupulous promoters from promoting dubious enterprises and then abandoning them. At the same time, the imperial administration took steps to facilitate the great expansion of credit, pressing firms to accept shares in the railroad industry as collateral for loans.

Efforts at re-regulation were temporary, at best. The 15 January 1860 edition of *Le Moniteur*, the official state newspaper, published a letter from Emperor Napoléon III to Finance Minister Achille Fould. It argued that French growth was restrained by legislative hindrances not shared by Britain and other states neighbouring France (Dougui 1981). The letter was likely aimed at preparing the ground for the emperor's next big move: a free trade agreement with Britain. In 1860, France and Britain signed the Cobden-Chevalier free trade agreement, increasing the economic linkages between their two economies. The origins of the treaty themselves are a tale of paradoxical relationships between "frenemies." After an assassination attempt on Napoléon III in 1858, another invasion panic had struck Britain. The French press had played up the fact that the assassin, Italian nationalist Felice Orsini, had used a British-made bomb in his attack.[59] The British government had then launched an enquiry into the country's relative naval strength. The enquiry had indicated that Britain had fallen behind France in steamships, greatly threatening British dominance.

Strangely, the events would bring the two countries together. In his 1862 book, *The Three Panics*, Richard Cobden had contended the futility of naval arms races and contested the figures on French naval strength. His preferred means of avoiding conflict was to foster trade. At the encouragement of William Gladstone, the chancellor of the exchequer, Cobden visited France to convince the emperor to sign a trade deal. Privately, Michel Chevalier gave Cobden indications that the Napoleonic government would be open to just that so long as the proposal was bilateral.[60] Officially, Napoléon III's ministers Rouher and Persigny presented the emperor with arguments favourable to reform, further stressing the risk of imminent war with Britain. Having reserved the power to sign trade agreements himself, Napoléon III soon approved the Cobden-Chevalier trade agreement over the objections of protectionist interests in the country.

Despite this agreement, economic rivalry between Britain and France persisted. Indeed, the debate in France over the adoption of free trade sparked considerable interest in how to invigorate French enterprise (Dougui 1981). Once Britain's company formation boom took off, French firms found themselves at a disadvantage. British firms operating in France could enjoy the benefits of limited liability, whereas it remained difficult for French firms to obtain the same privileges. In 1861, Auguste Vavasseur, a lawyer for the imperial court, advocated the replacement of the *société en commandite* with free access to the limited liability *société anonyme*. President of the Tribunal of Commerce of the Prefecture of Seine Georges Denière made similar arguments for the liberalization of French company law. Voices inside the administration were joined by the French business world, which called for competitive equality with British company law. On the other side, a few voices opposed liberalization – for instance, many in the Conseil d'État lamented a return to the rampant speculation of the early 1850s.

Business pressure led to an investigation into company law by the Corps législatif, the French lower house, which concluded that regulatory differences provided an advantage to English firms over French ones (Sherman 1974, 164). In August 1863, the French government authorized the creation of a new type of business, the *société à responsabilité limitée*, a limited liability corporation like the *société anonyme* that did not require authorization from the government, albeit subject to a capitalization ceiling. French policymakers appeared to agree that a mighty race among nations was taking place, and they meant to win it.

The initial market response to French liberalization was euphoric – in the months surrounding the debate and enactment of the 1863 law, the inflation-adjusted capitalization of the stock market tripled (Global Financial Data 2018). By 1864, however, the irrational exuberance driving the boom had become a frenzied panic driving down markets. During broadly favourable times, overleveraged financial firms fare well – many enterprises earn profits, and their ability to invest heavily serves them well. In lean times, however, such firms face a dangerous situation, with little capital to call upon when they are under duress.

The collapse of the Crédit Mobilier is a powerful example of the dangers of excess leverage, particularly when coupled with strong business–government linkages. In 1858, the Pereire brothers created the Compagnie Immobilière to manage their many construction activities. The firm underwrote the construction of the Grand Hôtel, with loans from the Crédit Mobilier and the Crédit Foncier. Through "creative" accounting practices, such as booking capital gains on land and buildings, the firm was able to give investors large dividends at the cost of maintaining the long-term fiscal solvency of the firm.

Politically, the Pereires sought to replicate an environment of loose credit well suited to their firm. When the 1855 election of Alphonse de Rothschild to the Banque de France undermined this objective, the brothers sought ways to work around the central bank. After France received Savoy in the settlement of the Franco-Austrian war of 1859, the Pereires tried to acquire the Banque de Savoie, which had the grandfathered right to issue notes. Their aim was to control a counter-institution that could force the French central bank to open the spigots. In this regard, they probably went too far – even many allies such as d'Eichthal and Chevalier denounced the move. Power also appeared to be shifting within the imperial court (which itself was more constrained by the legislature after political reforms in 1860). James de Rothschild had cultivated his own ties with Napoléon III, developing a friendly relationship with Empress Eugénie. Moreover, as the international engagements of the French Second Empire increased, its credit needs shifted from credit for industrial development to credit for sovereign lending, the latter being a Rothschild specialty. Some point to the 1862 hunt at Ferrières, where James de Rothschild hosted Napoléon III, as a sign that the times were turning against what Rothschild derisively called the "Credit Mob" (Ferguson 2000, 105–13).

Despite their waning influence, the Pereires found other ways to obtain capital. They merged their Compagnie Immobilière with Jules Mirès's Société des Ports de Marseille after Mirès was arrested for fraud in 1861 – a move made with the encouragement of the emperor. The Pereires' efforts to do to Marseille what they had done to Paris flopped. Haemorrhaging money, the Compagnie Mobilière threatened to bring down the Crédit Mobilier with it. The Pereires lobbied to double the capital of the Crédit Mobilier, succeeding with the help of the emperor. However, the problems at the Compagnie Mobilière were impossible to solve: the firm collapsed, forcing the Pereires into bankruptcy by 1867 (Davies 2016, 208–10). The problems in such a central firm spilled over into the larger economy. The Paris Bourse crashed in 1864, and, until 1868, French stock prices continued to fall (Global Financial Data 2018). The French real economy suffered too, with real per capita GDP falling 9 per cent from 1864 to 1868 (Maddison 2013).

Despite the protracted stock market crash, pressure to liberalize French company law continued. In 1867, the government passed an even more liberal company-formation law, allowing any company to form a *société anonyme* without the need for approval or any capital limits. In other words, France adopted a system of free incorporation even as its limited liability firms appeared to foster recurrent boom–bust cycles.

One important reason for the continued embrace of liberalization was how limited liability fit into the grand design of Napoleonic foreign policy. In spite of the obvious deficiencies of the French financial system, the French financial revolution enhanced the country's economic and political centrality. Napoléon III is often mischaracterized either as having an inconsistent foreign policy or as being a warmonger aiming to replicate the triumphs of his uncle. But, in fact, his grand strategy aimed consistently at replacing the Concert of Europe with a new institutional order centred on France (Cunningham 2001). He first sought to disrupt a balance-of-power system that had constrained French interests – breaking the Concert of Europe by separating Britain from Russia in the Crimean War. The next step was creating the Mediterranean system – a dense network of economic activity centred on France. The third was to be creating a political order capable of replacing the Concert of Europe, with France at its head.

The French government attempted to leverage its economic power in the 1860s to build just such an order. In 1863, after the Mexican government had defaulted on its debt, France intervened militarily, installing Maximilian, the son of the Austrian archduke, as emperor of Mexico. One set of motivations may have come from Michel Chevalier's desire to draw Latin America into the French sphere of influence. Napoléon III too, had shown interest in grand projects in the region, such as a canal in Central America, even before becoming emperor. French ambitions in the region may have been even more grandiose. In a world of free and open investment, such as that emerging in the 1860s, international investors faced a considerable source of worry: what if governments defaulted or expropriated foreign assets? The ability to protect global property rights had historically been exercised by those few states with the combination of strong naval power and extensive interests to protect. By 1863, France could claim to be such a power – exercising its influence to overthrow a profligate government.[61]

In addition to employing French martial power, the Second Empire embarked on a series of bold schemes for monetary unification, turning its growing financial prowess into a bid to seize a greater share of global structural benefits. In 1865, France turned to Belgium, Italy, and Switzerland with a proposal for a system of pegged exchange rates operating on a bimetallist basis (i.e., their money supply would consist of both silver and gold). The new Latin Monetary Union effectively traded on the French investment surge, drawing countries reliant on French capital into a French-led monetary bloc (Willis 1901; Gallarotti 1995; Einaudi 2001).[62] In 1867, the French government floated an even more ambitious scheme in an international conference.[63] Specifically, Napoléon III proposed a global currency based on a gold franc. Because the franc was already the basis of the Latin Monetary Union, it would be the natural currency to anchor the new monetary system (Gallarotti 1995). Although the proposal was rebuffed by Britain, it was a striking example of the aim of the Second Empire to establish itself as the leader of a new global order.

Napoléon III's grand ambitions were thwarted, much like those of his uncle. French military defeat in the 1870–1 Franco-Prussian War brought about the end of the Second Empire and weakened France. Deprived of Alsace–Lorraine and saddled with a considerable indemnity, the country was in no shape to launch grand schemes. Global monetary unification took place in the 1870s, but largely through the voluntary adoption of the gold standard and not the success of French monetary schemes.

The Origins of the Long Depression

Although the Anglo-French competition for global financial leadership had been peaceful, it was not without collateral damage. Corporate forms adopted for their ability to mobilize capital and exploit leverage spread around the world. The same flaws that plagued the Crédit Mobilier and Overend Gurney laid the foundations for an era of immense economic misery known as the Long Depression of 1873–96. Although economic growth continued through the era, it was often undone by collapse.

The era of limited liability brought about a profound transformation of the political economy of Britain and the world alike. Where Trollope's (1858) *The Three Clerks* had once portrayed financial speculation as a socially dubious if common activity, less than two decades later, Trollope (1875) depicted investment as *The Way We Live Now*. Instead of making their fortunes as hereditary landlords, members of the upper crust of British society participated in a kind of transnational feudalism, investing their fortunes in everything from Argentine municipal bonds to Indian railways. With all the world chomping at the bit for British investment, British institutions were elevated above the alternatives. The 1893 Gilbert and Sullivan musical, *Utopia, Limited* imagines a small island nation as its Princess, Zara, returns from her education in England. Inspired by English ideas, Utopia transforms itself to be more English, passing a bill declaring every Utopian to be a limited liability entity of their own – freed forever from responsibility.

Limited liability did not bring utopia to Britain. Britain suffered severe financial crises, including the Overend Gurney crash of 1866 and the City of Glasgow Bank crash of 1878. However, the relative lack of external competition allowed regulatory change to take place without concern over the loss of international position. In 1878, the City of Glasgow bank collapsed after its speculative investments in American railroads and Australian farms – masked to investors by fraudulent reports – failed (Checkland 1975, 470). With assets of £7.2 million against liabilities of £12.4 million, the failure of the bank represented a threat to the financial system as a whole (Collins 1989, 504).

Although the City of Glasgow Bank was an unlimited liability bank, its fraud was abetted by the weakening of reporting rules, and its collapse highlighted problems with the limited liability system. The seven directors of the bank held a mere 1 per cent of the bank's shares. As a result, they had less of an incentive to manage the bank cautiously or to ensure that potential shareholders could absorb losses (Acheson and Turner 2008). In this sense, the situation more closely resembled limited liability banks (which also had incentives to take risks since the directors would be held liable only for their holdings in the company). Other unlimited liability banks were directed by individuals with larger stakes and were not implicated by the collapse of the City of Glasgow Bank. The reaction of the stock market to the crash reflected this, with English limited liability bank stocks falling further than those of banks with unlimited liability (ibid., 249).

The collapse of the City of Glasgow Bank led to two sets of policy discussions, one regarding unlimited liability and another regarding the adequacy of reporting requirements. The Tory chancellor of the exchequer, Sir Stafford Northcote, viewed the central problem as one of unlimited liability. He feared that if people of limited means owned unlimited liability bank shares, they would be unable to cover debts in the face of bankruptcy. This view was similar to that of many editorialists, who believed that unlimited liability "only drives away wealthy men and substitutes them for those who do not have much to lose" (*Scotsman* [Edinburgh], 2 October 1880). While Acheson and Turner's (2008, 241) analysis of the occupational characteristics of major unlimited bank shareholders demonstrates that this was not true, this point was not contested in the debate over post-1878 reforms (Britain. Parliament 22 July 1879). To address this issue, Northcote implemented a system of "reserve liability," wherein banks would put aside a portion of capital as a fund with which to protect depositors.

The adoption of similar measures by the Crédit Mobilier led to disaster. Its early success had inspired many similar institutions to form in Germany (Fohlin 2007, 18–19). Some, like the Darmstadt Bank, were formed with explicit help from the Pereires. Deutsche Bank was established specifically to rival London in the finance of trade (Kindleberger 1990, 314). Liberal incorporation laws introduced in 1870 (Tilly 1989, 195), coupled with the inflow of French reparations payments after Germany's victory in the Franco-Prussian War, created conditions for a great boom, amplified by banking institutions inclined towards overleverage.

Loose credit conditions in Europe and the spread of large institutions able to overleverage themselves imperilled the American economy as well. American financier Duff Green had studied British and French financial developments in the 1850s and wanted to find a way to funnel European capital into American railroad markets (Green 1959). He established the Pennsylvania Fiscal Agency, which was later renamed the Credit Mobilier of America. The firm was taken over by the Union Pacific Railroad Company, which proceeded to use the agency as a front – overcharging the Union Pacific to build track to soak up a larger share of public subsidies. Congress was plied with bribes to keep the scheme afloat. Another financier, Jay Cooke, also sought to take advantage of loose credit conditions in Europe to finance railroad construction in the United States with his ambitious Northwest Railway (Kindleberger 1990, 319–23), while an allied firm bribed members of the Canadian Parliament to win a charter to build the Canadian Pacific Railway.[64]

The bubble burst in 1873, bringing down many. Comparing GDP per capita from peak to trough, the 1873 crisis saw incomes fall 6 per cent in Germany, 3 per cent in the United States, and 11 per cent in Canada, with slow recoveries in all cases (Maddison 2009). The excesses of the 1850s and 1860s were felt for a long time as well. The period from 1873 to 1896 is often characterized as the Long Depression – a protracted period of deleveraging in which prices tended to fall, bringing considerable hardship for debtors.

Conclusion

In the 1850s, the French Second Empire launched a financial revolution. Although that revolution failed to achieve stunning economic results, it enjoyed high-profile successes and enhanced the centrality of France in the global financial system. As incumbent global financial leader, Britain (particularly under the premiership of Lord Palmerston) was unlikely to take such a threat sitting down. Once confident of the superiority of the English "commercial spirit" and British regulatory institutions, Parliament not only instituted limited liability bankruptcy rules but also eliminated existing prudential safeguards. The seeming short-term success of these policies, and continued jockeying for global leadership, encouraged the governments of France and Britain to double down even further, while many countries abroad took similar steps. The simultaneous adoption of liberalized company formation rules and lax banking regulation produced a wave of severe banking collapses, including the French crisis of 1864, the Overend Gurney crisis of 1866, and the global crisis of 1873.

Chapter Four

The Interwar Battle for Financial Supremacy

The Wizard of Oz (1939) is the movie adaptation of an allegory about monetary policy, according to esteemed economic historian Hugh Rockoff (1990). Dorothy and her companions (a scarecrow representing farmers, a tin man representing the industrial worker, and a lion possibly representing perennial Democratic presidential candidate William Jennings Bryan) follow a yellow-brick road, cheered on enthusiastically by small, childlike people called Munchkins. At one point in the book, Dorothy skips sixteen times on one foot, and one on the other, wearing her silver slippers.[65] The number was the ratio of silver to gold favoured by free-silver advocates. Dorothy's journey was a representation of the then-salient political battle between American advocates of a gold standard and those favouring bimetallism.

Between 1878 and 1914, *many* countries followed the yellow-brick road. When the gold standard was disrupted by the First World War, great efforts were made to restore the old order. This chapter explores how those efforts went awry. Just as movie adaptations often depart from the book, the interwar gold-exchange standard was not like its predecessor. In 1913, American policymakers had finally overcome long-standing objections to an American central bank, aiming to achieve two objectives – combating financial panics and enabling the internationalization of the dollar so that New York might challenge then-dominant London as a global financial centre.[66] The objectives of prudence and primacy would soon find themselves at odds with one another.

Britain suffered considerable economic and material damage during the First World War. Forced to suspend the gold standard (effectively imposing capital controls), it was desperately short on gold. Initially, Bank of England Governor Montagu Norman sought to restore Britain's global financial primacy by encouraging the reserve use of sterling abroad. But American policymakers were not content to leave the field

Table 4.1. British and American Financial Reforms, 1879–1930

Development	British reforms	American reforms
Plateau, 1879–1918	**ca. 1879: Double liability rules for banks; capital minimums;** *gold standard constrains monetary policy* **1900: Companies required to make annual audits 1914: Defence of the Realm Act; gold embargo**	**ca. 1879: strong reporting requirements; numerous state-level laws; limitations on national banks;** *lender-of-last resort functions performed by voluntary clearing houses* *1890: Sherman Silver Purchase Act fuels bubble* *1900: Gold Standard Act commits United States to gold standard* **1908: Aldrich–Vreeland Act helps national banks form clearing houses 1913: Federal Reserve created** *1914: Victory of internationalists inside Fed commits United States to countercyclical monetary policy*
Competition, 1919–30	*1919–23: Bank of England encourages reserve use of sterling abroad* *1924: Return to gold at overvalued rate commits Bank of England to countercyclical policies*	*1925: Fed cuts rate to assist gold restoration* *1927: Fed cuts rate to assist gold restoration* *1925–29: Explosion of broker's loans without regulation*

to Britain. Under the Dawes/Young plan, they proposed to return the critical German economy to the gold standard, rebuffing an attempt to do the same on a sterling basis. Their thinking was that if Germany returned to gold, many other countries – including the British dominions – were likely to follow, forcing Britain to act decisively to salvage its international position. Despite the deterioration of the fundamentals of the British economy, key British policymakers such as Chancellor of the Exchequer Winston Churchill and Bank of England Governor Montagu Norman aimed to restore Britain to the gold standard at the overvalued pre-war exchange rate of $4.86. Critical to the decision was the desire to send a strong signal that Britain was "back" and ready to resume its role as the key global financial market. The problem was that the overvalued pound hurt British exports and undermined the British gold position. French policymakers played a spoiler role – France resumed the gold standard with an undervalued currency, allowing it to hoard gold.

In short, the major world economies returned to a world of free-flowing capital in a manner that guaranteed significant current account imbalances – with some countries running large surpluses and others running large deficits. American policymakers, such as New York Federal Reserve Bank (FRBNY) Governor Benjamin Strong, faced the dilemma of prudence versus primacy. For global financial primacy to mean something, other countries had to be involved in the global financial system. Strong responded, keeping interest rates low – even in the face of the bubble on Wall Street during the late 1920s.[67] When the bubble collapsed, Strong's successors similarly responded to external demands (i.e., the need to maintain America's gold reserve position) over domestic ones (i.e., the need to respond to the world's worst financial crisis in human history). The key developments of this chapter, and how they fit into the schema of the book, are summarized in table 4.1.

The (Financial) Pax Britannica

Late nineteenth-century Britain is the *sine qua non* of a plateauing lead economy. Absent external competition, it had been able to sustain strict financial regulations – resulting in somewhat slower growth. Although Britain's relative technological and military power was beginning to ebb, its emerging global economy, linked together by the gold standard, afforded it immense structural benefits. British financial leadership was relatively strong until the Panic of 1914 (Feis 1930, 3–17). Let us briefly recount the nature and extent of British power.

The new double liability banking rules implemented in 1878 fostered caution in the domestic lending activities of British banks. Baker and Collins (1999, 442) show a turn away from private-sector credit, falling from 74 per cent of bank assets in 1877 to 57 per cent by 1900. Instead, investors sought out international opportunities, such as utility stocks or public debt – particularly that of the newly developing Americas. As a result, British industry faced greater difficulties obtaining capital from banks and other traditional sources than their continental and American peers (Kennedy 1987; Edelstein 1982; Suter 1992).[68] The timing of this development was unfortunate. By the 1880s, the "railway age" was coming to an end, while new technologies held promise: steel, chemicals, and heavy engineering all lay at the bleeding edge of technology (Freeman and Soete 1997, 55–105). Although Britain was a successful innovator in many of these areas – for instance, developing the first synthetic dyes (Murmann 2003) – the United States and Germany exploited these new technologies more successfully. Steel production followed a similar pattern, with Britain leading at first, but falling behind by the end of the century. This generated a vicious cycle for Britain – the short shrift given to industry meant less growth domestically, which, in turn, pushed the attention of British investors further towards overseas opportunities.

Facing low returns at home, British investors sought high returns abroad. Foreign investment entailed risks and rewards of its own, as illustrated by the Barings Crisis of 1890. No foreign market was more exciting than Argentina, which was billed as "the next United States." At the head of those seeking to profit from Argentina's rise was the Barings Bank – a merchant bank nicknamed "the sixth great power." Throughout much of the nineteenth century, Barings was one of the few firms with a presence in Argentina. By the 1880s, the political reintegration of Buenos Aires, and the enactment of free-banking laws in the country, generated a stampede of capital flows, with investment rising from £25 million in 1880 to £150 million by 1890 (Ziegler 1988; Eichengreen 1999). However, by 1890, unsustainable lending by deregulated banks and runaway inflation had drained Argentina's gold reserves, pushing the Banco de la Nación to the brink of bankruptcy. Worse, unrest in Buenos Aires inhibited the Argentine government from reining in excesses. When investors began to doubt Argentina's ability to service its debt, pressure built on the reserves of the Barings Bank, coming to a head in 1890. The collapse of Barings precipitated a deep recession, despite a bailout orchestrated by the Bank of England. Although the Barings Crisis itself did not prompt major regulatory reform, modest changes did occur to rules around banking reporting laws by 1900 (Robb 1992).

Despite the crisis, Britain remained powerful. By the 1897 Diamond Jubilee of Queen Victoria, the British Empire ruled over 20 per cent of the world's land mass and nearly 25 per cent of its population (Britain. Census Office 1906). On a per capita basis, Britain was the richest country in the world (Maddison 2009). The British navy possessed 40 per cent of the world's capital ships, double the share of the next-biggest navy, France (Lee and Thompson 2017). At the dawn of the twentieth century, transatlantic telegraph cables were established, giving Britain control over the channels of information as well (Hugill 1999, 25–52).

Yet, of all Britain's capabilities, none compared to the structural power afforded it through its centrality to global finance. Defeated in the Franco-Prussian War, saddled with indemnity, and deprived of two of its richest provinces, France was in no position to revive the monetary ambitions of Napoléon III. Instead, the major currencies of the world acceded to the primacy of gold and, correspondingly, of Britain.[69] In a testament to Britain's capability, states turned to gold without British coercion. By 1879, the gold standard included Britain, Australia, Canada, Belgium, the Netherlands, Uruguay, Portugal, Switzerland, Denmark, Finland, Norway, Sweden, France, Germany, and the United States. Additional waves of joiners in the 1880s and 1890s would bring in Latin America, the Austro-Hungarian Empire, the Ottoman Empire, Italy, Spain, and much of Eastern Europe.

Network externalities were critical to the spread of gold. As each country joined the gold standard, the benefits increased to prospective joiners. When the United States held an election in 1896 between the pro-gold Republican, William McKinley, and the pro-silver Democrat, William Jennings Bryan, it took little effort to portray the gold standard as the sensible choice. One Republican poster displayed a couple outside the Democratic National Convention looking at pro-silver posters in China, India, Mexico, South America, Guatemala, and Japan. The tagline was a single word: "dubious."

London prospered immensely from the spread of the gold standard. It was inefficient to ship large quantities of gold across the ocean to settle national balance of payments. Markets believed that the pound sterling – defended to the hilt by a British Parliament dominated by the investor class – was as good as gold. Confidence in Britain's commitment to gold was immense – even if the country ran small current account deficits, expectations prevented devaluation of the pound (Broz 1997a). To some extent, the political economies of Britain, France, and Germany formed a mutually beneficial ecosystem. Lacking the same vote of confidence from global markets, the central banks of France and Germany maintained much larger gold reserves. In times of duress, they might bail out the British. In contrast to Kindleberger's (1973) notion that hegemons provide the public goods necessary to keep the international system afloat, British policymakers found it easier to outsource such tasks to others.

The universality of the British pound also made London the ideal place for the development of a market in trade acceptances. Importers and exporters often found it convenient to agree to make payments for deliveries at a future date. Banks could act as an intermediary, giving out acceptance notes that the recipient could use to withdraw funds later. The arrangement increased the scope for transactions because banks were more creditworthy than other parties. Banks, in turn, could reap substantial profits by undertaking many trade acceptance deals. Able to pool risk and specialize in knowledge about the creditworthiness of different traders, banks were less threatened than individual traders by non-payment of obligations (Broz 1999). Thus, British banks had access to a highly profitable market in which they faced limited international competition.

British investors possessed an additional advantage over others: their investments into the empire were protected by the empire. Remember the Lucas (1990) paradox? Lucas observed that investment typically flows from wealthy countries to other wealthy countries, even though the highest returns on investment exist in the developing world, because political risk is greater there. Nineteenth-century Britain had a solution to the Lucas paradox: the British military could protect British investments inside the empire. Even outside the empire, Britain's unparalleled naval power gave it incredible leverage – Britain could cut off access to the channels of global trade and investment to others.

Not only was Britain the richest country in the world, but it was also well placed to benefit from the rise of others. Despite periodic challenges (e.g., the Indian Mutiny of 1857 and the Boer War), the empire could be run on the cheap. For much of the latter half of the nineteenth century, the British army exerted control over 20 per cent of the globe with only 200,000 to 300,000 troops (Rasler and Thompson 1994, 196–7). The burden of empire was light – British debt as a percentage of GDP fell throughout the nineteenth century from 260 per cent in 1821 to 30 per cent in 1900 (Hills, Thomas, and Dimsdale 2010). Lest Britons question the moral justification of keeping millions under imperial servitude, British leaders were happy to renew the lease of life on the imperial cause. In 1897, Secretary of State for the Colonies Joseph Chamberlain (1897) declared that while past empires had run their empires for pecuniary advantage, the new empire operated with a sense of kindred spirit (in the case of the white self-governing dominions, like Canada) and noblesse oblige (in the case of territories with a majority non-white population). Although Britain was no longer the workshop of the world, at the end of the nineteenth century, Britannia's control over the vital networks of finance, information, and trade was stronger than ever.

The core of the Conservative and Liberal Parties supported free trade orthodoxy. The two parties often behaved similarly as they fought for the same swing voters, and Lewis Carroll satirized them in *Alice and Wonderland* as Tweedledum and Tweedledee. But as the nineteenth century wore on, the coalitions underlying British politics began to shift. The issue of Irish Home Rule divided many, particularly in the Liberal Party, with some favouring greater autonomy for Ireland and others steadfastly opposed. The Irish Question would see a rump of Liberal Unionists, led by Joseph Chamberlain, migrate from the Liberal Party to the Conservative Party. They would bring with them Chamberlain's enthusiasm for empire and desire for an "imperial preference" system – free trade inside the empire, tariffs for all others. The emergence of the heavy industries of the Second Industrial Revolution also split manufacturers. Whereas the textile mills had favoured free trade, the newer industries could benefit from some degree of protectionism. The growing trade union movement, and the expansion of the franchise too, portended shifting sands. In the 1906 election, the Conservative Party even campaigned in support of Chamberlain's protectionist ideas, albeit unsuccessfully (Irwin 1994).

The American Challenge to British Financial Leadership

The United States became the world's largest economy in 1872 (Maddison 2009). However, inadequate institutions prevented it from turning its bulk into a source of structural power – after the Bank Wars of the 1830s, the country did not even have a central bank. The story of the creation of the Federal Reserve contains within it the story of a rising power attempting to take on a leadership role in the global economy, with the structural benefits – namely, control over global acceptances markets – that such a role entailed.

Let us first survey the nature of American finance in the nineteenth century. Panics had beset the United States in 1873, 1884, 1890, 1893, and 1907. Since the Bank Wars of the 1830s, it lacked a central bank. When banks faced runs, their collapse ricocheted through the economy – each fall tightening credit markets further, worsening conditions for yet more financial institutions. Each year, agricultural harvests precipitated vast movements of capital from northeastern banks to interior ones to finance the harvest. The end of the harvest, in turn, prompted capital to flow back to the northeast. These capital movements frequently overwhelmed either the interior or the northeastern banks (Wicker 2000). The New York Clearing House, a voluntary association led by large bankers from New York City, could sometimes limit the damage from panics. However, most banks in the interior of the country received no such assistance from the Clearing House. During the Panic of 1893, 503 banks were forced to suspend operations, while the Panic of 1907 took down 73 (ibid., 4).

The absence of an American lender of last resort also had implications for the role of the United States within the global economy. Whereas many countries held British pounds in reserve, few held American currency. American commerce depended upon a quilt collection of bank notes from private banks, limiting the international role of American dollars. In particular, American financial institutions had no ability to engage in the lucrative trade acceptances market dominated by London.

Efforts to reform the American banking system evolved through the troublesome 1890s and 1900s. The dominant cleavage of the American Gilded Age was sectional, pitting the interests of different regions against one another (Bensel 1984). Monetary questions, such as whether the United States should operate on a gold or bimetallic basis, were a critical source of division. Agricultural interests in the south and west (not to mention silver mines) favoured bimetallism. Farmers hoped that the inflationary effects of adding silver to the money supply would raise the price of crops, making it easier for them to pay off debts (Rockoff 1990). In contrast, the wealthier northeast favoured a gold standard. The currency question divided politicians within the same party. In 1890, a Republican Congress, working with Republican President Benjamin Harrison, reopened silver production with the Sherman Silver Purchase Act. US gold reserves plummeted as speculators exchanged silver dollars for gold ones, prompting President Grover Cleveland, a "Bourbon Democrat,"[70] to end silver coinage in 1893. As the United States plunged into a depression, the currency question became the defining one in the 1896 election.

The populist, pro-silver Democratic presidential candidate, William Jennings Bryan, squared off against supporters of a gold standard, like President Grover Cleveland and Republican candidate William McKinley. A charismatic orator, Bryan crossed the country by train, delivering speeches to the masses replete with memorable lines like, "We shall not crucify mankind upon a cross of gold" (Bryan 1896) and folksy allegories using irrigation to explain monetary policy (Rockoff 1990). Flush with cash, McKinley ran a "front porch" campaign, showering the country with advertisements. He won the populous northeast and ultimately the presidency. Although the enshrinement of the gold standard in 1900 ended the currency question, debates about bank reform continued. New York banking interests favoured the creation of an asset-based currency and legal status for a system of national clearing houses, but legislative efforts to enact their proposal failed (Wicker 2005).

On 14 October 1907, shares of the United Copper Company reached all-time highs on the New York Stock Exchange (NYSE). F.A. Heinze and Charles Morse, a pair of speculators, were trying to corner the market on United Copper shares. The company crashed two days later, putting immense pressure on the network of financial institutions linked to the two men (Tallman and Moen 1990; Bruner and Carr 2007). By 21 October, the fallout had spread to the powerful Knickerbocker bank – depositors panicked as its president resigned. In Britain, such a collapse would have prompted action by the Bank of England. In the United States, however, the main response came from the New York Clearing House, then led by prominent New York banker John Pierpont Morgan. Although his stock ticker was spewing out disastrous results, he initially refused to bail out Knickerbocker. Rather, he proposed to rescue the Trust Company of America, which was in better shape. On 24 October, John D. Rockefeller ponied up $10 million to aid the rescue effort, and $25 million from the US Treasury followed. Morgan proposed an additional $25 million rescue fund, supported by other financial institutions (Bruner and Carr 2007, 94–100). He hosted directors of the leading banks in his opulent study on 2 November, locking the doors until those present contributed the necessary funds for the rescue (124). The Panic began to ebb.

The Panic of 1907 highlighted weaknesses in the American banking system, prompting public demand for reforms. Republican Senator and Chair of the Senate Banking Commission Nelson Aldrich shepherded a bill through Congress, allowing groups of national banks to create clearing houses. The measure was only a stopgap, however. He also launched a National Monetary Commission to address more long-term reforms (Wicker 2005, 42–52).

One way to reform the American banking system was to create a central bank, and one of the major advocates of such a course was Paul Warburg (Warburg 1930, 11–30). A recent immigrant from Germany, Warburg's advocacy was initially hampered by his imperfect command of English. However, he was also deeply intellectual, highly driven, and well connected – his family was linked to the powerful Kuhn and Loeb banking network (Chernow 2016).[71] Warburg was sceptical of the political prospects of wholesale reform. In one 1908 editorial, he called for the creation of a centralized clearing house, hoping to establish the germ of a European-style central bank in the United States. He argued that such a development would allow the country to finally "be respected as a modern and civilized nation."[72] Speaking before the National Monetary Commission, he added another element to his argument, emphasizing acceptances markets. He depicted the structural benefits earned by European, and mostly British, financial firms as an "annual tribute resulting from our primitive financial system" (Warburg 1910). A central bank could allow for the internationalization of the US dollar, setting the stage for an American role in acceptances markets.

Warburg also pushed the *Banking Law Journal* to conduct a poll of American bankers about the creation of a central bank, which found broad support. According to the poll, 60 per cent of banks favoured the creation of a central bank, with limited variation across regions. Support was highest in the Pacific region and New England at 73 per cent, but still above 50 per cent across the country (White 1983, 92). However, the poll had been vaguely worded, without clarifying whether the bank would be private or government-run. From the 200 detailed responses made public, it is clear that the nature of a central bank was a source of controversy. Western banks feared that a private bank would be beholden to Wall Street, while eastern banking interests preferred a privately controlled bank.

Warburg's ideas reached Nelson Aldrich. Through his own studies of European central banks as part of the National Monetary Commission, Aldrich had reached conclusions similar to Warburg's. Indeed, the pair differed mainly on one point: Aldrich thought that Warburg had not gone far enough (Wicker 2005). Due to the sectional divisions in the United States, however, Aldrich's endorsement was no guarantee of success. Progressives and populists despised him, seeing him as a bagman for large trusts. On the 16 May 1906 cover of the political satire magazine *Puck*, Aldrich was depicted as a giant spider, trapping legislation in a web stretching from the Capitol buildings to a Standard Oil well. He was linked by marriage to the Rockefeller family, and in command of a powerful political machine, so the depiction was not entirely unfair.

Aldrich invited a carefully selected group of attendants to the Jekyll Island resort in Georgia, where they designed a plan for wholesale banking reform. To avoid scrutiny by the press, the attendees were instructed to dress for a duck-hunting trip. They included Paul Warburg, who offered a link to the Kuhn and Loeb network as well as his own banking expertise. Henry Davison, a senior partner at J.P. Morgan & Co., linked the group to the Morgan banking network. Davison is often credited as providing the social glue to the Jekyll Island group, a vital role given Warburg's impatience with those who differed with his vision. Frank Vanderlip, president of National City Bank, was also in attendance. Vanderlip had authored a book, *The American Commercial Invasion of Europe* (1902), detailing the international possibilities awaiting American finance and industry. For him, reforming the financial system was an important goal (Cleveland and Huertas 1985, 54–71). Professor Piatt Andrew, assistant secretary of the Treasury, provided a link to the Taft administration with his attendance. Finally, Aldrich's secretary, Arthur Shelton, was also present at Jekyll Island (Lowenstein 2015, 109).

By most accounts, Warburg helped push the Jekyll Island group definitively towards a central bank (Broz 1997b; Lowenstein 2015). For instance, in a letter to him, Vanderlip refers to "your definite plan," noting that he was "greatly impressed" (Vanderlip to Warburg, 1 March 1910, Frank A. Vanderlip Papers, Rare Book & Manuscript Library, Columbia University Libraries, New York). Not only did Warburg convince other Jekyll Island attendees that a central bank could do a better job of preventing bank runs than the New York City Clearing House, he also made the case that a central bank could lay the foundations for American leadership in the global acceptances market (Broz 1997b, 1999). Indeed, immediately upon returning from Jekyll Island, Vanderlip made enquiries about the prospects of ramping up international banking operations (Vanderlip to Aldrich, 28 November 1910, Frank A. Vanderlip Papers). Following the meeting, Aldrich presented a bill proposing a private central bank with regional branches, in a concession to Midwestern bankers (White 1983, 91).

Warburg had also insisted that legislative efforts be supported by the creation of a league in favour of banking reform. A fund of $500,000 was created to support a Citizen's League for the Promotion of a Sound Banking System (Jacobs and King 2016, 64). It was to be headquartered in Chicago, giving it the appearance of a corn-fed, Midwestern institution. Officially, the league was simply a group of concerned citizens lacking a position on a central bank. Unofficially, however, it was completely aligned with the goals of the Jekyll Island group. League publicity materials listed a series of objectives matching the Aldrich Plan. One wonders how many actual citizens shared these priorities. For a moment, let us consider the implausible chorus: What do we want? "Legalization of acceptances of time bills of exchange in order to create a discount market at home and abroad" (Warburg 1930, 72). When do we want it? Now!

Just as the Jekyll Island coalition had settled upon a plan, the Republican Party was defeated in the 1910 House of Representatives elections. The setback dealt a blow to the prospects for a central bank. Many incoming Democratic members of Congress were aligned with the populist ideas of William Jennings Bryan and feared that New York would dominate any central bank. The new chair of the House Committee on Banking and Currency, Arsène Pujo, was particularly critical of what he called "the money trust." He created a committee to investigate the anti-competitive nature of the trusts, even calling upon J.P. Morgan to testify. Planning to retire, Aldrich wanted a bill creating a central bank as his swansong. But he was swimming against a powerful current: when he proposed central banking legislation, it was defeated.

The 1912 presidential election offered little hope for advocates of a central bank. Republican President William Howard Taft was sympathetic, but his electoral chances were slim. He faced a primary challenge from popular former president Theodore Roosevelt (under whom Taft had served as vice-president). After losing the nomination to Taft in the Republican National Convention, Roosevelt bolted from the party and launched a presidential campaign on the Progressive Party ticket. Warburg recounts one luncheon held to educate Roosevelt in the intricacies of banking issues, saying that Roosevelt came in knowing virtually nothing, but left seemingly won over to the Aldrich Plan (Warburg 1930, 77). Despite Warburg's impressions, the Progressive Party platform came out against the plan. On the Democratic side, Woodrow Wilson won the

Democratic nomination over William Jennings Bryan. Fearful of losing support from Bryan's backers, Wilson avoided taking a position on a central bank. In the ensuing election, Taft and Roosevelt split the votes of traditional Republicans, allowing Wilson to win the Electoral College in a landslide. The Democrats also took control of the Senate and the House, seemingly dooming the chances of the Aldrich Plan.

The campaign for an American central bank was saved by a mix of happenstance and foresight. When Pujo left Congress after the 1912 election, he was replaced as chair of the House Committee on Banking and Currency by Virginia representative Carter Glass. Glass knew little about economic matters (Lowenstein 2015, 164–78), so, seeking to prepare for his new job, he turned to Henry Parker Willis. Willis was a professor who had taught his children at Washington and Lee University and the author of *A History of the Latin Monetary Union*, a book ascribing the formation of the Latin Monetary Union to the imperialist aims of Napoléon III.[73] Willis was sympathetic to the goal of creating a central bank. Indeed, he had even authored some of the promotional materials for the National Citizens' League for the Promotion of a Sound Banking System, which was headed by his PhD adviser, James Laughlin.

Through Willis, Warburg was once again able to exert influence on policymakers. He was tasked with designing a central bank that would fit with the preferences of the Democratic Party (Warburg 1930, 82). At his insistence, Glass proposed a government-controlled central bank that would accept a broad array of bills for discount. The new plan also included fourteen Federal Reserve districts as a concession to Bryanites fearful of the undue influence of New York (White 1983).[74]

The Jekyll Island coalition broke apart: some members supported the Federal Reserve Act, some opposed government control, and others opposed the number of districts. Vanderlip expressed his opposition to the new scheme, proposing an alternative (Warburg 1930, 132). However, with the support of some congressional Republicans, most congressional Democrats, and the newly elected president, Woodrow Wilson, the bill passed (White 1983). While the Jekyll Island group was important in putting a central bank on the agenda, Democrats – including many Bryanite populists – were critical to the actual passage of the bill.

The precise nature of the newly created Federal Reserve System was still uncertain in 1913. Although supporters of lender-of-last-resort institutions and those desiring to internationalize the dollar agreed on the need for a central bank, their priorities differed. Domestic financial stability required a Federal Reserve willing to act counter-cyclically – providing liquidity when none was available and stamping out speculative bubbles before they grew too large. In contrast, internationalizing the dollar required a steadfast commitment to the gold standard to establish New York as the new centre of global finance. To play a role in the global acceptances market, the United States would have to remain open to inflows and outflows of capital, while the Federal Reserve would have to defend the exchange rate at all costs.

The first test of the relative importance of these two priorities came before the Federal Reserve's first meeting. The 28 June 1914 assassination of Austrian Archduke Franz Ferdinand set off a chain of events that pulled Europe into the First World War. Once war began, investors panicked – numerous countries experienced currency crises as capital outflows threatened their commitment to gold. Across the Old World, most countries responded by imposing capital controls to save their domestic economies. Treasury Secretary William McAdoo behaved differently, shutting down Wall Street for four months to uphold the American commitment to the gold standard (Sibler 2008). Once the United States was established as the only country maintaining gold convertibility, gold poured into the country.

Although the Federal Reserve Act itself left much open, the scramble for power inside the Federal Reserve would establish the dominance of an internationalist faction, committed to extending American financial power. Charles Hamlin, a twice-failed Democratic candidate for governor of Massachusetts, was appointed as the first chair of the Board of Governors of the Federal Reserve. Paul Warburg served alongside him, to the frequent consternation of the latter. In his diary, Hamlin wrote of Warburg, "I am about satisfied Warburg is absolutely out of sympathy with Reserve Act unless he can turn it into a vast system of centralization with N.Y. the predominating factor & that he is representing the wishes of the N.Y. banks rather than the people – in fact I suspect he has little sympathy with the people" (Charles S. Hamlin Diaries, vol. 2, box 356, folder 16, p. 67, Manuscript Division, Library of Congress, Washington, DC).

Although Federal Reserve Board members were divided on the priorities of the institution, its decentralized structure actually favoured the internationalists. As Warburg (1930) admits, the creation of multiple Federal Reserve districts amplified the importance of the FRBNY. Able to communicate easily with bankers in the largest financial centre in the country, the New York Fed effectively had a first-mover advantage. By acting first in the face of new information, it could determine how the rest of the Federal Reserve would respond.

Warburg insisted on the appointment of Benjamin Strong as governor of the New York Fed, a concession Hamlin granted, "altho we had reason to fear that choice might be attacked on ground that Strong would not have courage to withstand N.Y. capitalists influence" (Charles S. Hamlin Diaries, vol. 2, box 356, folder 16, p. 67). Strong was intimately connected to J.P. Morgan & Co., having been made a partner at Bankers Trust by his mentor, Henry Davison. When Strong's wife committed suicide in 1905, Davison took in Strong's three children (Lowenstein 2015, 64). Strong, in turn, was deeply devoted to his work. During the Panic of 1907, he had worked tirelessly alongside J.P. Morgan to avert a crash. He had similar views to Warburg about the prospects for the development of international banking operations, appointing an expert on the London bill market early in his tenure (Chandler 1958; Meltzer 2003, 74–5), while using his position to advocate broader interpretations of the Federal Reserve Act (Charles S. Hamlin Diaries, vol. 3, box 365, folder 17, p. 111). Strong also strongly favoured the maintenance of the gold standard, exhibiting a willingness to accept deflation (or inflation) to uphold the commitment to gold.

Within the Federal Reserve Board, debate ensued over the role of banker's acceptances outlined in the Federal Reserve Act. The act was vague on the question as some language on acceptances had been dropped in the course of legislative debate. Some members, such as Adolph Miller,[75] feared that such an allowance would have inflationary effects. Internally, Warburg released a memo arguing against this interpretation. But externally, he evangelized for the cause, declaring in a 1915 speech that "if our large banks individually open such credit for the European banks in England and on the Continent it would help the European countries involved; it would be good business for the American banks and it would be a great step in advance in establishing our American acceptances as a factor in world markets" (Warburg to Vanderlip, 17 June 1915, Frank A. Vanderlip Papers). Later, he evangelized about the prospects of New York supplanting London in a speech to the New York State Banker's Convention on 9 June 1916, declaring, "One of the most tangible results of the operation of the Federal Reserve System is the establishment and growth of the American banker's acceptance business" (Paul Warburg Speech included in letter, 16 June 1916, Frank A. Vanderlip Papers), while cheering American bankers for entering a field once monopolized by the Europeans.

Subsequent amendments to the Federal Reserve Act liberalized the rules governing acceptances. By 1919, firms could take on acceptance contracts worth as much as 100 per cent of their capital (Ferderer 2003). The new rules fostered rapid growth in the American acceptance industry, which grew from $250 million in 1917 to $1 billion by the end of the First World War (ibid., 670). After leaving the Federal Reserve in 1918, Paul Warburg continued to exert political influence, forming the

American Acceptance Council in 1919. Thus, the desires of the internationalists in the Fed to support New York City as a centre of global finance were supported by a growing industry.[76] At the same time, however, the institution's internationalist orientation undermined its ability to play the prudential role of combating speculation and softening the impact of crises.

The First World War and British Decline

All financial epochs rest on assumptions about the state of the world. Those assumptions rarely hold across all time and space. For the Victorians, particularly those sending investment capital around the world, peace was one of those assumptions. Great-power war was thought unlikely, and any war would be a war of manoeuvre, like the Franco-Prussian War of 1870 (House 1976). Despite the challenge of German naval construction, the British navy remained the strongest – surely Britain could continue to defend the sea lanes vital for world trade and global investment. And, after all, with the world densely linked by trade and investment, war would be so costly as to be unthinkable (Angell 1913, x–xi).

Belief in the impossibility of conflict is one of the oldest sources of bubbles. Time and time again, the outbreak of war bursts assumptions of perpetual peace, triggering financial panic. Austria–Hungary's 1914 declaration of war on Serbia acted like a giant margin call. Even as many reassured themselves that the war would be over by Christmas, markets were jolted. Investors sold securities in a frenzy, seeking the security of gold, spreading panic through the world's stock markets. Apart from the United States, which shut down its own securities markets, every country in the world was forced to suspend convertibility as investors redeemed bank notes and securities for gold (Sibler 2008). The Panic of 1914 delivered economic pain worse than a massive bombing campaign to the entire world – belligerent and non-belligerent state alike – even before the worst of the fighting had taken place.

Contrary to expectations of a war of manoeuvre, the First World War was a war of attrition. On the Western Front, both sides formed trenches, periodically sending men over the top to be slaughtered by machine gun fire. Along the mountainous border between Italy and the Austro-Hungarian Empire, soldiers were similarly compelled to advance against inhospitable terrain. Terrain offered more movement on the Eastern Front, but greater distances prevented a decisive defeat for Russia until 1917. Assembling the resources to arm millions of soldiers and maintaining a social order able to compel those soldiers to charge into near-certain death were beyond the capacities of the night-watchman state. As a result, every combatant state expanded its role in the economy during the war (Rasler and Thompson 1989; Tilly 1990). Moreover, Britain and France borrowed heavily from the United States to maintain their war effort. Gold flowed out of Europe, particularly to the United States and Japan (Bytheway and Meltzer 2016, 28–63).

In Britain, the expanded role of the state, coupled with the dislocations of the war, weakened the power of the financial sector. Fearing instability, Parliament shut down the LSE in 1914, reopening only under severe restrictions, maintained by the Defence of the Realm Act (Michie 2001, 143–69). The act required Treasury assent to any new issues of capital and share transactions. A broad role for government in banking persisted as well. After the Midland Bank took over the London Joint Stock Bank, the Treasury formed the Committee on Bank Amalgamations and prevented further mergers (Capie 1995, 397–8).

The liquidation of securities hit international finance particularly hard – the stock of British foreign investment collapsed during the war, even compared to other securities or the economy as a whole (see figure 4.1). While the political fortunes of international finance waned, however, the war strengthened the bargaining position of the British working class. To win the war, Britain needed ever more troops to go "over the top" and ever more workers to keep the army supplied. Generous political bargains were necessary to keep Britain fighting, while at the same time avoiding strikes. A war of attrition can be lost very suddenly if workers and soldiers refuse to serve. Following the immense losses in Verdun in 1916, French troops were close to mutiny. Failure to address the demands of the working class ultimately doomed Russia and Germany. In 1917, Bolshevik revolutionaries seized power in Russia after it had negotiated peace with Germany. In 1918, Germany sued for peace after the Kiel naval mutiny spread throughout the country.

In Britain, the Liberal government of Prime Minister Herbert Asquith faced pressure to balance the needs of fighting a total war with the precepts of British finance (Horn 2002, 37). When he proved unable to commit sufficient resources to the war, he was ousted, replaced by the more hawkish "national Liberal" David Lloyd George in a National Government coalition with the Conservative Party. The coalition represented a different sectoral alliance. Whereas industrialists had historically favoured the Liberal Party, and finance the Conservative Party, the new National Government was an alliance between both (Cain and Hopkins 1993, 2001, 409–63). Lloyd George aggressively pursued the war, sequestrating securities to finance new loans from the United States. As a result, Britain emerged from the war with a more

Figure 4.1. Bank Deposits, Market Capitalization, Foreign-Investment Assets, and GDP (millions of £2008), 1914–19

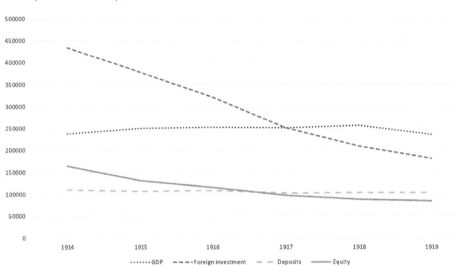

Sources: Foreign investment: Imlah (1958); market capitalization: Yale School of Management (n.d.); bank deposits: Capie and Webber (1985); GDP, GDP deflator: Officer (2020).

constrained domestic financial system. Although many countries maintained a nominal commitment to gold, capital controls prevented the proliferation of linkages that had characterized pre-war globalization. An embargo on foreign lending continued through the early 1920s (Atkin 1970). As a result, central banks and other lender-of-last-resort institutions could respond effectively to domestic needs. Tightly regulated, mired in debt, and increasingly closed, London emerged from the First World War unable to resume its pre-war role as the leading global financial centre. On the other hand, the United States sat atop a mountain of gold and had transitioned from the world's biggest debtor to the world's banker.

The Gold-Exchange Standard and Britain's Return to Gold

In this section, I begin by describing a decisive moment in world history. Winston Churchill, chancellor of the exchequer, sought the advice of the Treasury on whether to return to the gold standard. Few figures exerted more influence on Churchill than Bank of England Governor Montagu Norman. The exchanges between Churchill and Norman set the stage for an overvalued pound, resulting in global imbalances that led to the Great Depression, the collapse of the liberal global order, and the horrors of the Second World War. Let us first zoom in on that moment and then zoom out at the larger scope of British policy in the years following the First World War.

Montagu Norman was an odd figure in the staid world of central banking. Tall and raffishly dressed, his pointed goatee recalled a sixteenth-century courtier (Ahamed 2014, 23–33). He preferred the company of artists to bankers. For someone tasked with the leadership of an institution that strives for continuity and stability, Norman was rather volatile. Once a sickly child, and an uninspired banker in the family concern, he found a sense of confidence and purpose during his service in the Boer War.[77] A broken engagement in 1906 sparked the first of his many nervous breakdowns. Prone to bouts of euphoria followed by deep depression, he was once informed by psychiatrist Carl Jung that he would die in a few months from tertiary syphilis. Yet Norman did not die – he reinvented himself by accepting the life he had once dreaded. Thanks to his family connections to an august banking dynasty,[78] Norman gained a position as director at the Bank of England in 1907 and rose through the ranks, becoming governor in 1920.

On 2 February 1925, Norman jaunted up the white stone steps of the Bank of England. During a February day of 44 degrees Fahrenheit (*Times* [London], 3 February 1925), he might have mused about the possibility of disappearing on a cruise using his preferred pseudonym: Professor Clarence Skinner (Ahamed 2014, 217). Atop the stairs, he would have opened the massive black metal doors, adorned by lions holding keys. The historical record is uncertain, but ethnographies of English culture might lead me to imagine that, on his way to his office, he endured a series of conversations about the weather (Fox 2014, 35–50).

As Norman entered his office, he would have found a letter from Winston Churchill, then chancellor of the exchequer. His Majesty's Government was contemplating a British return to the gold standard at its pre-war parity of $4.86. Perhaps bitten by one of his own "black dog" days of depression, Churchill agonized about the decision, sending out a letter to Treasury and Bank of England employees demanding a response to the case *against* a return to gold. The letter noted that the question went beyond the "financial and currency aspects" of gold standard restoration and that the interests of "the merchant, the manufacturer, the workman and the consumer" might have conflicting interests over this question ("The Exercise," 29 January 1925, T172/1499B, Treasury files, TNA).

Norman must have contemplated Britain's position in the world – should the return to gold be delayed, or should Britain accept a weaker exchange rate reflective of the shocks of the war? Was it possible to restore what had been lost? His thoughts might have turned to Keynes's (1920, 11) nostalgic dirge for the lost civilization of the long nineteenth century:

> What an extraordinary episode in the progress of man that age was which came to an end in August 1914! ... The inhabitant of London could order by telephone, sipping his morning tea in bed, the various products of the whole earth ... he could at·the same time and by the same means adventure his wealth in the natural resources and new enterprise of any quarter of the world.

By 1925, that world lay in ruins. The war had cost the British Empire the lives of over a million people, and its dislocations had shut down the global markets. The gold standard – once a thread tying the world to London – had been severed by the violent convulsions of Europe's great powers. Untouched by war, the United States was usurping influence over the networks of trade and finance that had made Britain powerful. The face of Europe was reshaped – Germany was defanged, the Austro-Hungarian Empire had been carved up into a multitude of states, Italy was ruled by a fascist dictator, and the Russian Empire had fallen to a Bolshevik revolution. As new states formed, they often erected protectionist barriers, shutting their markets to British goods (Feinstein, Temin, and Toniolo 1997). Despite these changes, Norman sounded an optimistic note in his reply to Churchill, writing, "Given similarity without delay in respect of Free Gold, it is likely that tradition and experience will gradually set London as high as New York as an international centre" (Letter from the Governor, 2 February 1925, T172/1499B, Treasury files, TNA). Perhaps Britain could reclaim its place as the world's banker after all.

How did British policymakers come upon the disastrous decision to return to the gold standard at $4.86? If this chapter can accomplish one thing, let it be the eternal banishment of the gold standard fetish theory. The fetish theory asserts that Britain was in the thrall of a City–Treasury axis for which the restoration of the gold standard was automatic.[79] This perspective ignores a few central points. The gold standard of the 1920s was not the same as the classical gold standard. It was a gold-exchange standard, where multiple gold-linked currencies formed the reserves of most states. Policymakers frequently violated the "rules of the game" – for instance, by sterilizing gold inflows: taking actions to prevent gold inflows from impacting the money supply (Bordo and MacDonald

2003). Britain, facing a weak gold position throughout the 1920s, relied on other countries to hold sterling in reserve.

Viable alternatives to the gold standard existed. Keynes's critiques of Britain's return to the gold standard, for instance, received due consideration, even among those firmly in the City–Treasury axis. Empire free trade was also a potential alternative to a cosmopolitan vision of Britain, with considerable support inside the National Government coalition and, later, the Conservative Party (Cain and Hopkins 1993, 2001, 409–63). Empire free trade entailed free movements of capital and goods inside the empire, with tariffs for everybody else. A statutory link to gold might remain, but with most trade and investment taking place inside the empire, its implications would be limited. Effectively, the vision meant choosing a kind of regionalization over renewed globalization. Different versions of this position had been championed by figures from Joseph Chamberlain to Conservative press baron and powerbroker Lord Beaverbrook.

Advocates of $4.86 prevailed over sceptics because they believed that it could restore British financial primacy. Given the choice between half a loaf and an uncertain shot at a full loaf, British policymakers chose the latter. Perhaps naively, many policymakers thought that once the gold standard had been restored, tradition and experience would once again put London at the centre of global finance. The return of British dominance of financial markets like trade acceptances (i.e., the recapture of the structural benefits of global financial leadership), in turn, would boost the pound, making $4.86 easier to maintain. They gambled, knowing that restoration entailed significant risks – they were tethering the smaller British economy to a larger American one, prone to wild fluctuations. Let us examine the course of events leading to Churchill's folly.

On 14 December 1918, a month after Germany signed its armistice with the Entente Powers, Britain held an election. The National Government campaigned on promises to deliver for those who had contributed to the war effort. Returning soldiers were promised a land fit for heroes, and the franchise was extended to nearly every Briton. Deferring to the Conservatives, Lloyd George also argued for the post-war strategy of imperial economic union over inter-allied economic cooperation (Cain and Hopkins 2001, 445). The components of his National Government (i.e., Conservatives and National Liberals) won a crushing victory.[80] Asquith's Liberals were reduced to only a handful of seats, while Labour became the official Opposition for the first time ever.

The gold standard question was a critical one for the Lloyd George government. Lloyd George expanded social spending, hoping to ease the post-war transition with a boom. But these expansionary policies did not yield the results he had anticipated. As soon as the pound was allowed to float, it plummeted from a pre-war level of $4.86 to $3.20 (Sayers 1976). Nor did the real economy fare well – real per capita GDP fell 10 per cent in 1919 and another 6 per cent in 1920 (Maddison 2009). A parliamentary committee headed by former Bank of England governor Lord Cunliffe investigated the matter. Its report favoured deflationary policies[81] as a way to hasten the return to the gold standard. The report expressed concern over sterling's fall, although it held that increases to the discount rate should be sufficient to defend the pound. Time was of the essence, however, since a "more permanently adverse trade balance"… "would have been in the end disastrous to our credit and the position of London as the financial centre of the world" (Britain. Parliament 1918, 87).

Many American policymakers also favoured the restoration of the gold standard. In 1922, the United States was like a skilled gambler forced to play solitaire. Although it possessed the world's largest reserves of gold, and despite New York's growing role in global finance, the United States enjoyed few of the structural benefits that had typified British primacy because global flows of trade and finance were constrained. A world of free and open flows of capital could allow it to profit from its enhanced financial fitness. Benjamin Strong and Montagu Norman, both firmly in the gold camp, developed a deep friendship. The two maintained a constant correspondence, meeting as often as they could. Japanese central banker Inoue Junnosuke once recalled that he would never forget the happiness of Montagu Norman upon meeting Benjamin Strong after a long absence (Bytheway and Meltzer 2016, 115). Internationally, the two reached out to other central bankers to expand support for a gold standard world.

There were good reasons to be sceptical about the desirability of restoring the gold standard. Fresh from the success of his book *The Economic Consequences of the Peace*, and newly rich from currency speculation, John Maynard Keynes inveighed against the gold standard. Rather than advocating the pursuit of currency stability, he favoured using monetary policy to respond to domestic conditions. Although Strong and Norman considered Keynes's (1923) ideas "erratic," the two frequently violated the orthodox rules of the gold standard (Strong to Norman, 4 January 1924, 1116.4, Papers of Benjamin Strong, Jr., Federal Reserve Bank of New York). Under the classical gold standard, large inflows of gold caused inflation by expanding the money supply. Higher prices, in turn, led to outflows of gold as individuals substituted foreign goods for domestic ones. Strong sterilized the heavy gold inflows into the United States, preventing the new gold from circulating through the economy and raising prices. Of course, with so much gold sitting idle in the United States, it was more difficult for other countries to return to gold.

In many respects, the problems of the gold standard – which was effectively a global currency union – can be observed in currency unions today. It is always easy to blame deficit countries for their profligacy, but countries that stubbornly cling to current account surpluses are often just as culpable. The most successful currency unions resolve these issues with a measure of magnanimity. Consider, for instance, the currency union undergirding the second-largest country in the world – Canada. Oil-rich Alberta and auto-exporting Ontario lack synchronized business cycles, making it difficult to adopt a monetary policy that works for both. However, regularized interprovincial transfers and fiscal federalism can help offset divergence between the two, while the Bank of Canada keeps the system afloat. Like the euro today, the gold standard of the 1920s lacked regular mechanisms for coordinating between deficit and surplus countries (Blyth 2013, 51–92).

The lingering impacts of the First World War and its settlement posed a second layer of challenges to the global economy. The great powers at the Paris Peace Conference imposed harsh conditions on Germany, including a clause assigning it guilt for the war and a reparations bill of $12.5 billion (Ahamed 2014, 200). For Britain and France, mired in debts incurred in the conduct of the war, reparations offered a way out. However, Weimar Germany found itself unable to manage the twin burden of paying reparations and resolving the competing demands of a fractured society. It resorted to financing domestic economic activity through inflation. Reichsbank President Rudolf von Havenstein printed money to enable the German government to cover its costs. Even as hyperinflation rendered the mark worthless, Havenstein continued to prime the presses. Ironically, thanks to the strict central bank independence insisted upon by the British, the German government was unable to stop runaway inflation (ibid., 63). It would be difficult to engineer the recovery of European trade without fixing the German problem.

Policymakers from the major economies met at Genoa in 1922 to discuss plans to salvage the global economy. Although the attendees agreed on the idea of restoring the gold standard, competing Anglo-American interests necessitated a gold-exchange standard as opposed to the classical gold standard. Under a gold-exchange standard, currencies would be fixed vis-à-vis gold, although, in practice, multiple key currencies (the American dollar, British pound sterling, and French franc) would be used as reserves. The gold-exchange standard entailed far greater risks of instability since the stability of the entire system depended upon each key currency avoiding "exorbitant privilege" (Bordo and MacDonald 2003). British policymakers preferred a gold-exchange standard because they believed that London's history as the centre of global finance would encourage others to deposit badly needed gold in Britain, in exchange for IOUs (Cleveland and Costigliola 1977). American policymakers, including Benjamin Strong, expressed doubt about the viability of such a scheme. The United States sat atop a mountain of gold, so, naturally, it stood to gain from a classical gold standard. On the other hand, both British and American policymakers desired to restore a world of free-flowing capital, even on an imperfect basis. They believed that their own country would soon emerge as the dominant financial power, able to reap the lion's share of structural benefits from the system.

Political conditions in Britain offered limited opportunities for a smooth restoration. The Conservatives broke from the Lloyd George coalition, winning a tenuous majority government in 1922. Prime Minister Andrew Bonar Law, however, soon resigned due to throat cancer. His successor, Stanley Baldwin, called another election in 1923, which saw a minority Labour government under Ramsay MacDonald come to power, supported by Asquith's Liberals. Although Labour was a socialist party, MacDonald's chancellor of the exchequer, Philip Snowden, favoured a gold standard, as did Labour's coalition partners (Ahamed 2014, 326). Markets, however, were unconvinced of Labour's commitment to gold – and following the party's victory, the pound plummeted.

Despite these setbacks, the Bank of England undertook significant efforts to ensure that the new global economic system would operate on terms favourable to Britain. Enunciating his views in "Memorandum C," Montagu Norman sought to construct a bloc of countries with currencies tied to the pound (Peteri 1992, 253). He sought to fill the vacuum in Central and Eastern Europe caused by the decline of the mark and the franc – making efforts to influence the establishment of central banks and to assist in stabilization. Maintaining the primacy of sterling was never far from his mind in these endeavours. In one letter to the governor of the South African Reserve Bank, he was blunt about his goals, declaring, "All for the good of Sterling!" (Montagu Norman, quoted in ibid.). The problem for Britain was that it lacked the capital to motivate others to go with the pound. British policymakers frequently schemed to use American capital to underwrite their own ambitions. For instance, the British government floated a proposal wherein the Soviet Union might open its capital markets to foreign investment. The hope was that American capital would flow to the USSR through London, allowing the City to make a tidy profit and improving Britain's balance of trade in the process. The scheme fell apart due to Soviet reticence to pay the debts incurred by the Russian Empire, but is a useful illustration of the nature of British policy proposals. Although the Treasury and the Bank of England were happy to invoke orthodoxy when it suited them, they also entertained risky schemes when it served their larger goal: the restoration of British financial primacy.

Germany's ongoing difficulties gave Norman an unexpected opening. Although inflationary finance allowed the German government to make domestic payments, reparations were due in *gold* reichsmark, which could not be inflated away. In 1923, after Germany had failed to make reparations payments, French troops occupied the Ruhr region. The German budget deficit doubled, intensifying Germany's reliance on inflationary finance. Between August and November 1923, the exchange rate between the mark and the dollar went from 620,000 to 1 to 630 billion to 1 (Ahamed 2014, 41). Faced with a severe crisis, Gustav Stresemann of the centre-right People's Party formed a coalition government that included centrists, socialists, and Catholics. The new government settled on the idea of introducing a new currency, backed by land and fixed in quantity, called the rentenmark. It would be managed by Hjalmar Schacht and would effectively compete with the von Havenstein–managed reichsmark. The rentenmark was launched in October, amid revolutionary conditions: a young Austrian-born upstart named Adolph Hitler led the Beer Hall Putsch in Bavaria in November 1923. The fascist coup attempt failed, however, and the rentenmark supplanted the reichsmark. Finally, on 20 November, von Havenstein died of a heart attack, opening up the Reichsbank presidency to Hjalmar Schacht. Schacht was eager to restore the German currency on a gold basis; however, he would need help to succeed.

He reached out to Montagu Norman, receiving a warm reception. The two developed plans for a gold discount bank in Germany: Britain would provide Germany with credits to initiate the scheme as well as the credibility of an endorsement from the Bank of England. In addition, Britain helped quash French plans to create a central bank in the occupied Rhineland (Costigliola 1988). Germany, in turn, would operate the gold discount bank on a sterling basis. The scheme could hypothetically restart trade in Europe, while also assisting Norman's aim to create a vast sterling bloc.

Simultaneously, President Calvin Coolidge dispatched Charles Dawes to Europe to develop a plan to kick-start the European economy. Unfortunately for Norman, the Americans wanted to do more than just write cheques. Informed of the details of Norman's plans by his brother Max,[82] Paul Warburg was livid. He sent letters protesting against American exclusion from the gold discount bank scheme to the Dawes Committee's Owen Young,[83] declaring, "It is the question of whether the dollar shall permanently retain a predominant position, or whether we are willing to surrender financial mastery to the pound sterling for good and all!" (Peteri 1992, 254). The Federal Reserve Advisory Committee, of which Warburg was chair, issued similar warnings, urging the United States to use its great financial strength to help others restore the gold standard lest the world turn to sterling.

The Dawes/Young plan aimed to restart German reparations payments, which could assist Britain and France in repaying their own debts to the United States. Rather than reducing Germany's total obligations – an issue certain to incur French objections – the Young plan focused on reducing Germany's annual payments to manageable levels, based on the idea that Germans should pay a tax burden similar to that in France and Britain. The United States would provide Germany with a loan covering the first year of payments, while helping Germany return to the gold standard. Strong opined that, as an added bonus, the impending return of Germany to gold would force Britain to make the adjustments necessary to restore a gold standard world (Peteri 1992, 256).

The Dawes/Young plan accelerated the timeline for restoring the gold standard in Britain. The British dominions, particularly South Africa, which mined a large proportion of the world's gold, were eager to restore the gold standard (Costigliola 1988). For instance, Otto Niemeyer, the controller of finance for His Majesty's Treasury, warned that if Britain did not act soon, "a gold bill would for instance replace the sterling bill" (Niemeyer, "The Gold Export Prohibition," undated memo, T172/1499B, Treasury files, TNA). In June 1924, Philip Snowden launched the Chamberlain–Bradbury Committee, tasked to investigate whether to end the gold embargo, thereby freeing up British flows of capital.

Following the rout of Labour in the 1924 election, Conservative Stanley Baldwin became prime minister once again, commanding a solid majority. He appointed Winston Churchill as chancellor of the exchequer. A stalwart imperialist and a committed free trader, Churchill defied the strictures of British party politics. Indeed, he had abandoned the Tories for the Liberals before returning to his old political home. Of his frequent party-switching, he is reputed to have said, "Anyone can rat, but it takes a certain ingenuity to re-rat" (Halle 1985, 42). Churchill was pragmatic on the question of the gold standard. A friend of Lord Beaverbrook's, who was an inveterate foe of the gold standard, it is hard to write Churchill off as a pawn of the City–Treasury axis. Treasury papers clearly show that he was aware of the arguments against a return to gold. In January 1925, for example, Churchill sent a letter to Niemeyer, making the case that the gold standard was obsolete and that the requisite increase in bank rates would be disastrous for the economy[84] ("The Exercise," 29 January 1925, T172/1499B, Treasury files, TNA). Lord Bradbury, the joint permanent secretary of the Treasury, wrote that Churchill's views "have a spiritual home in the Keynes–McKenna sanctuary," with some "trimmings ... furnished by the Daily Express" (Lord Bradbury, quoted in Moggridge 1972, 64).[85]

Churchill also later enquired as to the validity of Keynes's argument in the *Nation* that a return to gold would tie Britain to a wildly fluctuating American economy (*Nation* [London], 22 February 1925, T172/1499B, Treasury files, TNA). Anticipating the problems of credibility inherent in a gold-exchange standard (Bordo and MacDonald 2003) and the "golden straitjacket" problem (Eichengreen 1995), Keynes had characterized Americans as living in "a vast and unceasing crescendo" (*Nation* [London], 21 February 1925, T172/1499B, Treasury files, TNA). He had argued that an economy expanding as rapidly as that of the United States was likely to experience temporary crashes (as Britain had in the nineteenth century). While it could weather these fluctuations due to its general upward trajectory, Britain would face dire consequences if it were tethered to the American business cycle by the gold standard. Churchill's notes on the article question the "spectacle of Britain possessing the finest credit in the world simultaneously with a million and a quarter unemployed" (Churchill to Niemeyer, 22 February 1925, T172/1499B, Treasury files, TNA).

The pro-gold Treasury view held that it was necessary to restore the gold standard as soon as possible, pegging Britain to its pre-war parity of $4.86. Sir Ralph Hawtrey, an economist espousing the Treasury view, wrote to Churchill in response to Keynes, arguing that the risks of being tied to a fluctuating American economy were "remote" because "if we and most of Europe are on a gold standard, the immediate effect of inflation in America will be exports of gold from America to us. These exports of gold will tend of themselves to stop the inflation" (Hawtrey to Churchill, 2 March 1925, T172/1499B, Treasury files, TNA).

To some extent, however, the argument that gold exports would cancel out inflationary effects was disingenuous. The United States could sterilize the effects of gold inflows (indeed, Benjamin Strong was doing just that). Churchill had earlier floated the idea of paying large amounts of Britain's debt to the United States in gold, so as to overheat the American economy and ease a return to gold, and the Treasury had noted this possibility (Cleveland and Costigliola 1977, 913). Otto Niemeyer said of Churchill's plan, "The United States could stand a good deal of this diet without swelling much" (Niemeyer to Churchill, 22 February 1925, T172/1499B, Treasury files, TNA), while Montagu Norman argued that the United States could sterilize the effects of over-payment (Norman to Churchill, 2 February 1925, T172/1499B, Treasury files, TNA). As to Keynes's concern about a vast, unceasing crescendo, even Niemeyer – who favoured a British return to gold – admitted that "there certainly are such dangers," adding that the United States was also "a growing competitor," but he saw the greater risk in Britain being the only country off gold (Niemeyer to Churchill, 22 February 1925, T172/1499B, Treasury files, TNA). In other words, even those advocating the Treasury view were aware of the possibility that a fluctuating American economy could have implications for British stability.

Although the Treasury and Bank of England were aware of the risks of a return to gold, another matter loomed large in their considerations: the restoration of London as the heart of global finance. A vital element of the Treasury view was the idea that once Britain had returned to the gold standard, investors would turn to London for acceptances. For instance, Niemeyer asked, "How are we to maintain entropot financial business, when no foreigner knows what a £ will cost him?" (Niemeyer to Churchill, 22 February 1925, T172/1499B, Treasury files, TNA). Montagu Norman was even clearer in his case for a swift return to gold: "Given similarity without delay in respect of Free Gold, it is likely that tradition and experience will gradually set London as high as New York as an international centre" (Norman to Churchill, 2 February 1925, T172/1499B, Treasury files, TNA).

The restoration of sterling also required painful deflation, which would put many Britons out of work. The Treasury view minimized the importance of these dislocations, however. Bank of England director Sir Charles Addis argued that "it [social disturbances] would not be too high a price to pay for the substantial benefit to the trade of this country and its working classes, and also, although I put it last, for the recovery by the City of London of its former position as the world's financial centre" (Moggridge 1972, 41–2). Niemeyer also waved away Churchill's concern that the vast gold reserves of the United States would grant that country too much leverage in a gold-exchange-standard world. He argued that the restoration of British exports and trade would actually reduce British dependence, while also noting that the British Empire was the biggest producer of gold in the world (Niemeyer to Churchill, "The Gold Export Prohibition," undated memo, T172/1499B, Treasury files, TNA).

Support for the restoration of gold extended beyond advocates of the Treasury view. Representatives from the British Federation of Industry – which stood to lose from the deflation necessary to restore the gold standard – nonetheless expressed the opinion, "Since this country is the international clearing house, both for money and goods, a general return to the gold basis by the principal trading countries would, in the opinion of the Federation, be greatly to our benefit" (British Federation of Industry to Bradbury Commission, 30 July 1924, T160 197/F7528, Treasury Files, TNA). In other words, if a return to gold restored London's centrality to global finance, such a move might be worthwhile, not just for finance but for industry as well. This is a powerful example of how the prospect of financial primacy facilitates broader political coalitions.

Two additional developments pushed Churchill to restore the gold standard at $4.86. Montagu Norman, following a long correspondence with Benjamin Strong, had received assurances that the United States would enact inflationary policies to ease the return to gold. J.P. Morgan & Co.[86] offered Britain credits to ease the transition back to the gold standard (Strong to Norman, 21 April 1925, Papers of Benjamin Strong, Jr.). In addition, the imperialist Churchill feared losing the dominions. Had Britain delayed its gold standard restoration, the United States might usurp the trading networks vital to the British Empire. In May 1925, Churchill wrote that "[if Britain did not return to gold] Australia would have trade with South Africa and all the Dominions would have trade with the United States on a gold basis" (Cleveland and Costigliola 1977, 927). Finally convinced, Churchill gave in to the Treasury view. Reassuring the chancellor, Norman told him, "I will make you the golden chancellor" (Norman, quoted in Ahamed 2014, 344).

In the coming months, the unofficial price of sterling rose as market expectations and the "dear money" deflationary policies of Winston Churchill and Montagu Norman ravaged the British economy. Later in 1925, Britain ended the embargo on gold, and capital flowed once more. With Britain and the United States back on the gold standard, many other countries followed suit – by 1928, 54 countries had fixed their currencies to gold (Eichengreen 1995, 189–90), aided by an accommodating stance from the Federal Reserve. The additional certainty provided by a global system of fixed exchange rates allowed for considerable expansions of global trade. Both New York and London banks financed a growing market in trade acceptances, peaking in 1928–9 at $1.7 billion and $1.6 billion, respectively (Eichengreen and Flandreau 2011).[87]

Although British economic policy in the 1920s had the superficial appearance of an orthodox strategy, in many respects Britain resembled Thailand or Argentina in the 1990s – a country liberalizing capital markets with an overvalued exchange rate. Britain encouraged numerous countries to hold sterling in reserve, giving itself structural benefits.

The extent of those reserves was not trivial – by 1928, 42 per cent of global reserves were held in the form of currency (Ruggie 1982, 390). The return to gold at a heavily overvalued exchange rate meant that sterling reserves held abroad could be redeemed for gold – of which Britain had little. Montagu Norman had pushed for a speculative bet of epic proportions: that experience and tradition would restore London to the centre of global finance. In fact, the overvalued pound depended on easy credit in the United States, a state of affairs that could not continue without disastrous consequences.

From Restoration to Depression

Gold standard restoration relied on accommodation by the United States. By lowering the discount rate and allowing American price levels to rise, demand for the dollar on currency markets would fall, while demand for other currencies would rise. The only way to maintain the pound at an overvalued $4.86 was punishing (and politically unsustainable) deflation, or the maintenance of easy credit in the United States. Other countries, most notably France, returned to the gold standard at undervalued rates. Following a long war against inflation, the Banque de France sought to build up its gold reserves. Not only could a wall of gold protect the franc, but gold reserves could also be used as a weapon to secure French foreign policy objectives – and even to set up Paris as a major centre of global finance (Kirschner 1997, 177–82; Mouré 2002, 183–4; Ahamed 2014, 368). The French quest for gold, and British reliance on easy money in America, generated a spiral – French policy depleted British gold reserves, a desperate Britain would beg the United States for easement, and the United States would be forced to follow suit, lest the system collapse.

The victory of internationalists inside the Federal Reserve had limited implications in the comparably closed world of the early 1920s. However, the procyclical implications of the Fed's policy orientation would become clear in the middle of the decade. It initiated a first round of cuts to the discount rate through 1924 and 1925 to assist the restoration of gold. With discount rates slashed from 4.5 per cent to 3.0 per cent, easy credit generated speculation in the United States. Florida, once commonly maligned as a malarial swamp, was being drained to give Americans an easily accessible vacation spot. Investors bought up Florida real estate – much of it still worthless swampland – in a frenzy. The stock market boomed, led by the glittering *wunderkind* of a new technological era – General Motors and its subsidiary, the Radio Corporation of America. By 1925, stock market capitalization in the

United States was double what it had been before the war (Ahamed 2014, 273). Some of this new investment was financed by broker's loans – money lent to customers by stockbrokers so that they could invest in the market (Galbraith [1954] 1997, 21). Should the bull market turn bust, a great many investors would be on the hook.

On the Federal Reserve Board, Adolph Miller sounded the alarm about an orgy of speculation (Wueschner 1999, 23–50). He feared that stock market activity was sucking money out of other sectors of the economy. Even before the Dust Bowl and the Great Depression wreaked havoc on American farming communities, they were experiencing hardship. Miller exhorted his neighbour, Commerce Secretary Herbert Hoover, to push for tighter monetary policy. Although Hoover favoured efforts to spark a European recovery, he was also suspicious of Britain.[88] Strong demurred, insisting that it was not the business of the Federal Reserve to combat bubbles. Hoover would angrily describe Strong as "having a mental annex to Europe" (Benjamin Strong, quoted in Barber 1988, 61). By 1926, at any rate, markets appeared to have levelled out.

Across the Atlantic, another golden moment was taking shape in France. The interwar political system there was deeply polarized between left and right. The left would rail against the pernicious influence of *les deux cents familles* – the two hundred families that allegedly monopolized the Banque de France and the French political system. The French right, in turn, was inclined towards virulent anti-Semitism and dark conspiracy theories. By the 1930s, a few years before the invasion of France by Nazi Germany, some on the French right would even declare, "Better Hitler than Blum," decrying the victory of Léon Blum, the Jewish leader of the centre-left Popular Front.

The year 1926 saw the collapse of the *Cartel des gauches* and the formation of a centre-right coalition government led by Prime Minister Raymond Poincaré. Over the next two years, Poincaré initiated a broadly successful program of currency stabilization. Aided by bourgeoisie relief over the ouster of the left-leaning *Cartel des gauches*,[89] the franc rose and then plateaued at close to one-fifth of its pre-war level (Mouré 2002, 129). Although Poincaré wanted to strengthen the franc further to ease debt repayment, Émile Moreau, the governor of the Banque de France, preferred to stabilize it at the attainable, devalued rate. The weight of opinion strongly favoured Moreau on this point, and on 25 June 1928, a new law returned France to the gold standard at a new, undervalued rate (101–45).

The combination of an undervalued franc and an overvalued pound was a disaster for the global economy. At the same time, France was enjoying growing relevance as gold poured in. The Banque de France built vaults 25 metres deep as a signal of its golden ambitions (Mouré 2002, 117).[90] French reserves did not consist solely of gold, however. As a result of Montagu Norman's tireless promotion of the pound sterling as a reserve currency, the Banque also held hundreds of millions of pounds. For years, perfidious Albion had thwarted French objectives and treated France with derision. When Norman met Moreau in 1926, for example, he offered no help to France. Indeed, he insisted on speaking English, although he was fluent in French and Moreau was unilingual. Following the meeting, Moreau wrote in his diary that Norman "is an imperialist seeking the domination of the world for his country which he loves passionately" (Émile Moreau, quoted in Ahamed 2014, 260).

By 1927, with the French reserve position on the rise, Moreau held the sword of Damocles over Norman's head. When Norman refused to renegotiate a 1916 French loan secured by gold, the Banque repaid the loan and took $90 million in gold reserves.[91] Next, the French converted $100 million worth of sterling notes into gold, further depleting British reserve assets. Norman appealed to Strong for assistance. Strong, recovering from illness and unable to travel to Europe, hosted a meeting with Norman, Schacht, and Léonard Rist[92] of France. Strong proposed another cut to the discount rate, reducing downward pressure on the pound. When he opened the spigots of loose credit, Hoover and Miller once again sounded the alarm, but were rebuffed by the Federal Reserve Board and President Coolidge, respectively.

Strong's gambit bought neither financial peace in Europe nor stability in the United States. In 1928, Britain and France squabbled over which should play the dominant role in the restoration of Romania to the gold standard. As the two countries fought, gold continued to flow out of Britain, intensifying pressure on Montagu Norman. Even Strong, visiting Norman and planning to retire as governor of the FRBNY, lost patience with his old friend. Strong died of a heart attack soon after, leaving the bank in the hands of George Harrison.

Strong might well have died with a sense of accomplishment. During his tenure at the FRBNY, he had led the United States from being a debtor country to reaching the apex of the global financial system. In a few short years, he had assisted in the restoration of the global gold standard. However, in 1928, the American economy was doing a bit too well. Between the cuts to the discount rate in July 1927 and October 1929, the S&P 500 stock market index more than doubled (Shiller 2000). In 1925, Hoover and Miller had been alarmed at $2.2 billion in broker's loans. By September 1929, the stock market was shored up by over $8.5 billion in broker's loans (Barber 1988, 71). The price-to-earnings ratio[93] of the stock market rose to levels unsurpassed until the dot-com bubble of 1999–2000 (Shiller 2005, 5). Tales abounded that even shoeshine boys and beggars were playing the market: a bubble of legendary proportions was afoot.

Although some in the Federal Reserve expressed concerns over a market truly out of control, they did not act decisively. In 1928, Senator James Strong, Republican from Kansas, proposed a bill adding price stability to the mission of the Federal Reserve. The bill was opposed by the entirety of the Federal Reserve Board, even the ordinarily inflation-averse Adolph Miller (Meltzer 2003, 534). Miller did, however, suggest that Congress take steps to reinforce the primacy of the Federal Reserve Board over the FRBNY. Benjamin Strong's death had left a power vacuum in its wake, limiting the ability of the Fed to respond to the bubble on Wall Street. In a reversal of the earlier debate, George Harrison pushed for increases to the discount rate, while Adolph Miller and his allies at the Federal Reserve Board pushed for moral suasion, using the bully pulpit to tamp down speculation (Eichengreen 1995, 217). Miller feared that raising discount rates would punish industry and agriculture instead of the financiers and spendthrifts he saw as driving the bubble. As a result, the Federal Reserve acted rather late – too late to suspend the powerful feedback mechanisms driving the unsustainable rise of the stock market.

Rising interest rates in the United States made domestic investments more desirable than international ones, prompting a crash in foreign lending. Gold inflows intensified, forcing much of the world to either copy the deflationary stance of the Federal Reserve or implement protectionist measures to limit gold outflows (Eichengreen 1995, 248). France, now stabilized with a weak exchange rate, joined the United States in vacuuming up gold from the rest of the world. While the Great Depression is often thought to have begun with the stock market crash of 1929, for many countries, the pain began earlier as their central banks raised interest rates to avert outflows of gold.

On Black Tuesday (24 October 1929), a panic broke out on the NYSE, with the Dow Jones Industrial Average crashing from a peak of 381.17 to under 200 by 13 November (Williamson 2020). While the Federal Reserve initiated open-market operations, its efforts were constrained by the fear that creating excess credit would once again spark speculation. Many in the newly elected Hoover administration and the Federal Reserve believed that a harsh correction was inevitable, even desirable. For instance, Treasury Secretary Andrew Mellon infamously argued that the United States needed to "liquidate labor, liquidate stocks, liquidate the farmers, liquidate real estate ... it will purge the rottenness out of the system" (Hoover 1952, 30). Contrary to his reputation, Hoover saw a role for government in fostering recovery. At the same time, he was convinced that private initiatives and sound currency were critical. At the Federal Reserve, there were additional institutional roadblocks to aggressive action. Despite possessing vast gold reserves, Federal Reserve notes had to be backed by at least 40 per cent in gold by law.

The other country with a strong reserve position, France, was committed by statute to an even more austere policy. Although France took in large amounts of gold from abroad, the Banque de France sterilized the inflows (Mouré 2002). Seemingly immune from the adverse conditions sweeping the world, French commentators referred to the country as "L'île Heureuse" (Ahamed 2014, 546). For everybody else, the situation was dire. A collapse in the price of primary products devastated the export position of much of the world. Debt service became intractable for major primary exporters like Argentina and Australia. Larger economies, like Germany and Britain, suffered radically dwindling reserves, forcing them to scramble for gold. In Germany, the discount rate stood at a punishing 7 per cent, strangling domestic credit (Eichengreen 1995, 395–445). Even with such high interest rates, Germany was unable to defend its reserve position. French fears that reparations payments would be renegotiated prompted a steady flow of gold from Germany to France.

Anticipating devaluation, investors pulled money out of those countries with the weakest gold positions in 1931: Austria, Germany, Britain, and Hungary. When difficulties in the Creditanstalt, a large Austrian bank, became public, the Bank for International Settlements made efforts to arrange $14 million in credit. The paltry fund ran out within a week, while efforts to create a second rescue fund were stymied by French demands that Austria renounce her customs union with Germany. Desperate purchases of securities by the Federal Reserve in April proved insufficient to stop the bleeding – in May 1931, the Creditanstalt declared bankruptcy, and Austria was forced to abandon the gold standard. The deep linkages between the Austrian and Hungarian economies meant that Austria's fall implicated Hungary, and a wave of banking collapses spread through that country. Speculators weighed in against the German mark next, as capital poured out of Germany. A desperate Reichsbank pleaded for a rescue loan of $1 billion, running up against considerable reluctance. Britain was tapped out, and France wanted Germany to abandon its efforts to renegotiate reparations payments. Efforts by President Hoover to declare a moratorium on reparations payments inspired intense opposition from the French government. Through the summer of 1931, the German mark collapsed, and Germany was forced off the gold standard.

By September 1931, a currency crisis had struck Britain. The Labour government of Ramsay MacDonald, elected in 1929, had responded to the Depression with largely orthodox measures to defend the gold standard (Ahamed 2014, 386). By 1931, however, MacDonald found his caucus unable to stomach the austerity measures that gold demanded. He and Philip Snowden broke with their own party, forming a National Government coalition with the Conservatives and Liberals. With the reserve situation now truly implacable, the coalition announced that Britain would devalue the pound, effectively leaving the gold standard. The $4.86 pound, purchased by years of high interest rates and punishing unemployment, was gone a mere six and a half years later. Yet, after Britain had abandoned gold, the sky did not fall. With the Bank of England free to provide liquidity to the banking system, Britain began to experience an economic recovery (Temin 1989).

Panicked investors now turned their sights on the United States. Although Americans possessed a mountain of gold, the now-devalued pound and a cheap franc rendered the dollar vulnerable. The Banque de France, too, steadily converted its holdings in other currencies into gold. Through 1931 and 1932, gold flowed out of the United States and back to Europe in large quantities. The Federal Reserve, initially able to undertake some rescue operations, was handicapped by the outflow. The statutory requirement that its notes be backed 40 per cent by gold meant that gold outflows greatly diminished the money supply of the United States. Afraid of undermining the dollar, the Federal Reserve avoided taking actions to expand liquidity. Instead, a banking panic swept through the country as depositors dashed to withdraw money from the banks. By 1932, nearly 8 per cent of American banks were in suspension (Wicker 2000). Saddled with blame for the greatest economic collapse in history, Herbert Hoover was defeated decisively in the presidential election that year. Upon taking office in 1933, the new president, Franklin Delano Roosevelt, promptly declared a banking holiday, took the United States off the gold standard, and soon signed into law an extensive set of new banking regulations.

The Great Depression devastated the American economy. With businesses and consumers unable to obtain credit, GDP fell 31 per cent, while unemployment rose to 25 per cent (Maddison 2009; United States. Bureau of the Census 1975, 126). Disastrous choices by American policymakers intensified the pain. In 1930, logrolling – trading favours in order to pass a bill – transformed initially modest efforts to protect struggling American farmers into the sweeping Smoot–Hawley tariff, which raised import duties. American protectionism invited retaliatory action from others. In 1932, the Ottawa Accords cloaked the British

Empire in a similar wall of tariffs. In Germany, the depression revitalized German revanchism. In the 1928 federal elections, Adolph Hitler's Nazi Party had received under 3 per cent of the vote; but, by 1933, it was the largest party, and Hitler had become chancellor. With the major Entente Powers mired in depression, and the liberal order shattered by trade wars and the scramble for gold, there was no political will among the great powers to stop German revisionism.

Conclusion

It is said that victory has many fathers, while defeat is an orphan. The historiography of the Great Depression tells a different story – many theories have been advanced to explain it. However, it is difficult to ignore the role of the gold standard in driving the world's economies to ruin. An overvalued pound and an undervalued franc produced large global imbalances, committing participants to heroic efforts to stay on gold. Further, the widespread use of reserve currencies, in addition to gold, meant that the viability of the system required the cooperation of the three major reserve currency countries. Accommodating efforts by the United States in 1925 and 1927 helped others return to the gold standard; however, they also drove it into a bubble of epic proportions. When the Federal Reserve finally moved to fight the bubble in 1928, the rest of the world was forced to adopt deflationary policies. When the great crash of 1929 hit, the gold standard was the critical vehicle transmitting economic pain abroad, while constraining American policymakers from saving the economy.

The thread linking all these critical policy mistakes – an overvalued pound, easy credit from the Federal Reserve in the 1920s, an undervalued franc, and the underwhelming response to the Great Depression – is the battle for financial primacy during the 1920s. British policymakers insisted on returning to gold at the pre-war parity of $4.86 because they believed that doing so would help restore London as the global centre of finance. Montagu Norman's efforts to promote the pound as a reserve currency made Britain vulnerable to currency speculation, even as it bought Britain some of the structural benefits lost in 1914. Benjamin Strong eased credit conditions in the United States to allow the world to return to gold, precisely because there was little benefit to the United States in being the only country on gold.[94] Moreover, American policymakers feared leaving the field to sterling in a world without gold – dramatic moves like the Dawes/Young plan came only *after* Norman appeared to have swung Germany into the orbit of sterling. French policymakers pursued a strategy of accruing reserves with an

undervalued franc because they represented a powerful tool by which
to influence debates over reparations. When collapse hit the major
economies of the world, most avoided actions to save their domestic
economies, instead maintaining their commitment to gold at great cost.
The flaws in a Federal Reserve designed to allow the United States to
contend for influence in a gold standard world rather than to respond
to domestic economic crises became clear when the limits on the creation of Federal Reserve notes hampered recovery.

Competing perspectives cannot explain the errors of the 1920s as
elegantly as those emphasizing power. Some argue that Britain's commitment to the gold standard reflected the near-religious power of the
gold standard idea. However, this account ignores voices agitating
against gold, from imperial federalists like Lord Beaverbrook to John
Maynard Keynes. Indeed, even Benjamin Strong and Montagu Norman
privately admitted that tethering Britain to a volatile American economy could prove disastrous. Another set of views focuses the causes
of the 1920s bubble on Wall Street, some implicating psychological
feedback mechanisms (Galbraith [1954] 1997) or Federal Reserve policy (Rothbard 1972). Archival evidence illustrates quite clearly that the
easy credit conditions maintained by the Federal Reserve were aimed
at shoring up the gold standard. Milton Friedman and Anna Schwartz
(1963) posited that the 1928 death of Benjamin Strong put the Federal
Reserve in the hands of amateurs, who proved unable to expand the
money supply[95] in response to the Great Depression. Meltzer (2003,
22), too, argues that Strong's death swung the levers of power in the
Fed to those, like Adolph Miller, whose thinking was dominated by the
Real Bills Doctrine. According to the Real Bills Doctrine, central banks
should provide credit primarily to productive activities like trade and
agriculture, while overall changes to the supply of money will have
no effect. Such thinking limited the range of securities through which
central banks might influence economy activity. Even if this view can
explain the initial hesitations to use monetary policy counter-cyclically,
the FRBNY favoured expansion, as did the chair of the Federal Reserve
appointed in 1930, Eugene Meyer. American policymakers were limited by the global scramble for gold in 1931 through 1933. The gold
standard was a yellow-brick road that led straight off a cliff.

Chapter Five

The Great Deregulation of 1980–2000

The 1987 film *Wall Street* depicts an American financial system run amok. It portrays Gordon Gecko, an unscrupulous businessman with a fortune built on insider trading, who schemes to take over Bluestar Airlines to raid its overfunded pension fund. When Susan Strange wrote of the same period, she characterized the Western financial system as a vast casino, where "rooms full of chain-smoking young men ... play by intercontinental telephone or by tapping electronic machines ... just like gamblers in casinos watching the clicking spin of a silver ball on a roulette wheel and putting their chips on red or black, odd numbers or even ones" (1986, 1). For all the awe that 1980s Wall Street inspired, global financial activity intensified by orders of magnitude in subsequent decades. Today, 1980s Wall Street seems as quaint a reality as workplace smoking or Bluestar's defined benefit pension fund.

In this chapter, I describe the transformation of American (and global) financial regulation from a tightly regulated system to a lax one. The Bretton Woods/Glass–Steagall era was the most stable era in financial history. Between the Second World War and the late 1970s, virtually no countries experienced financial crises. Yet neither system was to last forever. The key elements of Bretton Woods fell away in the 1960s and 1970s, as the United States sought to increase its ability to draw rents from its financial leadership (Helleiner 1996). On the other hand, reforming domestic finance proved more difficult. The Reagan administration deregulated S&Ls and appointed lax regulators to agencies like the SEC and the Federal Reserve. However, the broader campaign to reshape finance by repealing the Glass–Steagall Act encountered powerful resistance. The political genius of the Glass–Steagall system meant that there were diverse coalitions of bureaucratic and financial-sector actors opposed to reform. The determination of Reagan Cabinet members, such as Treasury Secretary Donald Regan, to reform the system were not enough – the coalition in favour of deregulation was simply too weak.

By the middle of the 1980s, external challenges to America's position as a financial powerhouse recast the regulatory debate. A surging Japan threatened to eclipse the United States in high-tech production and in finance. British financial deregulation under Margaret Thatcher produced a resurgent London. As American leadership came under threat, politicians and business leaders – including some in the SIA who had previously resisted reform – coalesced behind a competitiveness agenda that included substantial regulatory rollback. Despite the collapse of the recently deregulated S&L industry, and a developing world debt crisis spawned by imprudent lending by newly deregulated American banks, regulatory safeguards continued to be withdrawn. When Federal Reserve Chair Paul Volcker proved reluctant to reinterpret Glass–Steagall, he was outvoted by Reagan appointees in the Federal Reserve and replaced by the libertarian Alan Greenspan.

The opening up of regulations by the Fed drew the interests of different types of commercial and investment banks together, as each began to engage in the activities of the other. An enlarged political coalition yearning for financial supermarkets called for less deregulation, even as the competitive challenge from Japan receded (McCarty, Poole, and Rosenthal 2013; Witko 2016). During the tenure of Democratic President Bill Clinton, efforts at a regulatory rollback intensified. The Clinton years saw the elimination of bank-branching restrictions, the abolition of the Glass–Steagall system, and the legalization of derivatives trading. Progressive goals, like revitalizing economically depressed areas, were fused with a competitiveness agenda, substituting social programs for access to credit (Rajan 2010, 21–45). American policymakers used their influence within international institutions (such as the IMF) to promote neoliberal objectives like financial deregulation (Chwieroth 2010; Major 2012). The primary instance of increased regulation – the Basel Capital Accords – was the exception that proved the rule. The Accords were an Anglo-American ploy to limit Japanese competitiveness in banking, while prompting little change in the United States or Britain (Litan, Isaac, and Taylor 1994, 550–1).

Many commentators blame the 2008 financial crisis on the abolition of regulatory safeguards in the United States (United States. Financial Crisis Inquiry Commission 2011). These criticisms understate the problem: a global regulatory rollback made individual states more vulnerable to crises, while simultaneously amplifying channels for crisis contagion. In just a few years, the global economy was rocked by the 1997 East Asian crisis, the LTCM crash of 1998, Argentina's crisis

Table 5.1. American, Japanese, and British Financial Reforms, 1945–2000

	United States	Japan	Britain
Reconstitution, 1946–59	ca. 1946: Glass–Steagall; Bretton Woods; SEC governs securities	1946: Japan run by Supreme Commander for the Allied Powers (SCAP) 1951: SCAP ends; capital controls, securities–bank firewall persist	1947: Companies Act
Plateau, 1960–85	*1960: creation of the Euromarket* *1971–4: end of Bretton Woods, abolition of capital controls* **1975: CFTC created** *1980–2: S&L deregulation* **1982: Shad–Johnson Accord**	*1980: liberalization of capital controls* *1982: Bank Act allows banks to underwrite government bonds*	*1960: creation of the Euromarket* **1971: concealment banned, reserve ratios** *1979: exchange controls abolished* *1981: reserve ratios made voluntary*
Competition, 1986–2000	*1987: Fed reinterprets Glass–Steagall (5% cap)* *1994: Congress abolishes bank-branching rules* *1996: Fed reinterprets Glass–Steagall (25% cap)* *1999: Glass–Steagall repealed* *2000: commodity futures modernization liberalizes derivatives market*	*1986: creation of Tokyo offshore market* *1996: Japanese Big Bang*	*1985–6: Big Bang liberalizes stock market, formalizes regulation* *1990: joins ERM (constrains monetary policy)* **1992: leaves ERM**

and default, the dot-com bust of 2000, the financial crisis of 2008, and the eurozone crisis of 2010. Others contend that the role of deregulation has been overstated, pointing the finger at global imbalances instead (Chinn and Frieden 2011; Oatley 2016). In this account, the 2008 crisis was the product of cheap credit from saver countries in East Asia financing speculative bubbles in the United States. Yet these phenomena are more related than one might think. Both cheap credit and weak oversight encouraged poor investment decisions, while lax regulation amplified the effects of the eventual crash on the banking system. Table 5.1 summarizes the regulatory developments in the United States and its main challengers throughout the period in question.

An Era of Stability: Bretton Woods and the Glass–Steagall Era

The twin horrors of the Great Depression and the Second World War encouraged Americans to seek comfort and stability. In the 1920s, exciting technologies had been conceived, opening up new opportunities. By the 1960s, those technologies were being mass produced and made widely available. For instance, television allowed millions of Americans to watch comforting sitcoms and variety shows about good-hearted rural folk, like *Andy Griffith*, *The Beverly Hillbillies*, and *The Lawrence Welk Show*. The welfare state was ascendant, even if the raft of social programs included in America's New Deal (1930s) and later the Great Society (1960s) did not go as far as in other advanced industrial democracies. Pensions, welfare, health insurance, and permanent military mobilization each represented expanding frontiers for the Keynesian welfare (and warfare) state.

The Great Depression and its aftermath transformed the American financial system. Even in the depths of the crisis, many Americans had banked with the small, locally oriented S&Ls whose growth had been nurtured by the Federal Home Loan Bank Act. George Bailey, the protagonist of the 1946 film *It's A Wonderful Life* (and model for the "New Deal new man"), was a small-town banker. Although he aspires to be a worldly man, he sacrifices his desires to travel, instead anchoring the community by keeping his family's small bank afloat during the Depression. When the bank risks a run, it is saved by the small-town community it helped to create – social capital was performing the function of lender of last resort. After the Depression, the newly created SEC carefully monitored investment activity, rooting out fraud. The FDIC, in turn, insured ordinary depositors against the consequences of a bank run.

Many economists criticize Glass–Steagall as a Depression-era relic that needlessly repressed financial markets (Calomiris 2000; Calomiris and Haber 2014). Such criticisms miss the political genius of Glass–Steagall. By compartmentalizing the financial system, the act created a political ecosystem that resisted major reform for 45 years. If one wished to end interstate bank-branching laws, S&Ls would oppose reform. If one sector desired to deregulate the activities of commercial or investment banks, one or the other sector would lobby against reform to protect itself from greater competition. The bureaucracy overseeing the system, too, tended towards prudent, lawyerly enforcement of the rules. The prospects for an "iron triangle" relationship among legislators, regulators, and the regulated were diminished by the simple reality that banking was a boring, low-return industry. Cautious, well-regulated banks and capital markets monitored by a lawyerly SEC furnished large amounts of capital to expand production in the safe, well-established industrial behemoths of the Fordist era.

The Bretton Woods system, in turn, formed the basis of the international economic order for the non-Communist world. Its origins and nature tell us much about the influence of power over the construction of international regimes. In 1940, as Nazi bombers flew across the English Channel to blitz London, Germany and Britain were engaged in a debate over the economic future of the world. Nazi economic minister Walther Funk proposed a system designed to appeal to those exhausted by the crises of the old order – sound economies would come before sound currencies. Instead of the gold standard, a clearing union would resolve current account surpluses and deficits. Berlin, of course, would gradually overtake London as a financial centre, but the rest of Europe was to occupy a comparatively privileged role (van Dormael 1978, 5–7). The British ministry of intelligence dispatched one of its greatest assets – the now-renowned economist John Maynard Keynes – to defend the "old-time religion" of the gold standard and free trade. Keynes, however, did no such thing, suspecting that the propaganda value of such arguments would be negative. Instead, in his response to the German proposal, he co-opted the "New Order" proposal of a clearing union – arguing that Britain could do it better (7–10).

Four years later, the tides of war had turned, prompting the Allied powers to meet in the New Hampshire resort town of Bretton Woods to discuss the economic future of the world. Britain, of course, sent John Maynard Keynes – who would continue to advocate for an International Clearing Union (ICU) system. Under his proposal, trade would be denominated in the bancor, a new global currency. Countries running a bancor deficit would see their currencies depreciate against the bancor, while countries running a surplus would be taxed, with the proceeds going to an ICU reserve fund. In addition, Keynes pushed for a system of strict capital controls to prevent the kind of capital flight that had characterized the interwar period (Helleiner 1996, 25–50).

Despite Keynes's stature, the war had left Britain economically and militarily dependent upon the United States. Thus, the American representative, Treasury adviser Harry Dexter White, was in a position to dictate terms at Bretton Woods. White shared the broad outlines of Keynes's vision of a more regulated system – he had advocated some control over capital flows as early as his 1933 dissertation (White 1933, 301) – and continued to argue that most states should exercise some control over capital flows (Helleiner 1996, 38).[96] However, rather than acceding to Keynes's bancor, White insisted in ICU documents on a "gold-convertible currency." When asked what he meant by *gold-convertible currency*, he revealed that he was referring to the currency of the only country with substantial gold assets left: the United States of America. Thus, it was at Bretton Woods where the status of the US dollar as a global reserve currency was institutionally enshrined. A kinder, gentler global economic order is possible, but such an order is likely to reflect the interests of the most powerful states.

The Bretton Woods system saw the creation of two formal institutions – a World Bank concerned primarily with fostering long-term development and an IMF concerned with addressing short-term balance-of-payments problems. Although the order envisioned a kind of liberalism – expanded trade among states – it engendered the idea that states should insulate themselves against disruption. Most signatories implemented strict capital controls soon after. Marshall Plan aid, in turn, sweetened the deal of accepting American leadership for America's war-torn allies. Drawing on Karl Polanyi's call in *The Great Transformation* (1944) for a capitalism consigned to the organic nature of labour, Ruggie (1982) depicted the Bretton Woods order as a system of "embedded liberalism." Protected by strict capital controls, governments could use monetary policy to fight recessions without prompting capital flight and downward pressure on their currencies. Central bankers would be guided by the newly discovered Phillips (1958) curve, which posited a consistent relationship between unemployment and inflation. Full employment was achievable for all. Fixed, but adjustable, exchange rates and new rules established by the General Agreement on Trade and Tariffs promoted certainty around trade.

The new economic order achieved staggering success. From 1945 to 1973, the United States experienced the fastest rate of growth in its history. France experienced *Les Trente Glorieuses* (thirty glorious years), Germany had its *Wirtschaftswunder* (economic miracle), and Japan achieved 7.7 per cent real per capita growth (Maddison 2009).

Certainly, some chafed under the economic constraints of the New Deal era. Republican Senate Minority Leader Robert Taft ran for president in 1952 on a palaeo-conservative agenda that mixed free markets and isolationism. William F. Buckley sought to unite libertarians, conservatives, and anti-communists in his *National Review*. In academia, many classical liberals – from Friedrich Hayek to Gordon Tullock to Milton Friedman – wrote important works and came together in the Mont Pelerin Society. Those preferring a deontological case for unfettered capitalism could attend meetings of "The Collective," held at Ayn Rand's New York City apartment. From Rose Wilder Lane, who injected her libertarian beliefs into her mother's *Little House on the Prairie* books, to future chair of the Federal Reserve Alan Greenspan,[97] Rand's disciples enjoyed some influence. But their time was yet to come.

Despite its successes, the Bretton Woods system was not to last (Gowa 1983; Stein 2010). Its system of fixed exchange rates involved many countries pegging to the dollar, which, in turn, was pegged to gold. However, the economic fundamentals shifted dramatically between 1945 and the 1970s. In 1945, the United States – relatively unscathed by the Second World War – could export goods to the rest of the world, thereby enjoying a large current account surplus. In time, however, rapid growth and the restoration of trade meant that Japan, Germany, and France could export substantially more goods to the United States. Further, gold shortages in the early 1960s raised doubts that the United States would be able to maintain its commitment to gold at what was now the fixed rate of $35 an ounce. Britain, too, suffered difficulties maintaining the value of sterling – in 1957, rumours of a German revaluation triggered a currency crisis. Moreover, Britain's reliance on a captive sterling bloc was insufficient to restore London's role as a global financial centre (Helleiner 1996, 83–4).

The challenges of the dollar and sterling prompted policy responses. To expand the role of London as a financial centre without undermining the Keynesian welfare state, during the sterling crisis of 1957, British financial institutions began floating eurodollar loans (Helleiner 1996, 83). These were loans backed by dollar deposits of overseas residents, which could expand the ability of British institutions to finance trade outside the sterling area. In the United States, the presidential administrations of John F. Kennedy and Lyndon Johnson broadly encouraged the development of the Euromarket. Such a development was seen as likely to soften the blow of newly implemented capital controls; this was because US multinational corporations could still seek dollar financing through the Euromarket, while American banks could move their international operations to London, thus escaping New Deal regulatory restrictions (84–91). Yet perhaps most importantly for the United States, the Euromarket would increase the attractiveness of the dollar to foreigners, greatly expanding the structural benefits the country enjoyed, such as seigniorage (90–1).

In addition to the Euromarket, the gold pool was established in 1961 to forestall a speculative move against the dollar. The arrangement was an example of how powerful lead economies can rope others into serving their objectives through soft coercion. Gold-pool members pledged to hold on to dollars and reimburse the United States for half its gold losses (Eichengreen 2012, 51–62). The unequal arrangement encountered problems in 1965 as gold supplies began to dwindle and it came time for others to support the dollar; France dropped out of the arrangement, while Italy converted its dollar holdings into gold, even while still contributing to the pool. In 1967, finance ministers agreed to issue special drawing rights (SDRs), a new monetary unit created to supplement reserves. The SDRs were of limited utility, however, since they were accepted only in intergovernmental transactions or in transactions with the IMF. Moreover, they were difficult to create – requiring 85 per cent support in the IMF. By 1971, sustained American budget deficits, run to fund the expanded social programs of the Great Society as well as the war in Vietnam, coupled with increasing reliance on imported oil, worsened the American balance-of-payments situation further. Moreover, firms found it increasingly easy to evade capital controls and shift funds from one country to another (Goodman and Pauly 1993). The position of the Bretton Woods system appeared to be in question.

The perilous position of the dollar posed a political challenge for the United States. Inside the Nixon White House, Federal Reserve Chair Arthur Burns made the case for the orthodox position: the United States should raise interest rates, shoring up the dollar by attracting portfolio investment (Burns Diary, 8 July 1971, Arthur Burns Papers, Gerald Ford Presidential Library, Ann Arbor, MI). Politically, such a move was risky, evoking bitter memories for President Richard Nixon. In 1960, he had lost a presidential election to John F. Kennedy by the narrowest of margins, in part because fiscal and monetary restraint by President Dwight Eisenhower had depressed the economy. Nixon's Texan Treasury Secretary, John Connally, drawled a different tune from Burns: "Foreigners are out to screw us. Our job is to screw them first" (John Connally, quoted in LaFeber 1989, 612). Connally proposed that the United States allow the dollar to float, close the gold window, and apply an import surcharge until other states agreed to revalue their currencies. Nixon sided with Connally, making a surprise announcement of his intention to close the gold window on 15 August 1971 in what was termed "the Nixon shock."

Although America's major trading partners proved willing to renegotiate a new set of exchange rates at the Smithsonian Conference, Nixon preferred another option. Recalling the trilemma, states had to choose between two of the following three things: fixed exchange rates, free flows of capital, and monetary policy autonomy (Mundell 1963). By abandoning gold and allowing the dollar to float, the cost of maintaining fixed exchange rates would be shunted onto others. Moreover, Nixon could restore a world of mobile capital – a move he took in 1974, shortly before resigning amid the Watergate scandal. Nixon's move entailed considerable advantages for the United States. In a world of large capital flows, other countries would have to hold substantial reserves. Overwhelmingly, they were likely to accumulate the currency of the largest economy of the world: US dollars. As other countries held US dollars as reserves, they were effectively providing an interest-free loan to the United States,[98] which could be reinvested profitably, earning substantial excess returns (Helleiner 1996; Schwartz 2009; Eichengreen 2012). Although the United States would enjoy this exorbitant privilege throughout the dollar's reign, the need for other states to hold reserves would be increased substantially in a world of free flows of capital.

Free capital flows could serve other purposes as well. The possibilities for growth were limited in a mature economy like the United States. Indeed, by the 1970s, it had experienced a productivity slowdown. Patents, productivity growth, and wage growth ground to a halt (Romer 1987). Television depictions of American working-class families do a good job of approximating the boom of the 1945–73 period – and the subsequent stagnation. The Kramdens of the 1955 series *The Honeymooners* live in a cramped apartment, with no appliances (and no television set!). In contrast, the Bunkers of 1971's *All in the Family* own their own home, have all the latest appliances, and can play the show's title song on their piano. The blue-collar households of subsequent decades experienced relative stagnation. The Bundys of the 1987 *Married ... With Children*, the Connors of the 1988 *Roseanne*, and the Simpsons of the 1989 *The Simpsons* are materially indistinguishable (or worse off) than the Bunkers.

As governments floated their currencies, monetary policy became unmoored. Vote-seeking politicians cowed central banks into setting expansionary policies. Simultaneously, the cartelization of global oil production, with the formation of the Organization of Petroleum Exporting Countries, drove up the price of the primary fuel source beginning in the Fordist age. Inflation rose steadily across the global north, reaching double digits in every major industrial economy save inflation-averse Germany. The Phillips curve was in tatters, and monetarist economists like Milton Friedman (1977) appeared to have the best explanation: the Phillips curve assumed that economic actors expected no inflation, reflecting the experience of the era before the Second World War. The use of monetary policy to maintain full employment challenged those expectations. Unions and other economic agents were rational – if they experienced sustained inflation, they would expect greater inflation in the future. To maintain the real wages of their members, unions would demand higher wages. Private firms, in turn, would pass on the cost of higher wages to consumers by raising prices. An expansionary monetary policy risked rates of inflation that would spiral indefinitely.

Deregulation Stalls, 1980–6

In one episode of *The Simpsons*, the town of Springfield holds a bake sale to raise money for a statue of Abraham Lincoln. Unable to raise enough money, the town is forced to settle for a statue of Jimmy Carter with a plaque reading "Malaise Forever." The plaque references a 1979 speech in which Carter had described the "crisis of confidence" facing the United States. Spiralling oil prices, the Iranian revolution, and the simultaneous occurrence of inflation and high unemployment seemed to suggest that America's best days were past. Contrary to the popular depiction of President Carter passively accepting national malaise, however, he made two important policy decisions that would alter the course of the subsequent decade.

In 1979, Carter appointed Paul Volcker as chair of the Federal Reserve. Standing at 6 foot 7 inches, Volcker is a literal giant in the annals of monetary history (Treaster 2004, 79). Announcing interest rate policy (usually increasing rates) while surrounded by wreaths of smoke from cheap cigars, he has been described as having a "Delphic aura" becoming of his cryptic profession.[99] On banking issues, he was sceptical of financial innovations – once arguing in 2009 that the automated teller machine was the only positive financial innovation of the previous twenty years.[100] When it came to fighting inflation, Volcker delivered the tough medicine of high interest rates. The shock waves they created rippled through the global economy. Borrowing became expensive – my parents paid 18 per cent interest on their 1979 mortgage – with a depressing effect on the economy. By 1982, unemployment rates had exceeded 10 per cent (United States. Bureau of Labor Statistics 2020). At the same time, inflation finally began to ebb.

Inflation and the rate hikes meant to combat it threatened a vital segment of the American banking system: S&Ls. S&Ls were restricted by Regulation Q from raising interest rates above a certain ceiling. During periods in which inflation exceeded the interest rate ceiling, funds deposited in S&Ls earned a negative real return. Moreover, if other financial institutions offered depositors higher rates of interest, S&Ls would lose depositors to them. To solve this problem, while giving the Federal Reserve greater latitude to fight inflation, Congress passed the Depository Institutions Deregulation and Monetary Control Act of 1980. The act gave greater independence to the Federal Reserve, preventing politicians from coercing central bankers into politically convenient monetary expansions. Further, the act freed S&Ls from Regulation Q, while allowing them to invest in a wider array of securities. In *It's a Wonderful Life*, George Bailey assuaged panicking depositors in the

Bailey Bros. Building and Loan by declaring, "I-I-I don't have your money; it's in Tom's house and Fred's house." Bailey's equivalent in the 1980s might have instead stuttered, "I-I-I don't have your money, it's in Latin American sovereign debt."[101]

Although President Carter was open to financial deregulation, his opponent in the 1980 election, Ronald Reagan, was a true believer in the power of markets. He subscribed to the idea of supply-side economics – tax cuts can stimulate so much economic growth that they will offset any revenue losses (Stockman 1986, 53–6). Eliminating regulations – particularly financial regulations – was considered a vital pillar of Reaganomics (Niskanen 1988, 115–32). Reagan trounced Carter in the election, bringing into office the most market-friendly administration since the 1920s. Those familiar with the popular narrative of Reagan–Thatcher deregulation may think they know where this story is headed – surely it was "The Gipper"[102] who unleashed the creative destruction of the financial markets. In fact, the Reagan administration largely failed to overhaul the financial markets. Ideological convictions were insufficient to win the bureaucratic and political knife fight that characterized the push for financial reform. Only the realization, later in Reagan's second term, of the competitive challenges facing the United States was sufficient to break the impasse.

Reagan appointed Donald Regan as Treasury secretary. Regan was a hard-driving former marine and CEO of Merrill Lynch, a large investment bank. Although the two had met only briefly on two occasions before (one meeting consisted largely of Reagan joking about their similar names), Regan was a good fit for Reagan's philosophical goals. As CEO, Regan had lobbied the NYSE to end the practice of minimum fixed commissions for brokers, a system he later called "benevolent despotism," in contrast with a "democratized market" (Regan 1988, 147). Fixed commissions limited competition among brokers, allowing for the emergence of a cartel-like structure; and with decent returns guaranteed, brokers could make conservative, long-term bets. Finally succeeding in 1975, Regan opened up a wave of intense competition for commissions among brokers. The change was one of many that were transforming finance from a boring industry to a roller coaster.

In office, Regan had wide latitude to implement policy due to Reagan's passive leadership style. In Regan's telling, President Reagan "believed his campaign promises *were* his policy" (Regan 1988, 161). Although Regan would meet with Edwin Meese, counsellor and trusted adviser to President Reagan, this relationship was "disembodied" – the president's staff rarely referred to the president's thoughts or wishes (160). Regan favoured sweeping changes to the rules governing the financial system. He supported continued S&L deregulation, allowing the S&Ls to invest more widely. In addition, he wanted to abolish the Glass–Steagall system, enabling investment banks to engage in commercial banking and vice versa. Drawing on his own experiences with financial regulators, Regan wanted to simplify this alphabet soup (Federal Reserve, SEC, CFTC), while also changing the culture of the regulatory agencies. In place of a lawyerly SEC, he wanted regulators who were attuned to the concerns of businesses.

Although Regan continued the process of reforming the S&Ls initiated by the previous administration, he was unable to achieve a broader regulatory rollback. He managed the S&L deregulation process through the Depository Institutions Deregulation Committee, where he sought to leave the S&Ls with as few restrictions on their operations as possible (2 July 1982, box 147, folder 8, Donald T. Regan Papers, Manuscript Division, Library of Congress, Washington, DC). Regan was not alone – the United States Savings and Loans Association also favoured the deregulation of interest rates and increased ability to invest in a broader range of assets (29 June 1982, ibid.). In addition, there was bipartisan support for reform in Congress. At the same time, S&L deregulation impacted only a small subsection of the American financial system. Commercial banks were prohibited from securities trading activity, which was highly profitable. Investment banks like Merrill Lynch were also limited in their ability to engage in deposit banking and the insurance business.

Although abolishing Glass–Steagall was risky, it was not without some policy benefits. Deregulation opened up new opportunities for the deployment of capital. If commercial banks could underwrite securities, or if investment banks could take deposits, vast amounts of capital could be deployed in novel ways. The revolution in information technology also enabled the construction of more complex financial instruments, blurring the lines among commercial banking, securities trading, and insurance. On the other hand, deregulation posed significant risks. Opening up new opportunities for firms tends to lead to greater risk-taking, while, in the event of a downturn, the failure of large financial supermarkets posed immense risks of contagion (Mishkin 1999).[103] Joining the deposits of ordinary commercial banks to the riskier activities of investment banks could also create a set of banks too large and politically important to fail. Deregulated banks could reap large profits by taking on big risks, knowing that politicians would have to rescue them should their investments go awry. Moreover, the implications of newly emerging financial innovations were not well understood and lacked regulatory structures capable of measuring and accounting for their risks.

The abolition of Glass–Steagall was stymied by a distributional conflict *within* the financial sector and *among* the regulators. Large commercial banks were the strongest supporters of reform. Under Glass–Steagall, banks had underperformed relative to other financial firms – their share of assets in the United States had declined from 57 per cent in 1946 to 38 per cent in 1980 (Reinicke 1995, 58). Represented by the American Bankers Association (ABA), commercial banks could mobilize considerable resources. In addition, the banking lobby had a friend in Senator Jake Garn, the Republican chair of the Senate Banking Committee. A former pilot who would go on to represent Congress on the Space Shuttle Discovery, Garn had earthly priorities as well. As he authored legislation deregulating the S&Ls, his non-profit Institute of Finance at the University of Utah was being bankrolled by the junk bond industry.[104] Treasury Secretary Regan also favoured deregulation, although a less dramatic version, in which commercial banks wishing to underwrite securities would establish separate bank holding companies.

Some parts of the financial sector opposed abolishing Glass–Steagall. Smaller, rural commercial banks, represented by the Independent Bankers Association of America (IBAA), were unlikely to engage in securities underwriting and feared that loosening regulations might also expand interstate branching (Calomiris and Haber 2014, 283–330). The IBAA could count on Senator Fernand St Germain, the Democratic chair of the House Banking Committee, to advocate for their interests.[105] While a supporter of deregulation for S&Ls, St Germain opposed Glass–Steagall abolition. Investment banks, represented by the SIA, also opposed the abolition of Glass–Steagall, fearing increased competition from commercial banks. Although Republicans were more favourable to reform, those tied to the securities industry were reluctant to abolish Glass–Steagall.[106] Regulatory agencies also exerted influence over the debate. Paul Volcker at the Federal Reserve broadly opposed reforms on the ground that they posed risks to the larger economy, while the SEC was more open to reform. Turf war considerations were important to the position of both organizations, however. The SEC argued that it should regulate any newly liberalized securities trading by commercial banks. The Fed opposed this interpretation, instead arguing that it should remain the primary banking regulator (Reinicke 1995, 58–70).

In 1981, Garn introduced a bill that would allow commercial banks to underwrite municipal revenue bonds and manage mutual funds – a considerable expansion in the securities activities of banks. He received support from Regan, although Regan preferred that these services be offered through separate affiliates. Regan's insistence on a bank-holding-company model alienated the IBAA, whose members were small institutions, unlikely to create affiliates (Reinicke 1995, 58–70). Regan backpedalled on this requirement, but the IBAA remained opposed. St Germain pledged to kill any bills in the House Banking Committee. The holding-company proposal also prompted discord among regulators. The Federal Reserve feared that if banks could underwrite securities, the SEC would end up regulating them since its mission was to regulate all institutions underwriting securities. Faced with strident opposition, Garn scaled back his ambitions. In December 1982, he proposed a bill that bundled the deregulation of S&Ls with language allowing commercial banks to offer money market deposit accounts, which offered higher rates of interest to depositors maintaining a minimum balance of $2,500.[107] The bill, subsequently called the Garn–St Germain Act, was signed into law by President Reagan the same year.

With limited legislative progress, banks skirted Glass–Steagall by exploiting loopholes in the legislation and lobbying regulators. In 1981, Bank of America attempted to purchase Charles Schwab & Co., a prominent discount broker.[108] Making the case to regulators, Bank of America insisted that owning a discount brokerage would not constitute securities trading because Schwab simply took orders from investors. The Fed approved the acquisition, but specified that it distinguished between firms like Schwab and other securities underwriters. Elsewhere, investment banks like the Dreyfus Group acquired approval to operate an S&L in New Jersey from the comparatively liberal Office of the Comptroller of the Currency (OCC).[109]

Efforts to use regulatory arbitrage to escape the Glass–Steagall restrictions prompted Congress to seek clarification on the position of regulators over banking powers. The FDIC and OCC offered broadly liberal interpretations of the Glass–Steagall rules, which would allow commercial banks to expand their underwriting activities. Indeed, the FDIC proposed acceptance of broad securities-underwriting activities by state-chartered banks. In contrast, Gerald Corrigan (1983), president of the Federal Reserve Bank of Minneapolis, issued a statement clarifying the position of the Fed.[110] Corrigan stressed that while the central position of banks afforded them certain privileges, they must also accept limits on their ability to undertake risky activities. Accordingly, the Fed argued in favour of a moratorium on expansion of the banking powers of financial firms until Congress acted. The Fed's position was supported by the SIA and IBAA. Regan, although favourable to deregulation, preferred congressional resolution of regulatory uncertainty to the piecemeal regulatory turf wars that appeared to be underway (Reinicke 1995, 58–70).

Seeking to break the legislative impasse, Regan proposed legislation to allow banks to engage in securities trading through investment-banking affiliates, unified under a bank-holding-company structure. Predictably, the jealousies of competing regulatory agencies erupted. The SEC argued that if the affiliates of commercial banks were engaged in investment banking, it should be able to scrutinize them. The Federal Reserve balked at the prospect of losing turf to the SEC, while commercial banks opposed the measure due the burden of adhering to Fed *and* SEC rules. Thus, Regan's proposal alienated both opponents and supporters of Glass–Steagall. When Senator Garn proposed legislation in 1983 based on the administration's proposal, he faced opposition within the Senate Banking Committee from H. John Heinz, a Republican from Pennsylvania. A moderate who was closer to the securities industry, Heinz opposed dramatic reforms on the banking-powers issue. Instead, he announced that he would introduce a separate bill imposing a lengthy moratorium on new approvals. His support in the Senate Banking Committee was sufficient to credibly forestall Garn's plans (Congressional Quarterly 1984, 271–6). To give Congress sufficient time to debate, the OCC extended the moratorium on bureaucratic interpretations of banking powers until March 1984.

In 1984, the prospects for Garn's bill deregulating finance remained dim. St Germain expressed his principled opposition to a regulatory rollback, calling the bill "nothing less than a total reworking of the economic fabric of the nation" (Reinicke 1995, 75). The moratorium on new approvals was allowed to expire once again, prompting twenty-six banks to file with the OCC for the right to open out-of-state securities or insurance operations. However, Congress pressured the OCC to extend its moratorium on new approvals again. Meanwhile, the Continental Illinois Bank – a national bank with $40 billion in assets – collapsed in May 1984. In the House of Representatives, St Germain struck a sour note on deregulation: "When we are asked to endorse the movement of banks into fields even riskier than conventional banking, this type of incident does strongly suggest the need for careful analysis and caution."[111] St Germain introduced a bill closing the non-bank loophole without extending new powers to the banks, and it passed the House Banking Committee.[112] The move satisfied regulators' concerns about legal uncertainty, but challenged the deregulatory preferences of Garn and the administration. Although the Senate passed Garn's bill 89–5, St Germain used his leverage over the House Banking Committee to delay consideration until after the 1984 election (Congressional Quarterly 1984, 271–6).

With a long delay expected before Congress could act, the OCC allowed its moratorium to expire, and regulators scrutinized approvals once more. Although some approvals were granted and court rulings allowed the creation of discount brokerages, not all applications succeeded. For instance, the Federal Reserve rejected the application of Citicorp – a large commercial bank – to engage in securities activities. When Citi submitted another application, joined by Chemical Bank and J.P. Morgan & Co., the Federal Reserve dragged its feet. The recapitalization of the Federal Savings and Loan Insurance Corporation, which was being drained by the growing S&L crisis, was a higher priority (Congressional Quarterly 1987, 588–91). As before, the Fed's announcement was intended to put pressure on the Treasury and Congress to enact clarifying legislation. The Reagan administration, however, was distracted by the revelations of the Iran–Contra scandal.[113] Congress, in turn, was bogged down by a continued impasse. St Germain remained opposed to deregulation, and Garn preferred to allow regulators to slowly reinterpret Glass–Steagall. Further hopes of legislative action were dashed when the Republicans lost control of the Senate in the 1986 elections. William Proxmire, a Democratic senator from Wisconsin opposed to expanding banking powers,[114] replaced Garn as committee chair. In an interview signalling his views on banking reform, Proxmire said, "We've got to do everything we can to maintain the banking system we have. I think it's worked very well."[115] Glass–Steagall abolition appeared to be dead.

Regan had entered office determined not only to reduce regulations but also to change the way regulators behaved. As with the attempt to reform the banking system, competing interests quashed reform. Regan loathed the SEC, identifying his antipathy in an early memo. Noting that "one of the principal objectives to be encouraged by the Reagan Administration is the elimination of unnecessary regulatory impediments to capital formation," the memo argued that "the SEC can and does raise artificial barriers ... through regulations requiring excessive, unnecessary and costly initial registration and continuing disclosure requirements" (3 March 1981, box 169, folder 8, Donald T. Regan Papers). It advocated deep cuts to the SEC budget, reductions in disclosure requirements, and changes to leadership, which was "unsatisfactory either because of philosophic incompatibilities or competence" (ibid.).

To reshape the culture of the SEC, John Shad was appointed as chair. Not long after his appointment, he was confronted with a high-stakes turf war with the CFTC. The issue surrounded futures markets – markets in the future value of some stock or commodity. Futures markets had long been a staple of American agriculture, where they served an important purpose. Most farmers must borrow money to pay for land and equipment. Crop harvests are highly variable, and, in bad years, many farmers may experience hardship, even when their farms are viable over the long run. Futures markets allow farmers to hedge against risks like bad weather. Rather than directly selling their harvest, they can enter into contracts to deliver a certain amount of goods at a fixed price on some future date. Contracts can be traded by investors on an exchange, and they, in turn, can reduce their risks by entering into contracts with many farmers across different commodities. Commodity futures were traded aggressively in "the pits" of the Chicago Mercantile Exchange and the Chicago Board of Trade, where the synthetic nature of the market could make it prone to manipulation. In 1955, Vince Kosuga, an onion farmer and commodity speculator, managed to corner the national market on onions, eventually prompting Congress to ban onion futures trading (Lambert 2010, 41–3). By 1974, the US government had established the CFTC, a specialized regulator tasked with regulating these "future delivery" contracts. Such contracts are an example of a derivative – a security that *derives* its value from some other thing.

By the early 1980s, the emergence of an OTC market in different kinds of contracts was allowing buyers and sellers in the United States to trade more and more complex financial instruments such as futures, options, and swaps. As in agricultural futures markets, swaps allowed investors to trade on future outcomes. Unlike agricultural futures markets, however, swap contracts were untethered from the delivery of future goods. The CFTC argued that these transactions lay under its own purview and wanted to impose a strict interpretation of the Commodity Exchange Act.

Shad favoured a looser interpretation of the act because it fit Shad's ideological preferences as well as the view that new activities fell under the jurisdiction of the SEC.[116] The SEC drafted a study advocating the vertical integration of commodities and securities. Its position was that if an agency regulated the cash market for a particular security or commodity, it should regulate all derivatives related to that security or commodity. If that integration were implemented, the SEC would gain authority over OTC derivatives. Given Shad's support for the legality of swap contracts, the move would have allowed rapid growth in derivative markets. However, Treasury officials advised Regan to stay out of the dispute (Roger Mehle to Regan, 22 July 1981, box 169, folder 8, Donald T. Regan Papers). Instead, the SEC and CFTC were left to forge a compromise on their own. The Shad–Johnson Accord set up a preliminary agreement, erring on the side of caution by banning futures based on the performance of individual stocks or narrow stock indices. The agreement was not a long-term solution – it neither reined in the derivatives market nor gave traders assurances that swaps would be enforceable contracts. After contemplating the political capital necessary to open up a vast new financial market, Regan balked.

Regan also sought to alter the structure of financial regulation in the United States. While staffing changes could accomplish some shift in the behaviour of regulators, those changes could be easily reversed by subsequent administrations. Structural reform, on the other hand, could create bureaucratic interests invested in a particular style of regulation even after a government left office. Regan's efforts at structural reform failed completely. Citing the need to fight red tape, President Reagan approved a Vice-Presidential Task Group on the Regulation of Financial Services. The task group, which first convened on 11 January 1983, was headed by Vice President George H.W. Bush, with Don Regan as vice-chair (7 January 1983, box 148, folder 7, Donald T. Regan Papers).

The Treasury viewed the task group as a threat, potentially sidelining its own agenda. For instance, Assistant Treasury Secretary Roger Mehle exhibited fear that some within the group would undertake broad investigations that held the risk of "postponing or dissipating Administration deregulation proposals" (7 January 1983, box 148, folder 7, Donald T. Regan Papers). Vice President Bush was less dogmatically committed to the Reaganomics agenda – in the 1980 primary, he had criticized Reagan's economic policies as "voodoo economics" (Meacham 2015, 235). Mehle suggested that Regan focus the task group on reforms to regulatory structure rather than issues like Glass–Steagall. Regan appeared to follow this advice, warning Bush that the task group was "straying from its mission." He suggested further that the task group's broad focus created risks because opponents could reject its proposals on the grounds of "non-professional or inadequate research" (28 September 1983, box 148, folder 7, Donald T. Regan Papers). The Treasury was particularly worried about opposition from the Federal Reserve, whose expertise held sway in Congress (9 October 1984, ibid.).

Richard Breeden, a member of the task group, eventually arrived at a plan to create a powerful Federal Banking Agency that could shoot down legislation deemed detrimental to the stability of the banking system. Although the Regan Treasury was sceptical, it hoped that such a plan could supplant the Federal Reserve as primary regulator, thereby freeing banks from "its excessively theoretical and detailed supervision" (29 September 1983, box 40, folder 1, Donald T. Regan Papers). On the other hand, Treasury was concerned that an overhaul would hurt the ability of the Fed to resolve a far larger problem: the developing world's debt crisis. Developing countries in the 1980s were up against a perfect storm: American interest rates had been raised to unprecedented heights to combat inflation, while commodity prices had fallen from their heights of the previous decade. Many countries were forced to default on their debt as credit dried up. Although the

Fed's expertise would be vital to navigate the intricacies of global finance, the Breeden plan relied upon carving up the responsibilities of the Federal Reserve Board among other agencies, potentially adding *more* regulators (18 January 1984, box 148, folder 7, Donald T. Regan Papers). By the end of 1984, no legislation had been proposed, and the ambitions of the task group had been scaled back to recommending non-controversial changes so that Vice President Bush could declare his "mission accomplished" (9 October 1984, ibid.).

By 1986, the Reagan administration's intended financial regulatory rollback was a bust. At best, the administration continued the deregulation of S&Ls already initiated by the Carter administration, while marginally shifting the preferences of regulatory agencies. Legislative efforts to end Glass–Steagall and internal efforts to restructure the regulatory agencies failed. Two of the architects of Reaganomics, Council of Economic Advisers (CEA) member William Niskanen (1988) and Office of Management and Budget Director David Stockman (1986), concurred, stressing their inability to overcome political resistance. The Glass–Steagall system represented the equilibrium position of a dense political ecosystem: each component had both regulators and industry groups ready to defend the status quo. America's fragmented political institutions, moreover, gave actors many places to shut down change. The Senate, the House of Representatives, banking committees in either branch, the Federal Reserve, the SEC, the courts, and the administration all represented centres of power that could potentially forestall reform.

Competitive Challenges

Glass–Steagall was a politically robust system, characterized by a seemingly unbreakable equilibrium among investment banks, commercial banks, and S&Ls (Suarez and Kolodny 2011). However, it was vulnerable to external competition. Crafted amid a Great Depression that had decimated world trade and global finance, it had not been designed to buttress the global competitiveness of American financial institutions. External competition had played a minimal role before the 1980s: the United States had faced no viable contenders for global financial leadership. Let us consider the world of 1970: the second-largest economy, the Soviet Union, was a Communist dictatorship hostile to capital. Although it was a geopolitical challenger to the United States, it had no hope of challenging American financial leadership. The third-largest economy, Japan, possessed a GDP one-third the size of the United States. Western Europe matched the United States in economic bulk, but was politically disunited – although London exerted some pull due to its prominence in the Euromarket (Maddison 2009).

By the mid-1980s, America's position was slipping away. Dramatic economic growth had made Japan a peer competitor with the United States for global financial leadership. As the Japanese government began to deregulate its financial system (and as a rising yen made the assets of Japanese banks appear massive), the prospects for American finance grew even dimmer. Britain, though smaller than the United States and Japan, could also credibly threaten American leadership in many subsectors of global finance. Reforms implemented by the Conservative government of Margaret Thatcher, the Euromarket, and the acceleration of European unification made London an increasingly attractive place to do business. Strict regulations risked relegating American finance to a secondary position around the world, thereby undermining the foundations of American hegemony. Although neither Japan nor Britain supplanted the United States as lead economy, it is useful to review the extent of their rise in the 1980s.

The Rise of Japan

In 1960, Japanese Prime Minister Hayato Ikeda launched an incredible plan to double Japan's GNP over the next decade. The Japanese economy reached that goal in only seven years. Overall, between 1945 and 1980, real per capita GDP increased *tenfold* (Maddison 2013). Japan's growth was both qualitatively impressive and quantitatively impressive. Where once the Ministry of International Trade and Industry had forced IBM to share patents with Japanese electronics firms in exchange for gaining access to Japanese markets, by the 1980s, Japan was a leading producer of electronics (Encarnation and Mason 1990). Whereas the United States led the world in automobile production through much of the twentieth century, by the 1980s, Japan was the leading producer (Mitchell 2013). Even Japanese culture reached the American mainstream to an unprecedented degree in the late 1970s and 1980s. The Jedi knights of the popular *Star Wars* films were inspired by Akira Kurosawa's depiction of the last days of the samurai in *Seven Samurai*. One of the final roles of Orson Welles – director and star of *Citizen Kane* – was as a voice actor in *The Transformers*, a Japanese–American co-production. The *Teenage Mutant Ninja Turtles* may have eaten pizza in the dubious sanitary conditions of the New York City sewers, but they were trained by a Japanese sensei. Japan in the 1980s represented a different challenge to American leadership than the Soviet Union. With technological clout and great cultural appeal, it might conceivably have continued the succession of liberal global leaders who had been able to turn their country's economic strength into geopolitical power (Modelski 1978; Modelski and Thompson 1996).

As Japan approached the income levels of the United States and western European countries, economists foresaw the end of the high-growth period. Classical growth theory posits that GDP can increase in three ways – through more labour, more capital, and higher productivity (Solow 1956).[117] However, when an economy is at full employment, expanding the labour force does not increase GDP *per capita*. On the other hand, capital accumulation can increase growth in the medium run. With very high rates of saving, Japan built up large amounts of capital during the post-war period. However, in the long run, capital exhibits diminishing returns to scale. Imagine a coal mine full of workers with no tools. If the mine's proprietor gave each miner a drill (capital), output would increase with each new drill. But once every miner had a drill, the marginal gains from adding new drills would fall. If the mine's proprietor wished to increase output further, the miners might need a better drill, not more drills. Growth-accounting analyses of Japan tell a similar story of diminishing returns. The high-growth period was driven by capital accumulation and the movement of underemployed workers from rural agriculture to manufacturing – sources of growth that, by the 1980s, had been exhausted (Jorgensen 1988). Japanese economic policy needed to change, precisely because it had been so successful.[118]

Japan's post-war financial system was characterized by extensive regulatory oversight and limits to competition, but lax attitudes towards leverage. Before 1980, Japan had maintained capital controls, limiting the internationalization of Japanese finance. In addition, the Japanese banking panic of 1927 and the Allied occupation, led by the United States, had left a lasting imprint on the Japanese financial system – only twelve banks and four securities firms dominated the market. In addition, the Supreme Commander for the Allied Powers (SCAP) had separated securities and banking firms.

As in the United States, laws separating securities and banking activities had led to pronounced turf wars among the actors. Banks had initially maintained a privileged position, which Calder (2017, 49–58) characterizes as "the banker's kingdom." Large, long-term credit banks had mobilized the vast amounts of capital necessary to fuel the high-growth era. However, by the 1980s, the banker's kingdom was under threat. The need for large banks to funnel capital into heavy industry had diminished, and securities firms had begun to out-earn the banks (Rosenbluth 1989a, 101). The emergence of sustained Japanese budget deficits had opened up a new front on the banking-securities turf war – should banks be able to trade in government securities, or would that remain the preserve of securities firms? In addition, many ordinary Japanese savers had turned to the subsidized postal savings system to deposit their savings, posing additional challenges to Japanese banks (167–208).

Whereas reform debates in the United States were dominated by the jockeying of private-sector interest groups, bureaucratic actors in Japan exercised a great deal of influence over policies. Powerful government agencies like the Ministry of International Trade and Industry (MITI) and the Ministry of Finance (MoF) coordinated with big businesses. Rather than impose top-down rationalization, or legalistic oversight, bureaucrats often aimed to find out what firms were doing and how they could improve. Government agencies were staffed by highly skilled individuals – civil service jobs were prestigious, and civil service exams were difficult (Johnson 1982). Rather than being a terminal career destination, the MoF was a stepping stone to the legislature for numerous civil servants (Horne 1985, 200–1).

Post-war Japanese politics have long been characterized by inertial tendencies. Since 1955, the centre-right Liberal Democratic Party (LDP) has retained a legislative majority, apart from two, brief interregnums (1993–6[119] and 2009–12). However, the seeming continuity of LDP rule masks the factional divisions inside the party. Before electoral reforms passed in 1994, Japanese elections took place inside multi-member districts. Multiple LDP candidates stood in each district, with each LDP faction backing a single candidate to reduce vote-splitting. Faction leaders were highly influential in selecting the leader of the LDP (Schlesinger 1999). In return, prime ministers sought to keep the allied factions happy. With many legislative veto players, Japanese governments often deferred to the regulators (Tsebelis 2002). However, if the regulators were deadlocked, or if a policy had a marked impact on important constituencies, the LDP intervened decisively.

The most influential faction during the late 1970s and 1980s was that of disgraced former prime minister Kakuei Tanaka. His brief term (1972–4) had been marred with scandal: he resigned after reports that he had accepted bribes from the American aircraft company Lockheed. Despite the scandal, Tanaka was re-elected in his home district and continued to nurture a large retinue of allies. Unlike other factions that were united by ideological concerns, Tanaka's was held together by its successful practice of pork-barrel politics (Schlesinger 1999). An American visitor to Japan might gape in awe at the speed of Japan's legendary bullet trains. But they might miss the rather familiar pork-barrel politics that had extended expensive train lines to remote towns like the snowy hamlet of Urasa (ibid., 104). The Tanaka faction had strong support in rural areas due to its ability to acquire government funding for public-works projects. Strong ties to the construction industry gave the faction plenty of opportunities to recruit more members. Although too politically damaged to serve again as prime minister himself, Tanaka (and, after his death, a triumvirate of his acolytes) played a kingmaker role in Japanese politics. Thus, even as Japan adapted to the challenges of economic maturity, powerful interests desired to maintain the public-works state.

During the high-growth period, it had been easier to keep all LDP factions happy by sharing a growing pie. Slower economic growth meant slower growth in revenues, prompting Japan to run sustained budget deficits. Tax increases and spending cuts were difficult to implement in a political system with many veto players. When Prime Minister Masayoshi Ōhira tried to introduce a consumption tax in 1979, dissenting LDP legislators joined the opposition in a vote of no confidence against his government. The motion was successful, prompting a new election, during which Ōhira died of a heart attack. Fearful of a similar revolt, Ōhira's successors were highly constrained. They had to maintain the support of the Tanaka faction, with its demand for an expensive public-works state, while tax increases were politically unpalatable (Johnson 1986).

Rather than viewing private-sector actors, bureaucratic agencies, and LDP factions as separate entities, Calder (2017) characterizes each as being a participant in interlocking circles of compensation. Each cooperated to sustain mutual benefits, while deferring the costs of its preferred policies to the larger public. Critical in the dimension of finance was the overlap among the key actors in a financial circle of compensation, such as the major banks, the MoF, politicians, and the Bank of Japan (Calder 2017, 45) as well as those in an overlapping real estate circle of compensation (77). Although Japanese financial reforms of the 1980s appear modest in comparison with those in other countries, they represent rather significant steps in the inertia-prone context of Japanese politics. Reform debates crystallized in Japan around two axes, in particular – the liberalization of capital controls and the deregulation of the domestic financial system. Critical to the push towards reform was the emergence of new opportunities afforded by the country's economic clout.

Japan's economic success fostered new thinking about its role in the world. In the early post-war period, Japanese politicians had been guided by the grand strategic design of Prime Minister Shigeru Yoshida. The "Yoshida doctrine" emphasized a close alliance with the United States, minimal rearmament, and a focus on economic recovery, and it was a compromise between the competing desires of pacifists, idealists, and anti-communists on the one hand and those favouring engagement with Asia on the other (Green 2001, 11–17). By the 1970s, in light of Japan's growing economic clout, the Yoshida doctrine needed revision. In 1978, Prime Minister Ōhira, a member of Yoshida's faction, commissioned a series of study groups to investigate Japan's international role. Although Ōhira died before the reports were complete, his successor, Zenkō Suzuki, continued to read them.

No single figure impacted the content of those reports more than Yasuhiro Nakasone. Nakasone, a nationalist, sought a broader global role for Japan, complete with rearmament (Pyle 1987; Vogel 1996, 57).[120] Nakasone lobbied to become head of the Administrative Management Agency and then used his position to pack the study groups with allies. The participants included many advocates of a "neoconservative" agenda, aimed at repealing the regulations and government controls of the catch-up era (Pyle 1996, 71–4). Among the key contributors to the reports was the founder of Group 1984, an organization that criticized overregulation, likening environmental regulations to "witch-hunts," while proclaiming the dangers of the "British disease" (slow growth caused by excessive government intervention). This strain of thinking found many supporters, among them the chair of the Keidanren, Japan's most important business lobby.[121]

However, there was also a different thread to the reports, which spoke to Japan's destiny in a historical context. Where many American international relations scholars of that day were locked into a narrow game-theoretic debate over whether states cared more about relative or absolute gains, the study group drew upon more heterodox theories linking technological leadership to global political leadership. For instance, one frequent contributor to the project, Yasusuke Murakami (1992, 71–94), leans towards the works of Robert Gilpin (1981) and George Modelski (1978) in his *Anti-classical Political–Economic Analysis*. The view of history as a succession of global leaders, each vaulted to the top by their ability to capture the lead in technology, spoke to Japanese scholars and policymakers.

The Ōhira study group and its successors also suggested revision of the Yoshida doctrine in the face of American decline. Although the reports expressed support for rearmament, they saw such a course as politically costly. Non-military paths to global influence were preferable (Yasutomo 1989). Green (2001) describes the emerging Japanese policy of the 1980s as "reluctant realism." Still guided by the Yoshida doctrine, Japanese realpolitik involved the use of economic tools of influence. Financial liberalization was an important component of such a strategy. The liberalization of capital controls meant that Japanese firms could invest abroad, increasing Japanese influence. Banking and securities deregulation could increase the global competitiveness of Japanese financial firms. Internationalization of the yen could enhance reserve use of Japan's currency. All these changes, coupled with Japan's ability to recycle persistent current account surpluses into foreign aid, would give Japan a greater influence in international institutions like the IMF and the Asian Development Bank. Even if Japan did not become *the* dominant global financial power, it could become the primary financial centre in East Asia and the fastest-growing market in the world, earning immense structural benefits in the process (Gilpin 1987).

Critically, liberalization could abet the goals of Japan's domestic actors. The growth stoked by liberalization might increase government revenues without undermining the public-works state. Indeed, liberalization ultimately produced an explosion in Japanese land values – a boon to the real-estate-oriented Tanaka faction. Thus, when Prime Minister Suzuki announced that he would not run for re-election in 1982, proponents of the study group were in a good position to seize power. Nakasone, having used the study group process to nurture demand for a leader like himself, rejected a proposed alliance with the Fukuda faction (which supported strict adherence to the Yoshida doctrine), instead turning to the Tanaka faction (Endvall 2015, 144–6). Indeed, Nakasone appointed so many Tanaka faction members to Cabinet that his government was nicknamed the "Tanakasone" Cabinet.

A first reform debate involved the status of Japanese capital controls. By the 1970s, Japan was maintaining a substantial current account surplus, much to the chagrin of its trade partners like the United States. The liberalization of capital controls offered Japanese finance potential opportunities, and by 1978, American companies like Sears were seeking to borrow in Japanese markets (Rosenbluth 1989a, 56–7). However, bureaucratic jealousies stymied wholesale liberalization. A 1977 effort by Prime Minister Takeo Fukuda to end capital controls failed due to opposition by the MoF, which feared the loss of one of its most important powers. MITI, on the other hand, supported the liberalization (Solis 2004, 62–5). A consultative body aimed at reconciling the two positions recommended liberalization of current account and capital account transitions as well as the abolition of Japan's foreign-investment law. The MoF, however, would maintain the right to interdict capital flows under a broad range of circumstances (Rosenbluth 1989a, 57). In 1980, the Diet passed legislation putting the recommendations into law.

Despite liberalization in Japan, barriers persisted. One pathway to deeper reform would be to create a Japanese Offshore Market – eliminating withholding taxes and allowing a euroyen or eurodollar market to emerge in Tokyo. Absent restrictions, Japanese financial institutions could act as intermediaries between non-resident depositors and borrowers, earning the commissions befitting an international financial centre. Takeshi Hosomi, the vice minister of international affairs inside the MoF, had cultivated a group of young internationalist bureaucrats favouring an International Banking Facility (IBF), for which he advocated openly after leaving the MoF to head the Overseas Economic Cooperation Fund. In a 1982 speech he delivered after noting the rising degree of competition in international finance, Hosomi asked, "Why should Japanese financial institutions be under artificial restrictions?" (Takeshi Hosomi, quoted in Rosenbluth 1989a, 66).

There was considerable resistance to an IBF – the Tax Bureau of the MoF feared that it would lose revenue, the Bank of Japan feared that an offshore market would undermine its control over monetary policy, securities firms favoured only a limited IBF that retained their securities monopoly, while long-term-credit banks feared that such a move would undercut the distinction between short-term and long-term lending, thereby weakening their position vis-à-vis other financial institutions (Rosenbluth 1989a, 59–67). Against such political resistance, an IBF appeared to be a difficult proposition. However, the maintenance of barriers also entailed risks. The Reagan administration led a campaign to push Japan to liberalize its financial markets, with Donald Regan, in one speech to the Keidanren, pounding his fist and demanding "action action action" (Donald Regan, quoted in Rosenbluth 1989a, 75). Japan's massive current account surplus was seen as a political threat by the Reagan administration, and liberalization could conceivably reduce it.[122] Further, Japan's securities firms feared exclusion from British and American markets should protections remain.

The ensuing reforms in Japan may not have amounted to "action action action," but tangible steps began to be made towards internationalization. Japanese corporations were granted increasing access to euroyen bonds, allowing them to float bonds in a far less regulated environment. At the same time, regulators' fear of loss of control over the domestic money supply was leavened by a looming prize: increased international use of the yen in currency transactions allowed Japanese firms to engage in hedging against exchange risks. Hosomi's vision of an offshore Tokyo market came to the fore again in late 1984, with a large group of LDP legislators coalescing around a proposal for a Japanese IBF, while upholding the barrier between securities companies and banks. Although some legislators may not have fully understood the proposal – Rosenbluth (1989a, 85) notes that some of them may have believed that the Tokyo offshore market was a large construction project – support was strong (Rosenbluth 1989a, 78–89). Legislation creating a Japanese IBF passed in December 1986, with the new market attracting $115 billion in transactions in 1987 (albeit less than New York at $260 billion) (89). Although Japan's internationalization efforts were limited in many respects, they nonetheless represented large steps for a political system inclined to protect incumbents from competition.

The rollback of domestic financial regulations represented a second reform debate in Japan through the 1970s and 1980s. Banks were restricted from bond-trading a firewall enacted by SCAP, similar to the Glass–Steagall Act. By the 1980s, the environment faced by financial institutions had changed dramatically. The accelerating globalization of financial markets afforded greater opportunities for securities companies than banks (Calder 2017, 59–60). Growing Japanese budget deficits also enhanced the appeal of financial reform by creating a large market in government bonds. In 1980, the City Bankers Club, representing the twelve major banks, demanded the ability to trade in government securities (Rosenbluth 1989b). The banks faced opposition from Japan's four major securities firms, which resented the intrusion of new competitors.

The MoF interceded between the two industries, attempting to negotiate a compromise that would allow banks to trade in government securities, while imposing restrictions such as requiring them to acquire securities trading licences. When the City Bankers Club appealed to the government in response, Finance Minister Michio Watanabe deferred to the MoF. The MoF proposed a scheme granting banks access to the bond markets in exchange for prudential regulation: reductions of loans to any individual borrower to 25 per cent of their assets, while increasing disclosure requirements. The banking industry balked at the proposal, instead prevailing on the LDP to intervene. Speaking for the government, Chairman of the Policy Affairs Research Council Shintaro Abe expressed doubts that the MoF proposals could be passed as a bill, adding, "In a time when private sector vitality is essential, excess regulation is counter-productive" (Rosenbluth 1989b, 96). Over the objection of the MoF, the LDP prepared a bill opening up the bond markets to banks without additional regulations; it passed into law in April 1982.

Through the rest of the decade, the MoF and the government progressively relaxed restrictions on securities underwriting and repealed long-standing protections (Moran 1991, 103–12). Even some politically controversial legislation made it through. For instance, Japanese banks cheered the passage of a 1987 bill taxing interest income, which eliminated the subsidy to postal banks (Rosenbluth 1989a, 167–208). Although the MoF retained the authority to stop international investment operations by firms, it avoided doing so. This proved critical because even where strict Japanese regulations existed, financial firms could circumvent those rules by conducting what were essentially domestic Japanese transactions in the Euromarket (Mikuni and Murphy 2002, 152–3). At the same time, the Japanese banks maintained high leverage ratios, albeit masked by Japanese accounting principles. These rules counted stocks and property based on their purchase price, allowing firms to accrue substantial "hidden assets" as prices rose (Taniguchi 1999, 189).

The combination of financial liberalization and weak prudential regulations represented a ticking time bomb. Moreover, ties between Japanese firms and government actors risked moral hazard: should reckless investments enabled by liberalization threaten the survival of a well-connected firm, it could rely upon allies in government to rescue it. The intense loyalties fostered by LDP factionalism, in turn, could insulate corrupt politicians from the political costs of illegal activities. For instance, consider the 1986 Recruit Scandal. Despite the revelation that prominent LDP figures had illegally been given shares in a company that later soared in value, the party stayed in power (Schlesinger 1999, 233–7).

In retrospect, through much of the 1980s, Japan was in the midst of an unsustainable financial bubble. However, contemporary observers saw things differently. In an era characterized by a nascent revolution in information technology, Japanese leadership in semiconductors seemed to portend future Japanese domination. Japanese technological advancement amplified Japanese financial power. After liberalizing its capital account in 1980, Japan swung from being a net debtor to a net creditor, much like the United States in the First World War. As Japan became more economically central, Tokyo became an attractive place to do business. Between 1984 and 1989, the market capitalization of the Tokyo Stock Exchange increased *twelvefold*, leaping past the NYSE (Ibbotson, Carr, and Robinson 1982; French and Poterba 1991; London Stock Exchange n.d.; World Bank 2020).

Japanese banks, too, were on the rise. After the 1985 Plaza Accord, the appreciation of the yen enabled Japanese firms to recycle their profits into large purchases of international assets. Their ownership of such assets enabled Japanese banks to vault past the United States by 1986. By 1989, sixteen of the world's twenty-five largest banks were headquartered in Japan, with the largest Japanese banks owning five to eight times the equity of the largest American banks (Terrell 1990). The Japan of the 1980s seemed like an unstoppable juggernaut. Japan was beating the United States in high technology and using the proceeds of its industrial prowess to buy up every asset in sight.

A British Challenge

In contrast to the miracle economies of France, Germany, and Japan, post-war Britain was sometimes referred to as "the sick man of Europe." The dour sobriquet is an exaggeration – real per capita GDP growth in Britain chugged along at a solid 1.9 per cent a year between 1945 and 1973 (Maddison 2013). Nonetheless, it was a far cry from Britain's former prosperity. Once the centre of a vast global financial network, post-war Britain was more concerned with the "Macmillan Gap" – the idea that British banks had favoured overseas investment over British industry (Frost 1954). In 1945, despite the Allied victory in Europe, Winston Churchill was ejected by British voters in favour of Clement Atlee. Atlee's Labour government established an extensive welfare state in Britain, including stricter rules on financial firms imposed by the Companies Act of 1947. Geopolitically, post-1945 Britain proved unable to play an international role without American assistance – a fact decisively hammered home by the Suez Crisis. Later, Prime Minister Anthony Eden, working with the Israeli and French governments, sought to retake the Suez Canal and topple Egyptian President Gamal Abdel Nasser. In response, President Dwight Eisenhower blocked Britain from obtaining assistance from the IMF or the Export–Import Bank, even as Britain faced unsustainable reserve losses, unless Britain withdrew its troops. In the face of immense pressure on the value of sterling, Britain acceded to the demands (Kunz 1991, 116–52). Although the Euromarket still provided London with an important role in global finance, British finance was greatly diminished from its prior position (Helleiner 1996, 83–4).

While some Britons clinked pints of bitter to celebrate the achievements of the British welfare state, others lamented the Britain of council homes and nationalized railways. Some British Conservatives wanted to build a political machine capable of rolling back the welfare state. Restoring the global position of the City was a vital part of that agenda. The Tories had their first chance in 1970, with the election of Prime Minister Edward Heath. Heath had campaigned on the free market Selsdon Manifesto. Strident opposition from organized labour, however, pushed Heath to back down from his plans. Angry at the betrayal, Cabinet ministers Sir Keith Joseph and Margaret Thatcher plotted their rise to power, establishing a right-wing think tank, the Centre for Policy

Studies, while other Tory MPs formed the Selsdon Group to pressure future Conservative governments into staying on the right. In a letter to Thatcher, Joseph argued that he wanted to do more than "preach a materialistic greed of growth" (Joseph to John Wood and Arthur Seldon, 14 March 1974, Thatcher Papers, Churchill College, Cambridge). Joseph's fears of being cast as a Dickensian villain were well founded. Initially the pair's preferred candidate to challenge Heath, Joseph was forced to abandon his leadership ambitions after he gave a speech fretting that high working-class birth rates threatened Britain's "human stock." Thatcher replaced Joseph as the leading light of the movement, unseating Heath as Opposition leader in 1975 (following Heath's defeat in the 1974 election).

Capital controls (*exchange controls* in the British lexicon) were among the issues considered by Thatcher as she planned her rise to power. Capital controls insulated Britain from the destabilizing effects of large inflows and outflows of capital, reducing the fluctuation of the pound and freeing up the government to use monetary policy in the face of crises. On the other hand, controls prevented Britain from enjoying the benefits of capital inflows and outflows. The 1973 Selsdon Manifesto had described capital controls as reflecting an "out of date" "mercantilist philosophy" (Selsdon Group 1973). MP (and future junior minister) David Howell made the case for their abolition in a letter to MP (and future chancellor of the exchequer) Geoffrey Howe, who forwarded the letter to Thatcher. Howell argued that the status quo "weakens the position of the City of London as a financial and fund management centre" (Howell to Howe, 13 October 1977, Thatcher Papers).

In the elimination of capital controls, Thatcher had an issue that united her free-market ideological ambitions, the interests of the Tory-friendly financial sector, and the broad geopolitical goal of giving Britain a bigger share of global structural benefits. The day after Thatcher's 3 May 1979 election victory as prime minister, she received a memo from economist Douglas Hague outlining the advantages and disadvantages of capital account liberalization. Hague noted that the move would represent a free-market direction and that the City badly wanted it, but that the move would entail a large capital outflow (Hague to Thatcher, 9 May 1979, Thatcher Papers). Another, longer memo to now-chancellor Howe and Thatcher noted "persistent pressure from the merchants and bankers for liberalization," and it argued that Britain had stricter controls than most other advanced industrial economies. On the other hand, the memo also warned of "potentially volatile flows" and recommended only cautious liberalization (memo, George Richardson to Howe and

Thatcher, 11 May 1979, ibid.). Although Thatcher received favourable recommendations for abolition, the move entailed risks.

Other members of Cabinet advocated more radical reforms. John Nott, minister of international trade, argued that the chancellor's approach was "unduly timid" because British exchange controls were "more tightly controlled than in almost any other major western industrial country" (Nott to Howe, 25 May 1979, Thatcher Papers). In particular, Nott stressed that ending capital controls could increase the use of the pound in third-country financing, enhancing the role of sterling as a reserve currency. This was a fairly straightforward argument tying a liberalization agenda to potential structural benefits (Ikemoto 2016). Along similar lines, the financial secretary to the Treasury and a rising star within the Conservative Party, Nigel Lawson, later summarized the case for exchange control abolition in a memo, advocating that the controls be dismantled (Lawson to Howe, 4 October 1979, Thatcher Papers). In a conversation with Thatcher, Howe expressed a similar view, now advocating the elimination of controls. Seeking to assuage the fears of a reluctant Margaret Thatcher, he stressed that eliminating controls would allow Britain to invest North Sea oil revenues offshore, to make up for lost revenues once oil ran out (Cabinet Minutes, 17 October 1979, ibid.). Thatcher was finally convinced, agreeing to abolish controls "despite the risks involved" (ibid.).

On another question – the regulation of the LSE – Thatcher initially avoided a clear decision. In 1979, the London exchange was governed by internal rules: brokers were paid fixed commissions on trades, brokers and stockjobbers[123] were separate, and foreign firms were prevented from employing jobbers. These rules potentially ran afoul of the Restrictive Trade Practices Act, legislation aimed at breaking up cartels and promoting competition. The Stock Exchange Council requested an exemption from the act, warning that the sudden abolition of securities regulation could result in severe instability (Stuart Hampson to Tim Lankester, 18 October 1979, Thatcher Papers). In response to the request, Nott argued that an exemption for the stock exchange would be a political non-starter, while also undermining competition policy. In contrast, Howe argued that abolishing the rules risked economic turbulence and, further, that the Restrictive Practices Court was not set up to consider the wider implications of its decisions on the economy (Howe to Nott, 31 July 1979, ibid.).

Thatcher favoured a compromise that would deny an exemption for the stock exchange, while deferring a decision in light of the importance of adequate securities regulation (Stuart Hampson to Tim Lankester, 18 October 1979, Thatcher Papers). At the same time, a commission was established to investigate possible reforms to the financial system. Rather than being stacked by City bankers craving the return of laissez-faire, it was led by former Labour prime minister Harold Wilson and later by Professor Laurence Gower. Despite a desire to free up markets, Margaret Thatcher was more cautious than her "Iron Lady" reputation implied.

Cabinet discussion of stock market deregulation was delayed until after Thatcher's 1983 re-election victory. By then, the question of whether the LSE would be subject to the Restrictive Trade Practices Act loomed. Norman Tebbit, the new secretary of state for trade and industry, had negotiated a settlement with the exchange. If it abolished its old protective measures, the government would grant it exemption from its court case (memo, "Cabinet: The Stock Exchange," 25 July 1983, Thatcher Papers). The stock exchange capitulated, abolishing most of its critical restrictions (minimum commissions, the broker–jobber distinction, and rules against foreign firms). Margaret Thatcher also consulted with John Redwood on the matter. Redwood was a young Thatcherite stalwart considered as intelligent as he was conservative.[124] He emphasized the implications of reform for the City, identifying a top goal as "making dealing in London internationally competitive" (Redwood to Andrew Turnbull, 18 October 1983, Thatcher Papers).

The pending abolition of the LSE's internal regulations left open the question of what rules should be established in their wake. The old rules were a form of financial repression – they limited competition among actors to generate rents for insiders. At the same time, the separation of relevant actors (jobbers and brokers), high cost of individual trades, and limits on foreign firms from owning brokers kept the market small, reducing the implications of systemic failure. Freed from these restrictions, the stock exchange would become host to frenzied trading from new actors, with great potential for conflicts of interest.

One way to rein in these excesses would be to create a dedicated securities regulator, like the American SEC. Professor Gower supported a British SEC in his initial report (Gower 1985), a call echoed by the Labour Opposition in Parliament (Britain. Parliament. House of Commons 16 July 1984). However, the Thatcher Cabinet pushed for different options. In January 1984, Tebbit circulated a new draft of Professor Gower's proposals in Cabinet, which floated a plan for a hybrid regulatory structure. The LSE would be regulated by a new Securities and Investment Board, while implementation of the rules would take place within the exchange itself (Andrew Turnbull to Callum McCarthy, 18 January 1984, Thatcher Papers). Thatcher expressed broad approval of the plan, but sought wider consultation first.

Redwood weighed in again, expressing the opinion that he did not trust the staff of the Ministry of Trade and Industry, while saying of Professor Gower that his "chastity has never been broken by any spell of practical experience" (Redwood to Thatcher, 6 April 1984, Thatcher Papers). He argued that the proposed self-regulatory agencies (SRAs) would lead to a burdensome SEC system and a sprawling bureaucracy – the sort of red-tape monster that featured prominently in the nightmares of Thatcherites. Subsequently, he developed an alternative "minimal" regulatory proposal, limiting the role of government to ensuring competition and protecting against fraud. He stressed that British financial firms needed to be able to form "financial supermarkets" to compete with American firms. In his view, financial overregulation had allowed New York to outpace London in a vital sector of the economy, one that represented 13 per cent of British GDP (29 June 1984, ibid.).

Facing opposition to the Gower model, and seeing no support for an SEC-style regulator, Tebbit proposed a compromise. In a white paper, he set out a regulatory structure with fewer SRAs than the Gower plan and a clear right of appeal of SRA decisions. Redwood accepted the compromise, agreeing that this arrangement would still serve the principal goal of "keeping the City competitive" as the move represented a considerable reduction in the regulatory burden (Redwood to Thatcher, 16 October 1984, Thatcher Papers). Even the failure of Johnson Matthey Bankers that year failed to dampen the Thatcher government's determination to open up the markets. Indeed, Redwood argued that calls for increased regulation were tantamount to "witch-hunts" (Redwood to Andrew Turnbull, 12 December 1984, ibid.).

Internally, the Thatcher government united behind the reforms, passing the "Big Bang" deregulation legislation in 1985, with the reforms to take effect on 27 October 1986. Although the move was understood within the Thatcher government to be risky, optimism about the power of the markets, and pessimism about the prospects of the City without reform, limited these complaints. The Big Bang sparked a boom in the City. As figure 5.1 illustrates, between 1985 and 1989, the market capitalization of the LSE nearly tripled. With the Tokyo Stock Exchange rising at even faster rates, the threat to the position of the NYSE was clear. Even if London did not overtake the United States, it could play a spoiler role, forcing the re-evaluation of long-standing regulatory orders, lest the business of the world return to the City.

Figure 5.1. Market Capitalization of American, British, and Japanese Stock Exchanges ($US billions), 1980–9

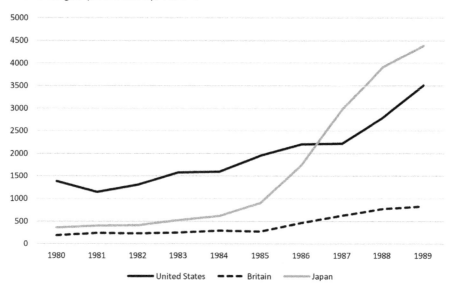

Sources: 1959–80: Ibbotson, Carr, and Robinson (1982); US and Japan, 1981–7: French and Poterba (1991); UK, 1981–7: London Stock Exchange (n.d.); 1988–9: World Bank (2020).

Competitiveness and the End of Glass–Steagall, 1986–2000

The rise of Japan, coupled with British reforms, threatened American financial leadership. In response, American policymakers and business leaders rallied behind a coherent agenda. President Reagan issued an executive order in 1983, creating a commission to explore the roots of America's sagging competitiveness. In its recommendations, the commission's report to the Finance Committee explicitly linked competitiveness and financial deregulation, recommending that the government "reduce disincentives to venture and other risk capital investments" (United States. Congress. Senate. Committee on Finance 1985, 14) and "reduce government intervention in the free flow of capital" (15). The following year, the Council on Industrial Competitiveness was formed, bringing together business leaders and academics to advocate for just such a pro-competitiveness agenda.

Whereas the ABA had previously argued for the abolition of Glass–Steagall on fairness grounds, after 1986, it emphasized international competitiveness. Its argument stressed that American banks were no less vulnerable to international competition than the automotive or semiconductor industry. If excess regulations prevented American banks from competing internationally, the results could be devastating for the position of the United States as the centre of global finance. For instance, in a Senate hearing, J.P. Morgan & Co. Chairman Dennis Weatherstone argued that the Glass–Steagall restrictions gave foreign banks operating in the United States an unfair advantage, while stressing that other financial centres were enacting reforms that would intensify those advantages (Reinicke 1995, 95–6).

The new argument attracted a broader coalition in favour of reform. Although Glass–Steagall repeal would open up the securities industry to competition from commercial banks, American financial leadership served commercial and investment banks in common. At the annual meeting of the SIA, some presenters began to speak out in favour of reform, to maintain American competitiveness internationally (Reinicke 1995, 96). Within the Federal Reserve, reports emerged stressing both the intensifying globalization of capital markets and the decreasing competitiveness of American finance within them (United States. SEC 1988; Terrell 1990). Even Paul Volcker admitted that it did not make sense that foreign banks operating in the United States were not subject to the same rules as American banks (Reinicke 1995, 93, 97). By the fall of 1987, William Proxmire had dropped his opposition as well – opening hearings by pointing out that fifteen foreign banks had managed to underwrite securities without incident.

In the House of Representatives, St Germain continued to oppose reform. With Congress unable to kill Glass–Steagall, proponents of deregulation found another channel by which to push their agenda: the Federal Reserve. Although the Fed cannot pass legislation, it interprets and implements laws. By reinterpreting Glass–Steagall, it could effectively reduce the impact of its provisions by allowing commercial banks to engage in some securities trading. Over time, liberal interpretations of Glass–Steagall could produce a convergence between different financial-sector actors, making it easier to reach political consensus.

While Chairman Volcker opposed reinterpretation of Glass–Steagall, his position within the Federal Reserve was increasingly tenuous. In March 1986, he had been outvoted on an interest-rate-cut decision by the Reagan appointees on the Federal Reserve Board of Governors (Funabashi 1989).[125] Although Volcker retained his position as chair and his main challenger, Preston Martin, resigned, the affair represented a significant vote of no confidence in Volcker. Later that year, the Federal Reserve Board addressed the question of how to interpret the Glass–Steagall Act. Volcker[126] was again outvoted by his peers, who voted to allow commercial banks to derive up to 5 per cent of their income from securities trading (Sherman 2009).

The following year, Volcker's term as Federal Reserve chair expired, allowing President Reagan to appoint someone more amenable to deregulation: Alan Greenspan. Since his days as a graduate student, jazz band player, and Ayn Rand acolyte, Greenspan had worked as a consultant, apart from a stint as chair of the CEA under President Ford (his former PhD adviser had been the Ford administration's Fed Chair Arthur Burns) (Greenspan 2008, 19–99). After serving with the CEA, Greenspan had finished his dissertation on housing bubbles, then returned to consulting. Testifying before Congress, he declared himself to be a "strong deregulator," echoing the competitiveness rationale for reform: "The important point, however, is that allowing American banking organizations to engage in expanded securities activities will make them more effective competitors in financial markets, both at home and overseas" (Reinicke 1995, 104). The argument was one Greenspan would make consistently in his tenure as Federal Reserve chair.

Rising support for deregulation did not mean that governments were indifferent about systemic risks. In the 1985 Plaza Accord and the 1987 Louvre Accord, the G5 leaders had attempted to devalue the dollar to reduce global imbalances (Funabashi 1989). Collaboration also took place on the issue of global financial regulation. American and British policymakers came upon a way to strengthen global regulatory safeguards while simultaneously enhancing their competitive position. Unlike American and British banks, however, Japanese banks were not subjected to strict rules governing leverage (Oatley and Nabors 1998; Singer 2007). They could invest heavily, while keeping little in reserve. Working together, American and British policymakers negotiated the Basel Capital Accord in 1988, which required signatories to maintain a favourable capital adequacy ratio[127] in case of a crisis. By emphasizing a regulatory approach that imposed stricter regulations in an area where Japanese laws were less stringent, American and British policymakers could nonetheless gain competitive advantages (Litan, Isaac, and Taylor 1994, 550–1). In other words, they were not opposed to regulation in principle, but rather opposed regulations when they threatened their countries' competitiveness.

In the short term, international coordination may have accelerated the growth of Japan's asset bubble (Mikuni and Murphy 2002). Appreciation of the yen was anathema to the preference of the MoF and Bank of Japan (BoJ) for a balance-of-payments surplus – an expensive yen was bad for Japanese exports. Monetary expansion could offset the upward pressure on the yen, but this would result in domestic inflation, while undermining efforts to weaken the dollar. Instead, the BoJ recycled a strategy that it had used in response to the Nixon shocks. It expanded the supply of credit heavily, while the MoF passed measures reducing capital gains taxes on land sales. As a result, much of the expansion of credit stimulated land sales, which ate up 30 per cent to 50 per cent of new lending (ibid., 138–9; Calder 2017, 60–1). Those selling land were typically wealthy, with a high marginal propensity to save. Thus, they deposited most of the proceeds from their land sales in the banks rather than increasing their spending. Banks could then repeat the cycle, lending to new borrowers. Thus, rather than stimulating generalized inflation, rising prices were concentrated in the real estate sector. Land purchasers saw that rising prices would enable them to borrow even more, using their land as collateral.

Continued speculative investments in land drove prices to absurd levels. One popular story claimed that, at the height of the boom, the Japanese imperial palace grounds were worth more than the combined real estate value of California (Economist 2007). The global financial regulations imposed by the Basel Capital Accords did little to slow the bubble. Indeed, most Japanese banks relied on a rule allowing them to count 45 per cent of their unrealized share price increases as tier 2 capital in order to maintain capital adequacy (Taniguchi 1999, 203). Despite the unsustainable nature of the bubble economy, it served the interests of influential stakeholders in Japan. The public-works state received soaring land prices, the export-oriented clients of the MoF and BoJ received continued balance-of-payments surpluses, and those seeking a broader global role for Japan within the confines of Japan's peace constitution got a roaring economic engine.

We know in retrospect that these policies had disastrous effects – when land prices crashed, panic ensued, and Japan plunged into one of the worst financial crises in history. Today, abandoned real estate developments, like the ghostly Nara Dreamland theme park, dot the Japanese landscape. Hayao Miyazaki's 2001 film, *Spirited Away*, offers a parable about the bubble era (Napier 2006, 301). After a Japanese family comes upon an abandoned theme park, the parents are transformed into pigs, while the daughter, Chihiro, is transported to a strange resort, where she must work as a cleaner to free them. The film's depiction of younger generations shackled by the avarice of previous ones unfortunately matches Japanese economic data well. Following the bubble era, Japanese economic growth never truly recovered, leading many to speak of the 1990s (and perhaps the 2000s) as a "lost decade."

Despite the hollowness of the Japanese boom, and the 1987 stock market crash, American policymakers remained concerned about challenges from abroad. Pressure to reform Glass–Steagall grew stronger, and even St Germain introduced a bill on banking powers. In 1988, the Senate passed legislation sponsored by Proxmire allowing banks to engage in a wide range of activities. Even business leaders outside the financial sector pushed for reform, with the National Association of Manufacturers offering its endorsement and a Senate Banking Committee poll indicating 77 per cent support for abolition among chief financial officers (Reinicke 1995, 108–9). However, the House of Representatives again proved a stumbling block. St Germain's legislation – already less sweeping than Proxmire's – also had to be approved by the House Committee on Energy and Commerce. Committee Chair John Dingell (Democrat from Michigan) was stridently opposed to the abolition of Glass–Steagall, once arguing that reductions in regulation would mean "a golden age of thievery."[128] The son of one of the architects of Glass–Steagall, Dingell was not inclined to legislate away his father's legacy. He used his leverage to demand only a limited expansion of banking powers. As negotiations between the committees collapsed, the legislative effort died.

Now close to retirement, Proxmire called upon the Federal Reserve to expand underwriting powers since Congress could not. Alan Greenspan happily obliged, doubling the limit on securities underwriting by banks to 10 per cent. By this point, the competitiveness case for abolishing Glass–Steagall had wide support. American banks had not only lost market share within the United States but were also less competitive internationally. Many Democrats on finance-related committees in Congress signalled their support for reform. In the House, Barney Frank indicated his view that since the Federal Reserve had acted, Congress would soon pass legislation (Reinicke 1995, 114). Senator Christopher Dodd argued, "It's unacceptable to most Americans that we should end up playing second fiddle to anybody in financial services" (117).

In addition, a new threat, complete with a timeline, loomed over the American banking sector. European Economic Community members were negotiating the creation of an integrated financial market by 1992. Not only could such a move greatly enhance the position of London vis-à-vis New York, but European policymakers were also discussing reciprocity: limiting the range of allowable activities by American banks in Europe to those permitted in the United States. By the end of 1989, even the SIA was ready to endorse the repeal of Glass–Steagall, stressing the pressing needs posed by "the global competition of the 1990s" (Reinicke 1995, 120). To sweeten the pot, investment banks wanted increased access to the banking market.[129]

However, the campaign to abolish Glass–Steagall was up against yet another headwind. The S&Ls, deregulated earlier in the decade, had taken advantage of new powers and lax oversight to make risky investments. In 1988, 205 S&Ls went bankrupt. In 1989, that number rose to 327, wiping out institutions with $235 billion in assets (United States. FDIC 2017). Since most of the failed institutions had FDIC protection, the federal government was on the hook for billions. Many S&Ls maintained close relationships with those in power, and their failure exposed dubious connections. For instance, Charles Keating, head of the ailing Lincoln Savings and Loan, prevailed upon five senators[130] – all of them recipients of campaign contributions – to discourage an ongoing investigation. The S&L failed later, and the ensuing bailout cost taxpayers $2.7 billion.[131] The failure of the Silverado Savings and Loan, in turn, proved embarrassing for the newly elected president, George H.W. Bush. His son Neil Bush had served on its board of directors, approving bad loans to business partners. Silverado was bailed out as well, costing taxpayers over $1 billion.[132] These costly bailouts dampened the appetites of the public towards financial deregulation.

Entering office in 1989, the newly elected president and his Treasury secretary, Nicholas Brady, supported the repeal of Glass–Steagall. Brady echoed the competitiveness argument offered by the ABA, stressing the need to do "something about this situation here where the top bank in the United States is 27th in the world" (Reinicke 1995, 121). However, efforts to re-regulate and rescue the S&L industry crowded the legislative docket in 1989 and 1990, pushing Glass–Steagall abolition to the back burner. By 1991, the cost of S&L bailouts had depleted the FDIC's funds, prompting interest in new rules governing deposit insurance coverage. Brady decided to take advantage of the situation by combining a proposal for new banking powers with efforts to reform deposit insurance, increase supervision of poorly capitalized banks, and eliminate branching restrictions. His omnibus proposal prompted fierce opposition from the IBAA, which opposed the elimination of branching restrictions. The small banks making up the IBAA did not want to have to compete against national behemoths. The proposal ran afoul of the preferences of the new Senate Banking Committee chairman, Donald Riegle, as well as John Dingell in the House. New amendments were attached to the bill under debate in the House, many of them unappetizing to the reformers (e.g., a moratorium on reinterpretation of Glass–Steagall by the Fed). Given the urgency of recapitalizing the dwindling funds of the FDIC, the Treasury was forced to step back from its insistence on including issues of bank powers in the reform debate. Legislative reform to Glass–Steagall had failed *yet again,* although reinterpretation by the Federal Reserve represented a partial victory.

The mercurial political environment of the early nineties opened up many potential avenues for American economic policy. In 1991, hot off victory in the Gulf War and the collapse of the Soviet Union, President Bush appeared to be unbeatable. His approval ratings reached as high as 89 per cent, remaining above 60 per cent for much of the year (Gallup 2018). These strong poll numbers discouraged many prominent Democrats, such as New York Governor Mario Cuomo, from running for president. A fairly obscure figure, Arkansas governor Bill Clinton, stepped into the vacuum and won the Democratic nomination. By 1992, however, the political landscape had shifted. Unemployment had surged to nearly 8 per cent by the middle of the year, with President Bush unable to reverse a sliding economy (United States. Bureau of Labor Statistics 2020). Bush visited Japan, intending to "talk tough" on trade to a perceived rival. Instead, he became publicly ill during a banquet, vomiting on the Japanese prime minister, Kiichi Miyazawa, and then fainting.[133] The image of the Japanese prime minister stroking the hair of a fainted American president seemed to embody a reality of American economic decline all too well.[134]

Despite the Japanese financial crisis, it was not yet clear that Japan had receded as a potential rival. In 1991, the Public Broadcasting Service series *Frontline* ran an episode on how America was "losing the trade war with Japan" (Koughan, Ewing, and Krulwich 1991). Many popular arguments circulated that were critical of the ability of American institutions to sustain competitiveness in the information age. One option, advocated by figures like Professors Robert Reich (Magaziner and Reich 1983) and Lester Thurow (1992), suggested adopting aspects of successful Japanese and German economic institutions. Industrial policy targeted at the bleeding-edge sectors of the future might help restore American competitiveness. Other works advocated the use of modest protectionism to advance American interests. For instance, Laura Tyson (1993) argued that the trade relationship with Japan was not reciprocal; by leveraging access to its large consumer market, the United States could negotiate more advantageous trade deals.

The 1992 presidential election saw the emergence of a three-way contest as Bush and Clinton were joined by the colourful Texas billionaire, Ross Perot. Perot made a credible, independent bid for the White House, running on a platform of protectionism and deficit reduction. While Bush defended free trade, Clinton was coy – supporting free trade, but stipulating the need for protections for the environment and labour rights. Following Clinton's victory in the general election, it was initially unclear what sort of president he might be. At times, he appeared to prefer the two more interventionist approaches to economic policy advocated by Tyson and Reich. Speaking after an economic conference in Little Rock, he discussed making strategic investments in research and development and training as the core of his economic strategy.[135] Further, he appointed Laura Tyson to head the CEA and Robert Reich – a friend since their days as Rhodes Scholars together – as secretary of labor.

Despite these appointments, Clinton was open to deregulation. Before the 1992 election, Clinton had been president of the Democratic Leadership Council, a group aimed at promoting centrist positions within the Democratic Party (Baer 2000). As Treasury secretary, Clinton appointed Texas Senator Lloyd Bentsen. Bentsen had received national exposure as the running mate of Democratic presidential nominee Michael Dukakis in the 1988 election. Former chair of the Senate Finance Committee, Bentsen was a conservative Democrat who was well respected on Wall Street. Clinton also brought the former co-chairman of Goldman Sachs, Robert Rubin, into the CEA. The libertarian Greenspan interpreted the appointment of conservative Democrats as a sign that Clinton was someone he could work with. Clinton, after all, was a fellow saxophonist – who better to build a new Jazz Age with (Greenspan 2008, 142–50)?

Greenspan possessed a powerful tool for influencing fiscal policy. He signalled to Clinton that interest rate hikes were likely, although serious efforts at deficit reduction could limit their adverse impact. For a president concerned with re-election, Clinton took Greenspan's words to heart. Considering the constraints that finance imposed on the administration, Clinton's political adviser, James Carville, opined, "I used to think if there was reincarnation, I wanted to come back as the president or the pope or a .400 baseball hitter. But now I want to come back as the bond market. You can intimidate everybody."[136] Robert Reich (1997) described a similar pattern in Clinton Cabinet meetings. Energetic, wide-eyed Cabinet ministers would propose measures to stimulate the economy, Bentsen would warn about deficits, and Greenspan would emerge from the shadows, warning of interest rate hikes. Protectionist inclinations inside the Clinton administration soon vanished as well. By the end of 1993, Vice President Al Gore was dispatched to defend the North American Free Trade Agreement in a debate on CNN's *Larry King Live* with Ross Perot.

With the threat of interest rate hikes undermining the desirability of industrial policy, financial deregulation became a more attractive option. In a letter to the president sent in 1993, Lloyd Bentsen argued, "The U.S.

banking system is facing secular decline," adding that removing restrictions could "expand productive lending, help distressed communities, increase U.S. competitiveness internationally, and improve the financial condition of the industry" (Bentsen to Clinton, 7 October 1993, Clinton Papers, James Marshall and Marie-Louise Osborn Collection, Beinecke Rare Book and Manuscript Library, Yale University, New Haven, CT). Bentsen attached a longer memo written by the comptroller of the currency, Eugene Ludwig, advocating the elimination of unnecessary barriers, including the rules limiting securities underwriting by banks and interstate branching restrictions.

In 1993, Congress opened discussion of legislation ending restrictions on interstate bank branching. Like Glass–Steagall, these were old restrictions that dated back to the Great Depression. The previous Republican administrations had not even considered such a move, fearing opposition from S&Ls and the IBAA. However, following the ravages of the S&L crisis, such institutions had little ability to influence Congress. Major banks, on the other hand, relished the prospect of interstate branching. A group of bank CEOs met with Rubin on 22 October 1993, perhaps expecting that they would have to push hard to win him over to their position. In fact, Rubin's briefing had urged him to support abolition of branching restrictions, arguing that the move was good for consumers and entailed few risks (Ellen Seidman to Rubin, briefing note, 18 October 1993, Clinton Papers). The administration gave testimony supportive of the legislation in Congress, which overwhelmingly passed the Riegle–Neal Interstate Banking and Branching Efficiency Act.

The end of 1994 saw the scope for financial deregulation expand even further. Congressional Democrats were massacred in the 1994 midterm elections, giving Republicans control of the Senate and House of Representatives for the first time since 1955. The Republicans had campaigned on a unified platform – incoming Speaker Newt Gingrich's Contract with America. Solidly conservative, the platform called for strict limits on spending, cuts to social welfare programs, cuts to taxes on capital, and tough-on-crime measures. If prospects for expansive industrial policy had been dim before, they were unthinkable after 1994. Staffing changes in the Clinton administration, and the balance of power in Congress, advantaged proponents of deregulation. Lloyd Bentsen retired as Treasury secretary and was replaced by Robert Rubin. Professor Lawrence Summers, a prominent economist, was brought in as deputy secretary. Critically, Democrats losing the House meant that John Dingell would no longer chair the Energy and Commerce committee.

The new chairman of the House Committee on Banking and Financial Services, Jim Leach, Republican from Iowa, took a swing at the

Glass–Steagall system with a bill allowing banks to underwrite securities and insurance contracts. Despite receiving indications of support from the Clinton administration, regulators, and *both* major banks and securities firms, the bill aroused objections from insurance companies. Like securities firms in the 1980s, insurance agents feared increased competition from commercial banks. Speaker Gingrich, after explaining to banking executives that "insurance agents can turn out more voters than banks can," sought to salvage the legislation by inserting a rider that indefinitely prohibited banks from entering the insurance business.[137] Although Leach was able to reduce the moratorium on insurance activities to five years, the restriction made the bill unappetizing, and legislative efforts failed again: Glass–Steagall appeared to be a legislative Lazarus.

However, regulators were happy to act, even though legislators were not. Greenspan advocated strongly for Glass–Steagall repeal, linking reform to American economic leadership. Speaking at a banking forum in New Orleans, he argued that the financial sector was being transformed by the information revolution, but that deregulation was necessary for the industry to reap the full benefits of those changes (Greenspan 1996). That December, Greenspan again reinterpreted the Glass–Steagall Act, allowing banks to earn up to 25 per cent of their income from investment banking (Sherman 2009).

Discussion of Glass–Steagall repeal continued, despite the earlier failures. Inside the Treasury, a memo circulated, discussing legislative strategies for Rubin and Summers (Jerry Hawke to Rubin, 11 December 1996, Clinton Papers). Rather than evaluating an ideal policy position, the memo considered how to maximize the administration's influence over the repeal of Glass–Steagall. It was assumed that repeal – now called "financial modernization" – was a desirable objective. A draft memo for discussion outlined the priorities for new legislation, among them: "to assure that U.S. financial institutions are fully competitive in international financial markets," "to encourage innovation," and "to secure for users the benefits of new advances in technology." Although the draft discussed risks to the global economy, it saw risk management as the answer. In other words, risk was seen as something knowable and calculable, despite the fact that the global economy was undergoing a period of unprecedented financial globalization coupled with a technological revolution.

The years 1997 and 1998 might have been a good time to consider the risks posed by the new financial order. In the 1990s, many East Asian countries had liberalized their financial systems. At first, capital rushed to finance rising economies in Southeast Asia. With credit freely available, many firms borrowed heavily to expand activity, triggering an economic boom. Strong government–business ties meant that moral hazards abounded in Thailand, Indonesia, Malaysia, and South Korea. Newly liberalized banks with friends in high places had confidence that governments would rescue them should their debt-fuelled expansion go awry. By 1997, speculators grew increasingly doubtful of the ability of Thai borrowers to service their debt, prompting many to short the Thai baht. When the Thai government devalued modestly, short-sellers grew even bolder, triggering a collapse, followed by rapid capital flight. Malaysia, Indonesia, and South Korea faced similar speculative attacks. A vicious cycle ensued: the lower the currencies of afflicted countries fell, the harder it would be to pay off US-dollar-denominated debt. Those afflicted by the 1997 East Asian financial crisis turned to the IMF for short-term credit – South Korea receiving what was then the largest IMF bailout in history. The strict conditions attached to the rescue helped prompt a political revolution in Indonesia, toppling the Suharto government. Malaysia balked at the terms of conditionality and retreated behind a wall of capital controls (Haggard 2000; Sheng 2009).

Warning signs flashed in the United States as well. In 1998, the hedge fund LTCM collapsed. LTCM was a *wunderkind* of the financial world. It was run by John Merriwether, alumnus of the legendary trading firm Salomon Brothers (Lowenstein 2000; Johnson and Kwak 2010, 53–4). Its board of directors included two Nobel laureates – Myron Scholes and Robert Merton had been awarded the Nobel Prize for economics for discovering a technique for valuing derivatives. The firm's strategy involved using new quantitative models to find profitable trades. However, LTCM was overleveraged, having made large bets on East Asia and Russia (which suffered a financial meltdown in 1998). When a firm borrows heavily to make investments, it has little margin for error – worse than expected results can force a firm to go bankrupt. The East Asian financial crisis of 1997 and the Russian financial crisis of 1998 caused LTCM to collapse, prompting a bailout by the Federal Reserve costing billions. Even if regulatory "modernization" was in order, financial innovations opened up new ways for firms to take risky bets. Successful modernization required new ways to observe those risks as they manifested – measures that were largely ignored by those seeking to reform the system in the 1990s.

Despite the 1997 East Asian crisis and the LTCM debacle, tantalizing prizes remained. New investment opportunities, such as liberalized emerging markets, dot-com companies driving a surging NASDAQ, and the burgeoning derivatives market made financial primacy increasingly valuable. Although the position of the United States was increasingly secure, competitive challenges remained. Japan had been chastened by the collapse of its bubble economy in 1989, but it was not yet obvious that it was in store for a "lost decade." In 1996, the prime minister, Ryutaro Hashimoto, had announced Japan's Big Bang – a program of aggressive deregulation aimed at enhancing Tokyo's position as a global financial centre (Horiuchi 2012; Royama 2012). London, too, remained an attractive alternative to New York as a place to do business. The intensification of the European project might have yielded considerable dividends for London as well.

The eurozone launched a new European currency, the euro, in 1999. Backed by the economic clout of continental Europe, the euro looked like it might be a serious contender against the United States dollar as the global reserve currency. Some American policymakers, such as Larry Summers, derided the value of reserve currency status as seigniorage benefits from "Latin American drug dealers" and "Middle Eastern mattress cash" (Summers to Rubin, 12 December 1996, Clinton Presidential Library, Little Rock, AR). On the other hand, Japan, the United States, and the European Union (EU) had begun issuing bills in very large denominations that were unlikely to be used in ordinary circulation (Cohen 2004, 75–81). The objective was to create bank notes that would be attractive to those holding reserves. The United States also maintained good relations with Saudi Arabia, at great cost, in exchange for Saudi Arabia's decision to denominate sales of oil (a large proportion of global trade) in dollars – effectively a Saudi vote for the dollar as reserve currency (Spiro 1999).[138] The primary advantage of holding the reserve currency was not direct seigniorage, but rather the influence it gave American policymakers and the edge it gave American investors. East Asian countries, wracked by a severe financial crisis, were desperate for reserves. High savings rates allowed them to accrue large dollar reserves, while providing the United States with cheap credit that could be reinvested profitably. Gourinchas and Rey (2007) estimated that American investors earned additional returns of 3 per cent during the period compared to their international competitors, thanks to the ability to secure such cheap credit.[139]

Reinterpretation of Glass–Steagall by the Federal Reserve may have also set in motion a degree of snowball effects encouraging further deregulation. Loosening the rules had not produced any obvious disasters yet. From a political perspective, momentum was also clearly in favour of deregulation. The fast-growing financial sector was able to donate more money than ever before. Donations to the financial sector by political action committees (PACs) in 2000 represented nearly a quarter of all PAC donations (Center for Responsive Politics

2019a). Moreover, the preferences of different types of financial firms were growing increasingly similar as banks engaged in more securities underwriting and securities firms in more banking.

Against a backdrop of continuing pressure for reform, Congress reopened legislative debate over the repeal of Glass–Steagall. As before, Jim Leach led the push in the House of Representatives, while Alfonse D'Amato sought to pass a bill in the Senate. Facing a tough re-election bid against House Representative Chuck Schumer, D'Amato needed cash to carpet-bomb upstate New York with negative ads.[140] The proposed bill, HR 10, was far more sweeping than that favoured by the Treasury. Leach and D'Amato were helped along by an extraordinary bet in favour of passage by Sanford Weill of the large insurance company The Travelers Group and John Reed of Citibank, one of the largest banks in the country. Weill and Reed sought to merge Travelers and Citibank in a deal worth over $70 billion.[141] Because Travelers was an insurance company and Citibank a commercial bank, the merger flagrantly violated the Glass–Steagall Act. Failure to repeal Glass–Steagall in a timely manner would mean chaos for two of the largest financial institutions in the United States.

Leach barely managed to pass HR 10 in the House in May 1998, by a vote of 214–213, one that cut across party lines (Republicans voted 153–72, Democrats 61–139) (United States. Congress. House of Representatives 2017a). However, it took longer for the bill to be considered in the Senate with the 1998 midterm elections fast approaching. A memo from Robert Rubin, written before a meeting with Weill and Reed, described how the battle lines on HR 10 were drawn (Rubin to Erskine Bowles, 22 September 1998, Clinton Presidential Library). The bill was supported by large banks and the Republican congressional leadership. Senator Paul Sarbanes, ranking Democrat on the Senate Committee on Banking, Housing, and Urban Affairs (CBHUA) also supported HR 10, fearing losses in the 1998 congressional elections as Democrats ran against the headwinds of scandal. Earlier that year, news of an affair between President Clinton and White House intern Monica Lewinsky had produced a media feeding frenzy.

On the other hand, there were reasons to oppose the bill as well. Some Democrats feared that it would undermine the Community Reinvestment Act (CRA), which encouraged banks to lend to underserved communities. Some Republicans on the CBHUA, such as Senators Phil Gramm and Richard Shelby, feared that the bill would extend the purview of the CRA to new institutions. Some small bankers and insurance agents were also inclined to oppose the bill, fearing increased competition. The administration signalled that HR 10 would be subject to a presidential veto despite another internal memo describing strong support for the bill from the ABA, the SIA, Merrill Lynch, Citigroup/Travelers, Nations Bank/ Bank of America, insurance groups, and even the IBAA (Lisa Andrews to Rubin, 22 September 1998, Clinton Presidential Library).

Despite widespread expectations of Republican midterm gains, the Democrats picked up four seats in the House of Representatives in 1998, while maintaining the status quo in the Senate. Alfonse D'Amato, however, was defeated in his re-election bid, making Phil Gramm the new chair of the Senate CBHUA. Gramm was a friend of the financial sector. When he ran for president in 1996, his campaign had been one of the best funded – raising $63 million, much of it from financial firms (Center for Responsive Politics 2019b). However, it is unlikely that finance was trying to win over a future president by backing Gramm's presidential ambitions. By his wife, Wendy's, own telling, he was charisma-deficient. Upon meeting him, her initial reaction had been "Oh, yuck!"[142] Rather, the emerging financial supermarkets backed him in hopes of currying favour with the next Senate banking chair. Thus, Gramm could be expected to push hard for a bill like HR 10; the real question was whether the Clinton administration would veto it.

Inside the Treasury, Larry Summers had concerns about financial modernization: he wanted to know whether new legislation would bring hedge funds closer to the federal safety net and whether the 1997 East Asian financial crisis should temper the administration's views on financial modernization (Richard Carnell and Gregory Baer to Rubin and Summers, "Rethinking Financial Modernization Legislation," 14 November 1998, Clinton Presidential Library). A memo to Summers and Rubin addressing these issues reported that the effects of new legislation were ambiguous on whether hedge funds (like LTCM) would be able to access the American financial safety net, and it noted that while the previous financial modernization bill "would have facilitated the creation of large financial conglomerates, it made no systematic effort to constrain the potential for such entities to be seen as too big to be allowed to fail." Despite their seriousness, these concerns were insufficient to garner opposition to Glass–Steagall repeal from the Clinton administration.

Congress returned to the question of financial modernization in 1999, with different legislation considered by the House and Senate. The Clinton administration strongly preferred the House bill, drafted by House Banking and Financial Services committee chair Jim Leach and ranking Democrat John Lafalce. In particular, Gramm's Senate bill was seen as troubling because it would restrict the operation of the CRA (Robert Rubin, Gene Sperling, Bruce Reed, and Larry Stein to President

Clinton, 1 March 1999, Clinton Presidential Library). Many Democrats feared that the CRA would become irrelevant following the elimination of Glass–Steagall unless access to the new powers granted to financial institutions were conditioned on CRA compliance. A second line of critique emphasized the dangers of mixing commerce and banking, citing the problems in the East Asian economies during the 1997 crisis. However, Congress had been showered with money by firms eager to see a Glass–Steagall repeal. In July, Gramm passed a bill in the Senate on a party-line vote, while the House passed an identical bill without objection. A veto remained the last tool by which the Clinton administration could shape the process of financial modernization.

The White House prioritized CRA preservation over considerations of systemic risk. The CRA had a constituency within the Democratic Party, while concern over systemic risk did not. Clinton had long favoured a "new markets" agenda, aimed at increasing access to credit for underserved communities, including distressed urban areas and rural Appalachia.[143] An administration memo providing background on the financial modernization bill reported that over sixty community groups had sent letters to the president expressing the need for a financial modernization bill that would preserve the role of the CRA ("Background on CRA Issues in Financial Modernization," 20 September 1999, Clinton Digital Library, Clinton Presidential Library, Little Rock, AR). The backgrounder suggested that Gramm was open to compromise, but that he wanted to eliminate CRA requirements for small banks; a "sunshine" amendment disclosing CRA agreements to the public; and a "have and maintain" provision, allowing financial firms to enjoy the benefits of Glass–Steagall abolition so long as they maintained a satisfactory CRA rating.

Gramm proved willing to negotiate, pushing for infrequent CRA compliance checks on smaller banks and sunshine rules. A compromise bill combining Glass–Steagall abolition with CRA-preserving concessions to President Clinton went up for a vote in the Senate. In the debate, Gramm received plenty of assistance from the Democrats. Chuck Schumer, for instance, sounded more like Alan Greenspan when he declared, "If we don't pass this bill, we could find London or Frankfurt or years down the road Shanghai becoming the financial capital of the world."[144] The conference report sailed through the Senate in a 90–8 vote (United States. Congress. House of Representatives 2017b). As the bill moved to the House of Representatives, a lonely John Dingell took the floor to urge his colleagues to vote against repeal. He reminded his colleagues of the immense cost of the S&L bailouts, that new financial supermarkets would be "too big to fail," and that the confused regulatory structure would be unable to prevent a serious crisis (United States. Congress. House of Representatives 1999). Most of Dingell's colleagues saw things differently: the conference report passed 362–57 and was passed into law by President Clinton (United States. Congress. House of Representatives 2017b). The principal regulatory order that had anchored the American financial system since the Great Depression was dead.

A celebratory Sandy Weill commissioned a four-foot-wide wooden etching of himself, emblazoned with the title "The shatterer of Glass–Steagall."[145] Weill may have given himself too much credit. Competitiveness concerns and grand ambitions had awoken reform in Japan and Britain in the 1980s. Competitiveness concerns had reshaped the interests of those initially opposed to reform, to a degree that had enabled a bureaucratic workaround of Glass–Steagall. A little laxity had become a lot of laxity as financial firms became more similar, larger, and more politically influential. Competitiveness concerns had likewise sustained pressure for deregulation, even in spite of the election of a presidential administration that might have been hostile to it.

Indeed, we have evidence of *another* regulatory reform under consideration around the same time as Glass–Steagall: the rules governing derivatives trading. Here the critical decisions were made within the Clinton administration, with competitiveness featuring prominently. Let us return to an obscure corner of the financial regulatory infrastructure: the CFTC.

CFTC Chair Brooksley Born was a respected lawyer and friend to First Lady Hillary Clinton. Charged with regulating swap contracts traded in the OTC derivatives market, the CFTC had front-row seats to the ways in which derivatives were transforming the American financial landscape. Many of these changes sparked alarm at the CFTC as swap contracts were taking place with little oversight. In one high-profile case, Bankers Trust sold interest-rate-swap contracts to clients that would yield returns if interest rates remained low, but massive costs if interest rates rose. A review of tapes found Bankers Trust employees referring to the ROF ("rip-off factor"), the amount that firms could earn by foisting dubious securities on unsuspecting customers. Misled clients including Procter & Gamble and Gibson Greeting Cards launched lawsuits.[146] Not only did derivatives markets represent a great opportunity for fraud, but a vast, unregulated derivatives market also posed immense risks to the system by itself. What were the implications if a single firm were on the hook for more insurance contracts than it could pay out on? Who would quantify the exposure of participants to these new risks? Could ordinarily conservative investors such as pension funds or municipal governments end up engaging in high-risk markets? With some of these concerns in mind, the CFTC prepared a concept release calling for clarification of the Commodity Exchange Act to address the risks posed by new derivatives.

Before the concept paper was released, Born discussed it with the principals of the President's Working Group on Financial Markets (PWG) on 21 April 1998. In attendance was Robert Rubin, Larry Summers, Alan Greenspan, and SEC Chair Arthur Levitt – the very heart of the Clinton administration's economic team. The handwritten minutes of the meeting show an overwhelmingly negative response to the CFTC proposal. Rubin insisted that the move "raises uncertainty over trillions of dollars of transactions" (Presidential Working Group Minutes, 21 April 1998, Clinton Digital Library). Greenspan argued that just as past regulatory anomalies had created the eurodollar market, so the "OTC derivatives market could flee to London." Noting the potential for uncertainty or competitive losses, both Rubin and Summers suggested an alternative to CFTC regulation, to be determined in the future. The day after the release of the CFTC concept paper on 6 May, Rubin, Summers, Greenspan, and Levitt signed a joint letter declaring their "grave concerns" (United States. Department of the Treasury 1998).

During the following year, the PWG met to discuss how to manage uncertainty in the OTC derivatives market, delivering a report to Congress in November 1999. The report, while noting the failure of LTCM, sought to reduce systemic risk "by removing legal obstacles to the development of appropriately regulated clearing systems." In other words, the regulators *were* the risks. The document strongly emphasized the implications of derivatives markets for American financial leadership, highlighting the risk that "legal uncertainty ... if not addressed, could discourage innovation and growth of these important markets and damage U.S. leadership in these arenas by driving transactions off-shore" (Summers et al. 1999). The report recommended excluding a large range of non-agricultural financial products from the oversight of the CEA, effectively curtailing the role of the CFTC in favour of the SEC, with its broader acceptance of swap contracts.

The House of Representatives passed legislation largely implementing the PWG's recommendations, the Commodity Futures Modernization Act, the following year in a 377–4 vote. Even Bernie Sanders, an independent democratic socialist, voted in favour of the bill (United States. Congress. House of Representatives 2017c). Senate legislation was delayed until the eleventh hour of the 106th Congress because Gramm sought to limit derivatives regulation even further. For instance, he exempted energy derivatives from regulation, much to the benefit of Enron – an energy-trading firm, where his wife served on the board of directors.[147] Gramm passed the bill by attaching it to a large appropriations bill, which passed unanimously. The legal uncertainty surrounding derivatives trading was banished. Firms rushed to take advantage of these new options, with the notional value of derivatives in insured commercial bank portfolios rising from $26 trillion in 1998 (United States. Department of the Treasury. OCC 1998) to $145 trillion by 2007 (ibid., 2007).

Free from regulation, capital poured forth and markets surged. The initial public offerings of new information-economy stocks, like Pets. com, were enthusiastically promoted by investment banks. The biggest prize of all, America Online, merged with Time Warner in a $165 billion deal marrying the capitalism of old with that of the new.[148] One book audaciously predicted that the Dow Jones Industrial Average would hit 100,000 by 2020 (Kadlec 1999). When the NASDAQ doubled between August 1999 and March 2000, such predictions did not seem crazy (Williamson 2018). Even those unable to play the stock market could find incredible investment opportunities. Some rushed online to trade beanie babies – stuffed animals that could be worth up to thousands of dollars. Each instance of amazing returns convinced even more people that a true golden age had arrived.

Investors were like new lovers, infatuation blinding them to the warning signs. Pets.com had virtually no revenues, beanie babies were low-quality, mass-produced toys, and high returns came with high risks. The NASDAQ crashed, falling from a high of 5,046.86 in March 2000 to 1,114.11 by October 2002 (Williamson 2018). The crash exposed numerous instances of outright fraud facilitated by lax regulation. Enron, which had traded energy derivatives hedged with other derivatives *that it owned,* collapsed after it became clear that its reported profits were fraudulent. The weaknesses underlying the economy were treated as a case of a few bad apples. Congress passed, and President George W. Bush signed, stronger corporate disclosure laws in 2002, but they did not turn their attention to the broader questions of systemic risk. Indeed, the SEC loosened its interpretation of leverage rules at around the same time.

Faced with a severe stock market crash and the 9/11 terrorist attacks, President Bush urged Americans to go out and spend. Congress passed tax cuts, the expansion of Medicare Part D (the Medicare prescription drug benefit), and a military build-up coupled with two simultaneous wars, all of which deepened the deficit (Chinn and Frieden 2011; Oatley 2016). Alan Greenspan cut interest rates to very low levels, keeping them there even after the economy had recovered from its recession.

American consumers did their patriotic duty and spent, driving the savings rate down to a low of 1.9 per cent by 2005 (United States. Bureau of Economic Analysis 2018). Together, these moves produced an enormous current account deficit. In an ordinary economy, such a deficit would have produced substantial downward pressure on the US dollar; however, because the United States was the world's money-centre economy, reserves remained desirable abroad. A glut of savers in Asian countries recently faced with collapse was happy to take on reserves.

Deregulation and cheap credit afforded by these global imbalances presented American financial firms with a no-lose proposition. Unlike the financial institutions of the previous era, new financial supermarkets were large enough that their actions had systemic consequences for the American economy. At the same time, they remained *small* enough that they could envision scenarios where they won through zero-sum schemes, such as the creation of financial instruments that masked the risks to the purchaser.[149] The data necessary to monitor the systemic risk generated by the burgeoning derivatives market, or the implications of this risk for the leverage ratios of financial firms, were not being monitored.

Despite these growing risks, few sounded the alarm. When prominent economist Raghuram Rajan (2006) argued, at a gathering of economists celebrating the retirement of Alan Greenspan in Jackson Hole, that finance had made the world riskier, his views were summarily dismissed.[150] Rajan argued that funds had strong incentives to adopt risky strategies (particularly ones that failed to hedge against unlikely events) to maximize returns, both because they wanted to attract clients and because herding was normalizing higher risk levels. New derivatives, rather than reducing risks, may have merely redistributed risks – converting plain-vanilla risks into more complex and volatile ones. Rajan lamented the fact that banks might be ill equipped to provide liquidity should some of the tail events occur.

Rajan's warning proved prescient. Investment banks devised new mortgage-backed securities called collateralized debt obligations (CDOs) that combined individuals from different tranches of risk.[151] The idea was that by combining risky and safe borrowers, the security would be more likely to deliver a positive yield. Heroic assumptions about the robustness of housing prices (which had crashed even in recent memory) informed the models. Mortgage brokers happily lined up borrowers, many of whom might previously have been denied a mortgage. But these brokers were originating mortgages because they planned to distribute them, not because they believed that the borrowers represented a good risk (Bhidé 2009; Gorton 2010). Teaser rates – initial low rates of interest that jumped after two years – were a common lure. Some of these subprime borrowers may have figured that, in an environment of rising house prices, they could renegotiate once the higher rates hit, but most were simply ordinary people doing what good, civic-minded people were "supposed" to do.

Milton Bradley's board game, The Game of Life, is probably the most succinct representation of the American dream. Much in the game is uncertain – college attendance, family size, and whether one invents a new mousetrap. But everybody has to take on a mortgage. Many investors were happy to purchase CDOs, many of which had been rated as low-risk ventures by credit rating agencies (many of whom were paid by the companies whose assets they rated). New derivatives, such as CDSs, which paid off lenders in the event of a default by borrowers, further assuaged investors (while earning the firms acting as insurers hefty fees).

By 2006, mortgage brokers – who were even signing up prospective borrowers with no jobs or income – had exhausted the supply of individuals willing to take on mortgages. House prices started to dip. With the period of teaser rates ending, and house prices falling, many borrowers were forced to default on their loans. These events were thought to be virtually impossible in the quantitative models underlying CDOs, which crashed in value as borrowers defaulted. The collapse directly implicated those financial institutions with the greatest exposure to subprime mortgages, such as Bear Stearns, Lehman Brothers, Merrill Lynch, and the government-sponsored entities, Freddie Mac and Fannie Mae. The decline in value of many CDOs at once, in turn, would be a disaster for firms like AIG, which had floated large amounts of CDSs, viewing them as something akin to free money (Sorkin 2010, 297–325). Massive losses incurred by those holding toxic assets raised questions about the ability of financial firms to meet their margin calls, as eyes turned to the government for help.

By March 2008, the Federal Reserve and the Treasury had orchestrated the rescue of Bear Stearns, an investment bank with heavy exposure to subprime mortgages – providing financing for a takeover of the firm by JPMorgan Chase at $2 a share.[152] But there was more than one bear in the woods. Treasury Secretary Hank Paulson, former CEO of Goldman Sachs, unsuccessfully tried to use the same playbook with other weak links in the American financial system. He turned to the "Oracle of Omaha" – billionaire investor Warren Buffett – to invest in the ailing Lehman Brothers (Paulson 2010, 175). However, Lehman Brothers' CEO, Dick Fuld, failed to offer attractive terms to Buffett, demanding $54 a share as Lehman's stock traded in the $40-to-$50 range. Despite the lack of a rescue for Lehman, calm fell upon the market – stocks were down, but only modestly (Williamson 2020). By September, the 2008 election contest was in full swing. President Bush, his approval rating at a paltry 33 per cent (Gallup 2018) following two terms of war, market turbulence, and disasters like Hurricane Katrina, probably wished he could slump through the last few months of his presidency without another crisis. Events soon dictated otherwise.

Shares in the firms most exposed to the subprime crisis took a beating through the summer, with events coming to a head in September. While the Treasury bailed out Fannie Mae and Freddie Mac, it was reticent to assist others. Dick Fuld continued to reject offers from other investors, holding out hope for assistance from the Fed (Paulson 2010, 219). He demanded $25 a share from Bank of America as Lehman stock sat at $18.32 during that summer (Sorkin 2010, 394), and he later rejected an offer of $6.40 a share from the Korean Development Bank (440). Fuld's stubbornness is a perfect illustration of the folly of the mega-mergers of the previous two decades: the knowledge that Lehman's collapse would be catastrophic gave him every reason to demand a rescue.

By 13 September, a last-ditch effort floated by Jaime Dimon for the major financial firms to kick in $1 billion apiece to absorb Lehman's toxic assets, financing a takeover by the British bank, Barclays, fell apart (Sorkin 2010, 632–90). Lehman Brothers filed for bankruptcy on 15 September, triggering imminent collapse for AIG and Merrill Lynch. Merrill Lynch was purchased by Bank of America the same day – a deal orchestrated under pressure from the Fed. In a press conference held that day, Paulson attempted to clarify the stance of the Treasury, declaring that he did not take "moral hazard" lightly (Paulson 2010, 315). However, the following day, the Treasury bailed out AIG at a cost of $85 billion (Sorkin 2010, 754), and Paulson would soon seek $700 billion from Congress to rescue the American financial system (Paulson 2010, 357). Initial rejection of the bailout by Congress on 29 September triggered one of the highest-percentage crashes on the NYSE in history. Even as the carnage on the markets prompted Congress to approve the unprecedented rescue, markets declined for months. Despite an extensive stimulus package, and even larger monetary expansions, unemployment hit 10 per cent, and recovery was slow (United States. Bureau of Labor Statistics 2020).

The implications of the crash were not confined to the United States either – many firms around the world held American mortgage-backed securities or had engaged in similar activities themselves. When leading financial actors vie for primacy through deregulation, they place their seal of approval on risky policies. Others, whether through imitation or competition, adopt similar measures. By 2008, the short-term liabilities of the Icelandic banks had exceeded 211 per cent of the country's GDP.[153] Across the Atlantic, it became clear that Greece had used derivatives to mask its debt load when it applied for membership in the eurozone. As global credit markets froze up, unsustainable policies that had been facilitated by debt were no longer viable. Regions prone to running large current account deficits, such as Ireland, Italy, Greece, Spain, and Portugal, collapsed.[154] Hamstrung by the European Central Bank (ECB), which was dominated by Germany, and unable to devalue their currencies, depression struck the eurozone periphery. Indeed, in the end, though deregulation wrought immense misery to millions, it did *not* threaten the global position of the United States as the apex money-centre economy. Collapse actually *increased* desire for a globally accepted reserve currency like the US dollar, while chastening prospective competitors like the euro. Today, networks of financial flows still cast the United States firmly in the centre of the system (Oatley et al. 2013).

Conclusion

The global economy of the late twentieth century was the scene of one of the greatest deregulations of all time. Facing increasing costs to the maintenance of the Bretton Woods system and declining industrial strength by the 1970s, American policymakers returned to a world of free-flowing capital. Other reforms to the banking system proved more difficult to enact in the 1970s and early 1980s, despite the deep commitment of President Reagan and Treasury Secretary Regan to free up market ideals. Deregulation was stymied by opposition from bureaucrats, securities firms, and those fearful of the risk of crises.

As America's exorbitant privilege grew, other countries strove to obtain similar benefits for themselves. With rapid growth, Japan became a viable contender for global financial leadership. Given the factional divisions inside the Japanese LDP, deregulation was an appealing option. Financial deregulation could appease the public-works state without tax increases, while expanding Japan's international profile without overt remilitarization. Britain's economy was smaller, but London's past financial glory cast a long shadow. The government of Margaret Thatcher possessed strong ideological commitments to free-market ideals, but the promise of restoring London's former role in global finance remained a powerful motivation for reform.

Japanese and British reforms pushed the United States towards the deregulation of domestic finance. Fears of foreign competition were critical in shifting the attitude of the SIA towards Glass–Steagall, allowing an opening for the Federal Reserve to allow commercial banks securities-underwriting powers. Not only did the opening by the Fed allow financial firms to converge in their interests, it also facilitated substantial growth in the political clout and systemic importance of key financial firms. The popular story of powerful financial firms lobbying for lax regulations would have been impossible without the opening of 1987. Each step in this process – the end of bank-branching restrictions, the repeal of Glass–Steagall, the liberal framework established for derivatives markets, and the *lack* of regulation of new financial innovations – increased the snowball effect of the growing power and influence of the financial sector. Even as warning signs flashed – the 1997 East Asian financial crisis, LTCM, the dot-com crash, Enron – politicians of every ideological stripe turned a blind eye. Competitiveness concerns created an opening for the champions of deregulation, while deregulation shifted the policy environment into one that was more and more friendly to risk-acceptant activity. The result was the worst global financial crisis since the Great Depression.

Chapter Six

Conclusion

I have shown that positional competition for global financial leadership drives waves of deregulation and financial crisis. Declining lead economies seek to enhance their structural advantages by liberalizing global financial flows. In time, the very structural advantages gained by the lead economy become the stakes of an intense regulatory competition among states. Other factors, such as the pulling and hauling of interest groups or the battle of economic ideas, doubtlessly influence financial regulation as well. However, positional competition provides a powerful systemic impetus towards under-regulation in periods where global financial leadership is up for grabs.

I have also presented considerable evidence to support the existence of a decline–deregulation tendency in the global economy since at least the mid-nineteenth century. In every instance where the lead economy began to experience relative decline, its leaders opted for financial liberalization and deregulation. Prospective challengers responded in kind. Very similar processes of regulatory competition immediately preceded the three worst crisis waves of the modern era: the Long Depression of 1873–96, the Great Depression of 1929–39, and the modern crisis wave.

Archival accounts strongly support the notion that policymakers in declining lead economies *and* their prospective challengers were aware (whether directly or indirectly) of the benefits of global financial leadership and actively sought to preserve (or obtain) them through deregulation. British policymakers and the business press underwent a sea change on the issue of financial regulation between the 1830s, when Britain stood ahead of the rest, and the 1850s, when France appeared to be making considerable gains. Key figures such as Prime Minister Palmerston and Robert Lowe were clearly concerned about British global competitiveness vis-à-vis France. French policymakers, in turn, were inspired by the Saint-Simonian vision of using massive investment banks to construct networks of infrastructure, commerce, and capital centred on France. Napoléon III sought to create a Mediterranean system, culminating in his proposal of a universal currency based on the franc. Financial institutions modelled on the French Crédit Mobilier spread around the world. Even Britain finally shed its long-standing opposition to limited liability corporations. Those very same institutions took on large risks simultaneously and were often at centre stage in the serious financial collapses that would plague Europe and America for decades.

The defeat of Napoléon III in 1870 vanquished France as a contender for global financial leadership, thereby ensuring British primacy. Much of the world adopted the gold standard in the late nineteenth century, effectively endorsing the pound as the global reserve currency. Even as Britain fell behind Germany and the United States in industry, London's role in global finance was unchallenged. However, precisely because the prize of global financial leadership (e.g., control of the acceptances markets) was desirable, American policy entrepreneurs, such as Paul Warburg, sought to usurp London's role. Key figures in American finance and politics met at Jekyll Island in 1910, aiming to combine the goals of modernizing the American financial system and internationalizing the dollar. Archival evidence is clear on the importance of that latter goal. Promoting the global role of the dollar meant a strong commitment to the gold standard, which precluded using the Federal Reserve as a tool to combat panics – if a country has a fixed exchange rate, it cannot effectively use monetary policy to combat financial crises.

The First World War battered British financial leadership and forced Britain to impose capital controls. After the war, British policymakers considered whether to restore the gold standard. Once again, archival evidence shows that alternatives, such as a floating currency and an imperial economic bloc, were seriously considered. A key reason that British policymakers favoured the restoration of a global gold standard at the pre-war parity of $4.86 was that it represented the clearest way to restore the primacy of London. They did not select it because it was the safest course – even Montagu Norman, the quintessential champion of the Treasury view, considered Keynes's argument that gold standard restoration would tether Britain to the wild fluctuations of the United States to be essentially true. Moreover, Britain and the United States agreed to create a gold-exchange standard, wherein the currency of either (and, to some degree, of France) would jointly play a reserve role.

The scheme was far less stable than the gold standard of the nineteenth century – it required three central banks to adhere to "the rules of the game." Ultimately, wild speculation on Wall Street, facilitated in part by a sustained period of low interest rates in the United

States (intended to aid British return to the gold standard), created a massive bubble. When the Federal Reserve moved to burst the bubble, it triggered gold outflows in nearly every other economy, exporting hard times. Even as the panic on Wall Street grew worse, the commitment of American policymakers to the gold standard prevented serious action to inject liquidity into a failing economy. The result was the most severe economic calamity in history.

The deregulation of the late twentieth century followed a similar course. Although the Glass–Steagall system fostered financial stability in the United States, by the 1970s and 1980s, American leadership was under strain. Falling behind technologically, the country liberalized capital flows in the 1970s, expanding the reserve role of the US dollar. By the 1980s, however, Japanese and British competition for financial leadership posed a serious challenge. Archival evidence supports the notion that policymakers in both challengers were interested in expanding the global roles of their own countries and in potentially supplanting the United States at the centre of global finance. Faced with the prospective loss of American financial leadership, long-standing foes to financial deregulation, such as the SIA, shifted their stances, allowing first a bureaucratic solution and subsequently a political one. By the end of the 1990s, the United States had ended the long-standing Glass–Steagall system and liberalized the derivatives markets, ushering in a new era of financial speculation. Today we are living with the deleterious side effects of those decisions.

There are important differences between each of these episodes. In the 1850s and the 1980s to 1990s, regulatory competition was dominated by changes to the rules governing financial institutions. In the 1920s, regulatory competition was characterized more by the liberalization of capital flows – although that financial liberalization limited the ability of regulatory institutions to act (e.g., the gold standard weakened the ability of the Bank of England and Federal Reserve to play a lender-of-last-resort role). The kinds of economies engaged in economic competition have also varied across historical epochs. The competition of the 1850s pitted a broadly liberal, market-driven economy against an authoritarian state with a bank-dominated financial system. Each sought to loosen capital flows through different means, with Second Empire France relying on many informal as well as formal measures. When one considers the prospect of US–China competition, Second Empire France may be the most relevant historical analogue. The competition of the 1920s featured a battle between two liberal, market-driven economies, while that of the 1980s was a bit of a mix, with Japan deviating from the classic model of such an economy.

It is also fair to say that the episodes of financial folly explored in this book differ in magnitude, success, and consequences. This is to be expected: whereas some policy environments contain powerful forces promoting inertia, others have few constraints. Moreover, all exercises in risk-taking are not the same. Indeed, many financial reforms that led to disaster in the past – such as limited liability – are indispensable today, now that markets and regulators better understand what is going on "under the hood."

Let us turn first to the question of the magnitude of deregulation. Who deregulated most, and who moved least, during periods of competition? Using Appendix 1 as a guide, the most aggressive deregulator was 1850s Britain, while the most circumscribed deregulator was 1980s Japan. The former involved not only the reform of company formation laws and the introduction of limited liability but also the removal of a number of prudential safeguards. On the other hand, in Japan, the biggest changes involved greater international exposure and modest changes to the distinctions between banking and securities firms. That each of these cases might occupy the opposite ends of the spectrum makes a certain amount of sense. British prime ministers are famously unconstrained – although, admittedly, Lord Palmerston did have to contend with a more fragmented system of factions than other prime ministers in the same time period. Japan in the 1980s, on the other hand, contained powerful inertial tendencies. Moreover, its pacifist constitution dampens pressures to aspire to global domination (even of a financial nature).

Of course, there are serious limitations to an approach that simply counts reforms. Financial regulatory orders are more than the sum of their parts, and comparably small changes can be transformative. Inertia in the face of rapid market changes – such as that characterizing Japan in the 1980s – can be as dangerous as barrelling in risky directions. One useful gauge of the degree to which governments moved on the stability–growth axis is financialization, which should capture the intensification of financial intermediation in eras of competition. Thus, I include a simple measure of the increase in stock prices relative to changes to GDP from the initiation of deregulation to the crash. For instance, in the case of the United States, one might look at the growth of stocks relative to the economy from 1987 to 2008. A stock market that far outpaces the real economy is a sure-fire sign of financialization – and perhaps of a set of financial reforms that have intensified intermediation without necessarily triggering growth.

Table 6.1 summarizes the key cases – in all instances, there was evidence of greater financialization, ranging from a slight increase in the

Table 6.1. Comparing Episodes of Deregulation

Case	Ratio of stock price growth to GDP growth	Real growth per capita, deregulation to peak (%)	Real growth per capita, deregulation to crisis trough (%)	Per capita GDP decline in crisis (%)
1850s–60s Britain	1.60	1.3	0.9	−1.8 (1866) −1.5 (1878)
1850s–60s France	2.04	1.5	0.6	−8.8 (1867)
1910s–20s Britain	1.15	2.3	0.6	−6.6 (1929)
1910s–20s United States	2.36	2.1	−2.6	−30.8 (1929)
1980s–90s United States	1.89	1.8	1.4	−5.6 (2008)
1980s–90s Britain	1.98	2.1	1.7	−6.1 (2008)
1980s–90s Japan	3.21	3.4	n/a	n/a (1991)

Sources: Stock prices: Acheson et al. (2009); global financial data: Taylor (2016); GDP: Jordà, Schularick, and Taylor (2013), Maddison (2009); GDP per capita: Maddison (2013).

case of 1920s Britain to much more in the case of 1980s Japan (and, to a lesser degree, 1920s United States and 1850s France). This, too, makes a good deal of sense. British reforms in the 1920s were rooted in an incorrect assumption that London would resume its place at the centre of global finance almost automatically.

A second question might be to ask whether deregulation successfully stoked growth and salvaged financial leadership. In a qualitative sense,[155] Britain staved off the French challenge in the mid-nineteenth century, while the United States staved off the challenge from Japan and Britain in the 1980s and 1990s. On the other hand, by the 1930s, the United States had usurped Britain's financial leadership. Quantitatively, the period from the initiation of deregulation until the pre-crisis peak has also been characterized by above-average growth.[156] However, each period of major deregulation has been followed by a severe financial crisis. If, instead, one selects the trough of a financial crisis as an end point, the growth record of deregulated financial systems is decidedly below average. The main outlier, Japan, did not experience negative real growth in the face of the collapse of its financial bubble, but it *did* see two subsequent decades of near-zero growth.

One takeaway from this data should be that the pattern of decline and deregulation characterizing the global financial system is a problem. The mutual striving of all great powers for the spoils of economic leadership leads each to adopt a position on the trade-off between growth and risk that is suboptimal in the long run. Although the removal of safeguards appears to stoke growth, this appearance is too often a fleeting sugar high.

Although competitive deregulation is ultimately self-destructive, it is not clear how to rein in the impulses faced by each actor. Even if prudential doctrines prevail and interest groups favour regulation, the presence of great rewards will produce intense competition. The development of international institutions and regulations has not done much to reduce this process. Indeed, insofar as international institutions can influence policy, they increase the value of being powerful enough to shape institutional rules. The Basel Capital Accords, for instance, did little to prevent the 2008 financial crisis – but they were useful as a club for the United States to use against a rising Japan.

Ikenberry (2001) imagines the prospect of a far-sighted, Rawlsian hegemon that might establish institutions that diffuse its advantages so as to preserve itself in the expectation of future decline. Yet the "veil of ignorance" theorized by Rawls (1971)[157] presupposes a choice made by free and equal individuals, whereas decisions about world order are made by states with decidedly unequal power. Even if a benign global leader were to come along, forgoing advantages would only hasten its decline, not forestall it. Absent structural advantages, it is only a matter of time before technological diffusion and economic catch-up produce viable challengers. Although I do not have a solution to the tragic nature of interstate financial competition, surely the first step is to identify the problem.

American Twilight?

Is the past prologue? Critics might ask, "Why should we expect these events to occur again?" My answer to this criticism is that the processes driving regulatory competition are still here – in fact, they are stronger than ever. The global financial system is far more integrated than at any point in human history. The United States is central to the network of finance in a way that no other country has replicated. Indeed, Rey (2015) argued that the business cycles of countries with liberalized financial markets so closely follow the United States that the old trade-off among capital mobility, monetary autonomy, and fixed exchange rates has been effectively whittled down to just the first two. In the past, some of the countries engaged in competition, such as Britain and the United States in the 1920s, were on broadly friendly terms, even as they competed. China and the United States have a more awkward relationship – one is authoritarian, the other democratic. Both represent military threats to one another, and many American allies have territorial disputes with China. The stakes of lost primacy are likely to be even higher than in the past. In the remainder of this concluding chapter, I ask whether American decline is likely and, if so, what the implications are for global financial stability.

The crash of 2008 was supposed to be a humbling moment for America – a bitter harvest for a hubristic hegemon. The reality was more confusing. In many respects, the short-term effects of the financial crisis shored up American structural leadership, even as the material underpinnings of American structural power became weaker than ever. It is in precisely this setting that prospective challengers will have incentives to overturn American financial leadership.

During the 2008 crisis, the US dollar retained its position as the global reserve currency, while its primary competitor – the euro – was undone by the economic contradictions of the eurozone. Faced with an economic crisis, the ECB was unable to simultaneously balance the needs of the current account deficit–prone eurozone periphery (Portugal, Ireland, Italy, Greece, and Spain) with those of the northern European surplus countries, most notably Germany. Lacking monetary autonomy, and with inflation-averse Germany holding the reins of the ECB, the eurozone periphery was forced into deep austerity measures, enduring Great Depression–like unemployment levels (Blyth 2013).

A fiscal union – regularized economic transfers from surplus to deficit countries – might help coordinate business cycles within Europe. However, the developments of recent years raise doubts as to whether such a project is politically feasible. A wave of populism has swept across Europe, strengthening a host of politicians sceptical of the European project. On the left, there are those who see it as a Trojan horse for neoliberalism and austerity. For instance, Greek Prime Minister Alexander Tsipras was elected in 2008 on a platform of reversing the austerity measures imposed on Greece, even holding a referendum to reject the conditions of a Greek bailout. On the political right, hostility to migration has fuelled the rise of a second set of far-right Eurosceptic parties. In some cases, such as Hungary, the far right is in power. In other cases, such as Austria, the far-right Austrian People's Party has inspired centre-right parties to adopt similar stances. Finally, the successful Leave vote in Britain's Brexit referendum means that the world's second-largest financial power has left the EU. However, it may be too soon to write Europe's epitaph: if Frankfurt or Paris supplants London, and if French President Emmanuel Macron succeeds in his bid for a unified European bond market, the EU's clout will expand inordinately.

The other challenger to American financial leadership, China, will be a contender in the medium run. Certainly, much has been made of its growing influence – by some measures, it may even possess the world's largest economy, with a competitive position in many emerging high-tech sectors (e.g., 5G networks).[158] President Xi Jinping's ambitious One Belt, One Road initiative envisions a modern silk road stretching across Eurasia, aligning broad swathes of the continent to the Middle Kingdom. China is the dominant figure in the BRICS group, which collectively exerts considerable influence in global economic governance and which is even creating its own parallel institutions (e.g., the New Development Bank) (Roberts, Elliot Armijo, and Katada 2017). In the wake of the financial crisis, China took on a massive position in US bonds, leading many to comment on growing American dependence on China. In addition, the four largest banks in the world are Chinese institutions (Mehmood 2017). There *are* a number of reasons to believe that China will be a significant player in global finance in the years to come.

It takes time to transform economic bulk into structural power. The United States surpassed British GDP in 1872, but it did not supplant Britain as the world's financial centre until the 1930s (Maddison 2009). Breathless accounts that China "used more cement in three years than the U.S. did in the entire 20th century" miss the realities about the nature of the contemporary economy.[159] The big profits lie in owning intellectual property, not in manufacturing and construction. Although China's clout in international organizations is impressive, the BRICS lack the cohesion of the G7 and might easily find itself divided. India and China, for instance, maintain numerous territorial disputes, while growing Chinese influence in Central Asia threatens Russia's influence. Like Wilhelmine Germany or France in the eighteenth and nineteenth centuries, competition between regional and global agendas poses a challenge for the creation of a coherent grand strategy.

Moreover, China's most recent effort to liberalize its financial system was a bust. The Shanghai Composite Index soared, only to crash in the summer of 2015.[160] Nor was China alone – Brazil and Russia have experienced considerable economic pain in recent years. In addition, the process of internationalization limits China's influence over its own banking system. Many of the largest Chinese banks have American branches, meaning that they must adhere to *American* regulations. There may also be limits to China's ability to convince international investors of its ability to protect property rights. On the one hand, there have been many high-profile corruption scandals. On the other, the regime's own anti-corruption program has been criticized by many for its selectivity – targeting prospective political rivals, not corrupt officials. Large swathes of China's elite want other options – Chinese applications for the American EB-5 visa (the Immigrant Investor Visa

Program) far exceed the China quota – and absent capital controls, it is likely that much capital would join them.[161]

The United States also enjoys a commanding lead in military power over the rest of the world. To some extent, the focus on military spending understates America's advantage – although its military spending is more than triple its nearest challenger, it makes up only 3.3 per cent of American GDP (World Bank 2017). In addition, the United States has a major qualitative advantage in its possession of a peerless navy and air force, granting it unmatched power projection capabilities. Its monopoly on power projection fosters many mutually enriching relationships. For instance, the United States trades protection and access to the global commons to Saudi Arabia in exchange for Saudi denomination of sales of oil in US dollars, effectively voting for the dollar as a global reserve currency. The American position in international institutions, likewise, remains strong. The United States maintains its ability to effectively veto structural changes to the IMF, and the presence of the BRICS bloc may even enhance American influence in some respects because it enables American policymakers to play off the G7 minus the United States against the BRICS.

The combination of significant advantages with tenuous material underpinnings is a dangerous foundation for the global system, however. The United States is not merely falling behind China and others on indicators of economic bulk but is also lagging in some high-tech sectors. China now leads in the export of many important high-tech goods, such as solar panels, and recently surpassed the United States in patents per year. A number of eminent economists, from Robert Gordon to Larry Summers, have opined that American productivity growth is apt to be slow for some time. Nor is the United States educating scientists – American students perform dismally on international standardized tests like the PISA, and 42 per cent of STEM (science, technology, engineering, and mathematics) workers in positions requiring PhDs are foreign born (United States. National Science Foundation 2016). Those figures are testament, in part, to the continued prestige of American universities, but one wonders how long that source of strength can continue. As China and India grow wealthier, they will increasingly be able to construct institutions of higher learning that keep their brightest minds at home.

American policymakers are increasingly unable to sell a coherent geopolitical agenda to voters. Slow growth means that American politics has increasingly taken on a zero-sum quality, empowering those who appeal to entrenched interests or racial divisions. Consider the failure of the Trans-Pacific Partnership (TPP). A bold scheme to create a high-standard free trade zone encapsulating 40 per cent of world trade, the TPP would have extended American structural power. Deep antipathy to the agreement on the political right and left, however, scuttled its implementation – by the 2016 election, even Hillary Clinton, who had negotiated the TPP as secretary of state, declared her opposition. As in Europe, rising opposition to immigration undermines the long-term economic fortunes of the United States. In a world of seven billion people, many of whom have access to decent schools, a country of 350 million people cannot stay ahead indefinitely.

In the wake of the last great financial crisis, the Dodd–Frank Act created a new regulatory order. It created a Financial Stability Oversight Council to oversee "systemically important" financial institutions; a consumer protection agency was developed to prevent consumers from being exploited by financial institutions; while capital requirements were increased as well. The presidential administration of Donald Trump has already considered moves to eliminate the "systemically important" designation, alongside efforts to curtail the consumer protection agency. Where John Maynard Keynes once warned of "animal spirits" driving speculation, House Financial Services Committee Chairman John Hensarling declared, "We want for the animal spirits to move in our economy, to let freedom ring."[162] On 24 May 2018, Congress passed a second bill, raising the asset threshold for banks to qualify as "systemically important" from $50 billion to $250 billion.[163]

Unlike the Glass–Steagall system, Dodd–Frank does not appear to have been successful in creating a political ecosystem to support its prudential aims. Should external challenges to American financial leadership mount – and they will – policymakers seem likely to restart the tragic cycle of regulatory competition and crisis once more.

Distinguishing Between Stringent and Lax Regulation

Table A.1 summarizes some of the relevant questions that one would have to ask to assess the banking system of a given country. It would be useful to know, for example, whether banks are subject to strict prudential rules, with good oversight and clear rules limiting their leverage. Are firms limited by restrictions on their scope or specialization (and do these restrictions separate risky activities from less risky ones)? Finally, we might also ask whether mechanisms exist that push firms to internalize systemic risk.

Table A.1. Types of Banking Regulations

	Less stringent	Intermediate	More stringent
Prudential regulations	Weak oversight, few effective restrictions on bank leverage	Moderate oversight, moderate restrictions on bank leverage	Strong oversight, clear provisions limiting leverage and ensuring strong reserves
Scope/specialization	Few limitations on banks' size, scope, or specialization	Moderate limitations on banks' size, scope, or specialization	Strong limitations on banks' size, scope, or specialization
Risk internalization	No mechanisms to ensure private internalization of systemic risk	Moderate mechanisms to ensure private internalization of systemic risk	Strong mechanisms to ensure private internalization of systemic risk
Reporting	No reporting requirements; or ineffective requirements	Some reporting requirements, with some loopholes	Strong reporting requirements

Table A.2. Types of Securities Regulations

	Less stringent	Intermediate	More stringent
Risk management	No management of activities likely to impact systemic risks	Some management of systemic risks, but shortcomings (e.g., failure to keep up with market innovations)	Dynamic and active intervention to prevent activities exacerbating systemic risks
Company formation	No restrictions on company formation; wide access to all corporate forms	Moderate restrictions on company formation, particularly riskier corporate forms	Strong restrictions on company formation, particularly riskier corporate forms
Reporting	No requirements on companies to report information	Some reporting requirements, with some omissions	Strong reporting requirements

Securities markets, too, are subject to regulation in most countries. A more stringent policy environment might feature dynamic efforts (e.g., responding to financial market innovations) to prevent firms from engaging in activities with systemic risks, some restrictions on riskier corporate forms, and good supervision and accounting requirements. Once again, some of these types of reforms might be more common in particular eras than others. For instance, regulations on corporate forms, such as access to limited liability protections, were important historically but are not as common today.

A third set of considerations involves how an economy responds to crises once they occur. A more stringent economy might have a lender-of-last-resort institution, albeit one that is subject to penalty rates (to address moral hazard problems) and committed to counter-cyclical action. On the other hand, an arguably worse situation than even the absence of a lender-of-last-resort institution would be the presence of one committed to procyclical policies. A procyclical lender of last resort would provide credit in good times, risking the creation of bubbles, while yanking it away when it is needed most. Lender-of-last-resort institutions could be procyclical for many reasons – it could have to do with how they are regulated and staffed, or it could have to do with related institutions, such as commitments to a fixed exchange rate that prevent adequate responses to domestic economic conditions. For instance, Eichengreen (1995) attributes the disastrous monetary policy of the United States in the 1920s to the restrictions imposed by the gold standard.

Table A.3. Types of Lender-of-Last-Resort Institutions

	Very Lax	Somewhat lax	Moderate	Somewhat stringent	Very stringent
Lender-of-last-resort policy	No penalty rates; commitment to procyclical monetary policy	No lender-of-last-resort institutions	Weak, mostly private lender-of-last-resort institutions	Strong lender-of-last-resort institutions, but weak penalty rates	Strong lender-of-last-resort institutions, clear penalty rates, and commitment to counter-cyclical monetary policy

Table A.4. Capital Controls

	Less stringent	Moderate	More stringent
Lender-of-last-resort policy	No restrictions on flow of capital	Moderate capital controls, capital controls with exceptions (e.g., IBFs)	Strict capital controls

Finally, states may take different approaches to the regulation of their capital account. Some states may impose strict restrictions, preventing capital from flowing into and, more frequently, out of the country. Other states may opt for very few restrictions on the flow of capital, whether by explicit legislation or simply through lax enforcement of capital controls. However, many countries occupy a middle range between the two, and some may have capital controls that are limited in various ways. For instance, a country might maintain capital controls while also segmenting part of the economy as an international business facility (IBF) subject to fewer rules.

Notes

1 Paul (2011) argues that the South Sea Bubble was a rational bubble – that is, investors were responding to genuinely good prospects as opposed to behaving irrationally.

2 Since some countries experience different types of financial crises simultaneously (e.g., a banking crisis and a currency crisis), a crisis may appear multiple times, so a number greater than 1 in the data would be theoretically possible.

3 Prominent recent works include Barth, Caprio, Jr., and Levine (2006); Grossman (2010); Eichengreen (2012); Admati and Hellwig (2013); Turner (2014); and Calomiris and Haber (2014).

4 Specifically, Admati and Hellwig (2013, 191) propose raising equity requirements from 3 per cent to 25 per cent. They are also critical of the practice of using risk-weighted capital since this can be gamed by banks, whose information is superior to that of regulators.

5 In this book, I will employ the term *lead economy* to mean leadership in a particular constellation of power subsystems, following the tradition of the leadership long cycle (see Modelski and Thompson 1996; Reuveny and Thompson 2004). The lead economy is the biggest global capital exporter and the biggest high-technology exporter for a similar conception of leadership. Due to its technological and financial prowess, it also tends to dominate in high-tech military capabilities, such as power projection. Following my definition, I consider Britain to have been the lead economy from the eighteenth century until the Second World War, followed by the United States, which holds that role today. Although it is possible for the positions of states to diverge across these power subsystems, the correlation between them is frequently strong, and it would be a mistake to conceive of financial or monetary power in a vacuum (Strange 1988; Cohen 2015).

6 Some might ask, Why leadership and not hegemony? I believe that *hegemony* is distinct from the phenomenon I am describing. First, the bar for hegemony tends to be fairly high. Kindleberger (1973) considered waning American hegemony in the 1970s to be sufficient to explain the Nixon shocks. Wallerstein (1984, 40) considers American hegemony to have ended in 1967. Second, most definitions of hegemony emphasize preeminence in domains of power (e.g., territory, raw GDP) that are not necessary conditions for a state to exert global economic leadership. The distinction is more than esoteric. Nineteenth-century Britain and the twentieth-century United States clearly satisfy most definitions of hegemony and leadership. But there are historical cases where notions of hegemony and economic leadership clearly diverge. For instance, Modelski and Thompson (1996) consider Portugal to be the leading power of the sixteenth century because of its control over vital trade routes, whereas Spain had larger armies and controlled more territory. Spain might have been closer to European hegemony, but it was Portugal that played a leading role in the world economy. The twenty-first century may well feature a similar dynamic to the sixteenth in that one power dominates finance, trade, and power projection, while another is larger in bulk power.

7 Although I am describing banks here, similar trade-offs exist for other forms of intermediation.

8 For key works on the links among capital markets, innovation, and growth, see Goldsmith (1969); King and Levine (1993); Freeman and Soete (1996); and Rajan and Zingales (2004).

9 Many economists argue that deregulation fosters growth (see Levine 1997, 1999; Calomiris 2000; Rajan and Zingales 2004; and Kaminsky and Schmukler 2008), that deregulation and/or expansions of credit undermine stability (Kindleberger 1978; Minsky 1992; Schularick and Taylor 2012), or both (e.g., see Ramey and Ramey 1995; Loayza and Ranciere 2006).

10 Although figure 1.2 depicts two political coalitions, one could easily represent more than two inside the same framework.

11 For an explicit description of how I classified more and less stringent regimes for the purpose of this book, see the appendix.

12 See, e.g., Kaminsky and Schmukler (2008).

13 In some ways, the contrast between the work of Vogel (1996) and Ostrom (1990, 2005) is instructive here. Vogel (1996, 19) notes that his definitions flow from an understanding of what regulation has looked like since 1975. On the other hand, because his work focuses on the regulation of many sectors of the economy, he must be sure that his terms generalize across those different policy domains. Ostrom (1990, 2005), on the other

hand, aims to develop a framework for understanding the governance of environmental systems (and common-pool resources, in particular). Thus, an important part of her institutional analysis and development framework stresses consideration of biophysical conditions. Such an inclusion would make less sense if she were studying financial regulation.

14 For instance, social-network-analysis techniques offer a quantitative window into the relationships among actors.

15 All uses of a dollar sign in this book denote US dollars.

16 For the quintessential guide to micro-prudential regulation, see Dewatripont and Tirole (1994).

17 For considerations of the potential benefits of a unit-banking system in the context of the debate over Glass–Steagall repeal, see Corrigan (1987); Bentson (1994); and Mishkin (1999). For some of the responses more critical of unit banking, see White (1986); Kroszner and Rajan (1994); and Calomiris (2000).

18 In this book, I distinguish between the Glass–Steagall system – a broad set of rules introduced in the Great Depression to regulate finance – and the more specific Glass–Steagall Act.

19 One controversial theory posits that, in addition to short-term business cycles, there are longer, forty-to-sixty-year cycles in economic growth; these are called Kondratieff (1979) waves after the Russian economist sent to prison by the Soviet Union for his conclusion. Different works have contested the precise cause of these long waves (see Van Duijn 1983, 59–146; Goldstein 1985), including variations in capital investment, innovation, capitalist crisis, and wars.

20 Before the Industrial Revolution, a similar process can be observed in the discovery of trade routes, with the succession of leadership going back to Sung China in 960 CE (Modelski and Thompson 1996, 142–77).

21 Specifically, investment data were drawn from Imlah (1958); Woodruff (1966); and Lévy-Leboyer (1976). GDP data were drawn from Maddison (2009). Figures were converted using Officer and Williamson (2020).

22 Although such an enquiry is beyond the scope of this book, more research cataloguing the transition from the Chinese-centric financial order described by Frank (1998) to that of the nineteenth century would be invaluable to our understanding.

23 Rosas (2009) argues that the propensity for socially costly bailouts is even worse in authoritarian regimes, whereas democracies are more likely to apply Bagehot rules.

24 The Rothschilds were not saints, but anti-Semitism is undoubtedly behind some of the antipathy they inspire. Financial crises often heighten anti-Semitic sentiments. The recent financial crisis is no exception: one

survey found that 25 per cent of Americans blamed Jews for the 2008 crisis a moderate or great amount (Malhotra and Margalit 2009).

25 These are funds invested exclusively in firms likely to reduce environmental impacts.

26 See chaps. 3 and 5, respectively, for fuller analysis of these episodes.

27 It might also be useful to measure centrality, as Oatley et al. (2013) do for more recent years. Unfortunately, granular data on foreign-investment flows are not widely available for the late nineteenth or early twentieth centuries (Twomey 2000). Additionally, some aspects of financial power do not generalize across historical eras. For all their imperfection, relative foreign-investment assets are a pretty direct measure of relative financial power that transcends particular time periods. Another objection might be that states with large gross assets may not possess significant net assets. Yet there can be power in being a debtor as well: the United States runs large current account deficits – in part, because it can, thanks to reserve demand for dollars (Eichengreen 2012).

28 And, indeed, the British saw the writing on the wall as early as 1931, with the publication of the Macmillan Report of that year.

29 The *haute banque* was comparable in form to English merchant banks, like Barings (Cassis 1991, 58).

30 One way to think of the Long Depression is as a period of prolonged deleveraging following the excesses of the 1850s and 1860s.

31 Even IPE scholars are not immune to cognitive dissonance. Few would hesitate to consider the combination of capital-market liberalization and overvalued exchange rates in 1990s Thailand and Argentina to be a risky endeavour. Yet there is a tendency to see Britain doing the same thing in the 1920s as, somehow, a conservative policy move.

32 The Japanese boom would turn out to be a bubble, but hindsight is 20–20.

33 In particular, there is debate over whether Glass–Steagall abolition prompted the 2008 crisis. Advocates of this view, including the United States Financial Crisis Inquiry Commission (2011), point to the creation of "too big to fail" institutions as one mechanism. On the other hand, some big-bank systems are relatively stable (Bordo, Rockoff, and Redish 1994; Turner 2014). My view is that Glass–Steagall was more of a *political* compact, using turf wars to prevent the financial sector from taking a united front. Moreover, even after its abolition, American financial firms never reached the relative size of big-bank countries like Canada and Britain. Rather, the United States was dominated by mid-sized financial firms, big enough to do systemic damage, but small enough not to internalize the systemic fallout of their actions.

34 That said, the rise of domestic political coalitions and economic ideas hostile to strict regulations can explain some of the persistence of lax

regulatory orders, even after competitive challenges recede. For instance, the late 1990s saw the United States continue to roll back regulations, even as its main competitors seemed to be vanquished.

35 In chap. 1, I argued that states tend to try the first strategy earlier and the second strategy later.

36 As the global economy expanded in the 1970s and 1980s, much of the debate over hegemonic stability theory (HST) came to focus on whether it could explain free trade rather than stability (Krasner 1976).

37 Some works characterize reserve-currency management as a burden, positing that countries face a dilemma between providing liquidity to the rest of the world and achieving domestic goals (Triffin 1960; Strange 1971).

38 A few countries (e.g., Panama) may even adopt the global reserve currency as their own for domestic use.

39 I do not claim that China lacked any external relations or impact in the nineteenth century. Indeed, McKeown (2008) points out usefully that our understanding of a very important global economic phenomenon – large-scale immigration in the nineteenth century – is skewed because of the tendency to ignore significant waves of migration inside Asia as well as the development of controls to keep Chinese workers out of the Americas. For an interesting, Chinese-centric perspective of the global economy from 1400 to 1800, see Frank (1998).

40 The contemporary tendency for advanced economies to produce goods, even high-technology ones, offshore disguises the fact that the vast majority of the value chain remains in the advanced economies. For instance, Kraemer, Linden, and Dedrick (2011) found that only about 2 per cent of the revenue of the Apple iPhone and iPad flowed to China, although both products were assembled there.

41 Some, such as Brooks (2013), posit that lobbying by economic actors and international regimes like the International Centre for Settlement of Investment Disputes means that intervention to protect property is obsolete. I believe this view is short-sighted. Global investment grew, initially, because of a consistent record of intervention to protect property rights by the United States (Maurer 2013). As capital markets grew large, capital became able to sanction violators, so even host countries came to prefer the courts for easy resolution of disputes. Yet this system is built on the threat of force by capital-exporting countries and continues to be so. Even today, there is substantial evidence that foreign direct investment follows US troop deployment (Biglaiser and DeRouen 2007) and that financial firms with greater exposure to the global South donate most actively to legislators willing to intervene on behalf of investors' interests (Lee, Florea, and Blarel 2019).

42 For instance, see Flandreau and Jobst's (2009) analysis of the spread of the gold standard between 1870 and 1913.

43 American high schools elect prom kings and queens at graduation. Based on my viewing of *Heathers* and *Mean Girls*, at least, some students take these contests very seriously.

44 Germany might be considered a challenger to Britain in the late nineteenth and early twentieth centuries due to its growing industrial and naval power. However, it never challenged British financial leadership.

45 Challengers might also initiate bouts of competitive deregulation themselves.

46 I refer to Louis-Napoléon by his regnal name (Napoléon III) only after his coronation as emperor.

47 Joint-stock banks were partnerships, in contrast to the private merchant banks that predominated in London. Drawing deposits from the public, and run in the interests of diverse capital subscribers, joint-stock banks could raise capital more widely than private banks. On the other hand, there was more uncertainty involved in their operation because it was not always clear how much capital the bank subscribers had on hand.

48 I note that the financial revolution of the 1820s and 1830s does not fit the schema of this book well since Britain deregulated without an external challenge. As noted in the introduction to the book, before the 1840s, financial globalization had not reached the kind of levels that would make the structural benefits of leadership possible. Moreover, global competition is not the sole factor driving regulatory outcomes. In this case, domestic politics appears most convincing – the political equilibrium inside the British policy environment shifted towards greater acceptance of risk-taking.

49 In the title of one important history of Napoléon III, Anceau (2012) describes the emperor as "Saint-Simon on horseback."

50 Under double liability, directors are held liable for losses, while ordinary shareholders are not.

51 The Second Empire also approved the creation of the Crédit Foncier, a large institution designed to finance mortgages.

52 When Fould retired in 1854, Isaac became president and gave his brother Émile the deputy position.

53 In terms of its democratic bona fides, the Second Empire is characterized by Plessis (1985) as undergoing two phases. In the first period, the regime was less democratic (though also more innovative), while in the second it grew more liberal.

54 The infamous Credit Mobilier of America was not affiliated with the French institution.

55 Real per capita French economic growth during the Second Empire grew at 0.95 per cent per annum, only slightly faster than during the 1840s

(Maddison 2013). Advanced industrialized countries tend to converge on growth rates of about 2 per cent per annum; however, growth rates in the nineteenth century were often slower.

56 Although a Whig, Palmerston could sometimes rely on backing from Tories on confidence votes.

57 One reason Cobden may have lacked a fear of France was his personal friendship with Michel Chevalier. Indeed, while British fears of French invasion were on high alert, Cobden wrote *The Three Panics*, using alternative figures to attack the view that France was a peer competitor to Britain in naval power.

58 Lowe and Palmerston were on good enough terms that Lowe was able to petition Palmerston to assist two of his friends, one man whom he believed had saved his life and another 40-year-old nephew leading a "bare subsistence" in academia (PP/MPC/1569, Palmerston Papers, Special Collections, University of Southampton).

59 To appease French sentiments, Lord Palmerston proposed a bill making it illegal for Britons to murder foreign citizens. The bill was defeated, a vote of no confidence in Palmerston. As a result, the Tory Earl of Derby took power briefly. He lacked a majority, however, so it was not long before a new election brought Palmerston back to power.

60 British trade policy tended to be unilateral. For instance, the Corn Laws were abolished in 1846 with no expectations of reciprocity from abroad.

61 The actual occupation of Mexico, however, turned out to be a costly disaster. French troops ultimately abandoned the country, and Emperor Maximilian was overthrown.

62 Flandreau (2000) is more sceptical of political explanations of the Latin Monetary Union, arguing that it also had substantial benefits for the participants.

63 In 1866, the Second Empire had also held a conference on international weights and measures, promoting a standardized set of measures.

64 A precondition for British Columbia to join Confederation, the Canadian Pacific Railway was a vitally important national project.

65 In the film version, the silver slippers were changed to red to better showcase the Technicolor technology. Green slippers might have been more appropriate to capture the monetary reality of the early twentieth century.

66 Mundell (1961, 1963) offers the classic explanation for why countries cannot simultaneously accommodate free flows of capital, use monetary policy to fight recessions, and maintain fixed exchange rates.

67 Some might contend that the events described in this chapter are not instances of regulatory rollback because there was no great repeal of long-standing statutes. Some measures might even be construed as

regulatory moves – after all, central banks provide regulatory functions, while acting as lenders of last resort. The problem with this interpretation is that central banks are what you make of them. A central bank that acts procyclically will make bubbles worse and crises more severe. However, a fixed-exchange-rate regime like the gold standard ensured just that. All countries face a trilemma – they may wish to have a fixed exchange rate, free-floating capital markets, and the ability to use monetary policy counter-cyclically, but can maintain only two of the three at a time. Opting for a gold standard and a world of open capital markets meant that central banks would be forced to adjust to international conditions, while ignoring domestic ones.

68 Bank conservatism was hardly the sole contributor to British industrial decline. As Capie (1995) notes, British industry had relied increasingly on non-bank sources of capital since the 1840s. On the other hand, the threshold of a new technological era is a bad time to face capital shortages.

69 Britain had operated on the gold standard since 1717 after Isaac Newton, then master of the mint, set the price of silver too high, driving silver out of the country. *De jure*, Britain adopted the gold standard in 1821.

70 Bourbon Democrats were more pro-business Democrats, favourable to the gold standard.

71 The two most powerful banking networks in the United States at the time was one surrounding J.P. Morgan & Co. and the other surrounding Kuhn & Loeb. Anti-Semitism was a factor in the separation of the goyim Morgan network from the Jewish Kuhn & Loeb network. Members of the two cliques even lived in distinctly different parts of New York City (Pak 2013, 80–106).

72 Paul Warburg, "Paul Warburg Urges a Central Bank," *New York Times*, 1 February 1908.

73 Henry Parker Willis was also Charles Kindleberger's doctoral adviser.

74 According to Warburg (1930, 1:102), Bryan initially pushed for *fifty* Federal Reserve districts.

75 Miller was the only economist on the Federal Reserve Board. Despite Miller's expertise, Hamlin describes him as being wracked with self-doubt, writing that Miller lacked practical knowledge and distrusted his own. Instead, Hamlin complained that Miller's views hewed close to those of the banks (Charles S. Hamlin Diaries, vol. 2, box 356, folder 17, p. 112).

76 See Frieden (1990) for a depiction of the broader sectoral battle between the internationalists and domestically oriented sectors in interwar American politics.

77 A decorated soldier, Norman was awarded the Distinguished Service Order.

78 His grandfather, George Warde Norman, referenced in the previous chapter, had been a long-standing director of the Bank of England.

79 Some versions of this story make much of the friendship between Benjamin Strong and Montagu Norman, and the large credit from J.P. Morgan & Co. aimed to speed along Britain's return to gold.

80 The Conservatives won a lower share of the vote than in 1910, but a great deal more seats thanks to vote-splitting.

81 Under a classical gold standard system, countries were expected to adjust prices in response to inflows and outflows of gold. Countries facing inflows of gold would experience inflation, while those facing outflows would have to endure deflation to maintain their exchange rates. The large decline of the pound since the First World War implied the need for a painful deflationary period.

82 Many of the Warburgs remained in Germany, where they were prominent in banking in their own right (Chernow 2016, 35–209).

83 Although Dawes was the pitchman for his mission to Europe, Young, a chairman of the board of General Electric, was the brains behind the Dawes/Young plan.

84 Churchill was not simply playing devil's advocate. For example, he hosted a dinner featuring speakers for and against the immediate return to the gold standard, including Reginald McKenna, chairman of the Midland Bank. Churchill also later invited Keynes to join the Other Club. There is ample evidence that Churchill agonized over the decision (and later regretted) to return to gold (Ahamed 2014, 317–51).

85 The *Daily Express* was owned by Lord Beaverbrook.

86 Now run by J.P. Morgan's son, Jack Morgan.

87 All figures are converted from pounds to dollars at the exchange rate of $4.86 per pound. Ferderer (2003, 670) puts the value of New York acceptances at $1.75 billion in 1929.

88 Hoover's experiences combating British efforts to cartelize rubber production had given him a dim view of British magnanimity (Hoover 1952, 81–4).

89 The *Cartel des gauches* had floated the idea of a wealth tax, an idea sure to inspire fear among the wealthy.

90 Despite the new vaults, a large amount of the physical gold that backed world currencies remained in London, with pallets marked for their respective countries.

91 Despite its preferable reserve position, France continued to owe money to Britain. Nonetheless, Britain's flimsy reserve position meant that it was vulnerable to moves against sterling.

92 Moreau did not attend, fearing that his inability to speak English would exclude him from the deliberations.

93 The P/E ratio of a company (or market) is the ratio between the market price of the company and its earnings per share. People paying large

amounts of money for shares that pay them limited dividends could be a sign of speculative buying. On the other hand, there may be cases where companies genuinely do have long-term earning potential that is as yet unrealized. For instance, Amazon took a long time to turn a profit, but is now a powerful behemoth.

94 In essence, British policy decisions were driven by competitiveness concerns, American ones by a mix of competitiveness concerns and a desire to maximize structural benefits.

95 Bernanke (1983) contests the role of the money supply per se. For him, the Great Depression resulted from the drying-up of credit resulting from the wave of banking collapses plaguing the country. Banks, by lending out to consumers, play an important role in expanding the money supply. Bank failures, however, limit banks' ability to do the same thing given the same amount of creation of high-powered money by central banks.

96 White's impact on the future development of American economic strategy was undermined by accusations of spying for the Soviet Union. However, he suffered a fatal heart attack soon into his trial, and his guilt or innocence continues to be debated. For instance, Craig (2004) makes the case that White did engage in some espionage, but that rather than aiming to subvert American policy, he had sought greater US–Soviet post-war cooperation.

97 At the time, Greenspan was a graduate student who also played in a jazz band.

98 Or a very low-interest loan, should foreigners prefer US government bonds.

99 See Leonard Silk, "The Mark of El Supremo," *New York Times*, 12 June 1988.

100 See Alan Murray, "Paul Volcker: Think More Boldly," *Wall Street Journal*, 14 December 2009.

101 Chile, Argentina, Mexico, Venezuela, and Brazil borrowed heavily from international sources, with foreign credit making up a majority of their total credit at the height of the 1982 Latin American debt crisis (Frieden 1992, 76).

102 This nickname referenced Reagan's portrayal of football player George Gipp in the film *Knute Rockne, All American*.

103 Some contemporary accounts contested the risks of intermingling securities and commercial banking (White 1986).

104 See Kathleen Day, "A Lobby's Decline and Fall: Bailout Erodes SL Industry's Clout," *Washington Post*, 28 July 1989.

105 For instance, S&Ls had lent over $1 million to St Germain, with no money down, so that he could purchase five International House of Pancakes franchises. See Howard Kurtz, "Draft Report Clears St Germain on Influence Allegations," *Washington Post*, 12 April 1987.

106 For instance, Alfonse D'Amato, Republican representative from New York and prominent Senate Banking Committee member, was more reluctant to favour reform than Jake Garn.

107 This would be $6,510 in 2020 dollars (Officer and Williamson 2020). See Leonard Sloane, "Your Money: Money Fund Bank Accounts," *New York Times*, 11 December 1982.

108 Whereas investment banks might actively manage the funds of clients, discount brokers simply take the orders of investors, offering no advice. On the emergence of discount brokers, see Thomas Friedman, "Bank Bids $53 Million for Broker," *New York Times*, 25 November 1981; Robert Bennett, "Nervous Banks Start Striking Back," *New York Times*, 10 January 1982.

109 See Associated Press, "Dreyfus Bank Allowed," *New York Times*, 8 February 1983.

110 In addition, the relative importance of the Fed's interpretation had been affirmed by a Federal Appeals Court decision, which argued that prior rulings had granted "insufficient weight to the expertise of the Federal Reserve Board."

111 Jean Lasalle, "US Rescue of Large Bank Stirs Criticism," *Los Angeles Times*, 22 May 1984.

112 See Kenneth Noble, "House Panel Approves New Limits on Banking," *New York Times*, 27 June 1984.

113 When Congress blocked funding for right-wing paramilitaries opposed to the Sandinista government in Nicaragua, senior figures in the Reagan administration sought another source of funding. In violation of sanctions, they sold weapons to Iran. The question of whether President Reagan was aware of the deal engulfed the administration.

114 It would be difficult to paint Proxmire as a pawn of the securities industry either since his campaigns were largely inexpensive and self-funded: he won re-election in 1982, spending only $62. See Adam Clymer, "Campaign Costs Soar as Median Spending for Senate Seats Hits $1.7 Million," *New York Times*, 3 April 1983.

115 "Banking System Seen as Sound," *Washington Post*, 23 November 1986.

116 Derivatives are a good example of how state intervention is often necessary to create the conditions (e.g., enforceable contracts) for markets to operate. The real regulatory debate is not always a question of whether to have rules or not, but rather whether to have lax ones or stringent ones.

117 Specifically, when Solow ran a statistical model on the first two factors, he found a large, unexplained residual, which he posited was driven by productivity.

118 Ironically, just as Japan sought to reform its institutions, many American commentators argued that the United States should adopt institutions more like those of Japan (Johnson 1982; Magaziner and Reich 1983).

119 From 1994 to 1996, the LDP shared power with the Japanese Socialist Party.

120 Later, as prime minister, Nakasone made a controversial visit to the Yasukuni Shrine, a monument to soldiers killed in the service of the Empire of Japan (including some convicted of war crimes).

121 On the other hand, administrative reform – particularly of finance – was likely to run up against the prerogatives of an MoF with strong desires to protect its turf (Vogel 1996, 58).

122 American preferences were complicated because greater access to Japanese markets could reduce the American current account deficit, while producing profitable opportunities for American financial firms, but increased use of the yen as the currency of international trade and finance might undermine the role of American financial firms.

123 Brokers interacted with clients, while jobbers actually made trades on the floor.

124 Redwood later unsuccessfully challenged Thatcher's successor for the Conservative leadership, John Major, whom he believed insufficiently conservative. After leaving politics, he worked in investment banking and chaired the Economic Competitiveness Policy Group. On John Redwood, see Andrew Roth, "John Redwood," *Guardian* (Manchester), 20 March 2001.

125 The vote was a critical one. The G5 economies had negotiated the Plaza Accord – agreeing to weaken the dollar relative to the Japanese yen and German mark to rebalance the global economy. An American interest rate cut was vital to the success of the accord. Volcker preferred to wait for his German and Japanese counterparts to adhere to their commitments first.

126 Volcker was not necessarily against the changes and had urged Congress to act (Meltzer 2003, 1206).

127 This is the ratio between a firm's capital and its risk-weighted assets.

128 Leslie Wayne, "Bank Barrier Resists Foes: Glass–Steagall Walls May Just Be Replaced," *New York Times*, 18 September 1991.

129 See Kurt Eichenwald, "A Reversal by Brokers on Banks," *New York Times*, 2 December 1989.

130 The senators – Dennis DeConcini, John McCain, Alan Cranston, John Glenn, and Donald Riegle – were subsequently nicknamed the "Keating Five."

131 See Richard Stevenson, "Lincoln Savings Official Pleads Guilty to Fraud," *New York Times*, 23 July 1991.

132 See Stephen Labaton, "F.D.I.C. Sues Neil Bush and Others at Silverado," *New York Times*, 22 September 1999.

133 See Michael Wines, "Bush in Japan: Bush Collapses at State Dinner with the Japanese," *New York Times*, 9 January 1992.

134 Although we know in hindsight that the Japanese challenge had subsided, it was not obvious at the time. In 1990, a Chicago Council on Global Affairs found that over 60 per cent of the American public and American leaders identified the economic power of Japan as a critical threat (O'Reilly 1991, 20). By 1994, 62 per cent of the public still identified "economic competition from Japan" as a critical threat, although that view had subsided among leaders (O'Reilly 1995, 22).

135 See *New York Times*, "The Transition: Excerpts from Clinton's Conference on the State of the Economy," 15 December 1992.

136 James Carville, "The Bond Vigilantes," *Wall Street Journal*, 25 February 1993.

137 Newt Gingrich, quoted in Keith Bradsher, "No New Deal for Banking: Efforts to Drop Depression-Era Barriers Stall, Again," *New York Times*, 2 November 1995.

138 Cohen (2010, 133) notes that the invasion of Iraq followed closely on Saddam Hussein's insistence on paying for Iraqi oil in euros. This perhaps illustrates American sensitivity to the petrodollar question.

139 See also ibid. (98–134); and Eichengreen (2012). In addition, Schwartz (2009) discusses how global imbalances, coupled with American housing policy, enabled the United States to experience differential growth faster than other developed economies.

140 See Leslie Wayne, "Signs of a Shift in Senate Stance on Bank Law," *New York Times*, 5 June 1998.

141 See Mitchell Martin, "Citicorp and Travelers Plan to Merge in $70 Billion Deal: A New No. 1; Financial Giants Unite," *New York Times*, 7 April 1998.

142 Wendy Gramm, quoted in Richard Berke, "Tough Texan: Phil Gramm," *New York Times*, February 19 1995.

143 See also Rajan (2010, 21–45), who argues that the subprime crisis was the result of efforts to make up for slowing growth and rising inequality using expanded credit.

144 Stephen Labaton, "Congress Passes Wide-Ranging Bill Easing Bank Laws," *New York Times*, 5 November 1999.

145 See Katrina Brooker, "Citi's Creator, Alone with His Regrets," *New York Times*, 2 January 2010.

146 See Floyd Norris, "Paving Path to Fraud on Wall Street," *New York Times*, 15 March 2012.

147 See Eric Lipton, "Gramm and the 'Enron Loophole.'" *New York Times*, 14 November 2008.

148 See Saul Hansell, "Media Megadeal, The Overview: America Online Agrees to Buy Time Warner for $165 Billion; Media Deal Is Richest Merger," *New York Times*, 11 January 2000.

149 Extremely concentrated banking systems, like the Canadian system, largely avoided taking the risks that characterized the American system. There may be a non-linear relationship between bank concentration and risk-taking, with specialized unit-banking systems and highly concentrated systems outperforming those in the middle.

150 See Justin Lahart, "Mr. Rajan Was Unpopular (but Prescient) at Greenspan Party," *Wall Street Journal*, 2 January 2009.

151 The arguments oft employed by conservatives, that the Community Reinvestment Act forced banks to take on subprime mortgages and that

Fannie Mae and Freddie Mac precipitated the crisis, cannot explain some stylized facts. For instance, recent research finds evidence that increases in access to credit also occurred for middle- and upper-income borrowers (Adelino, Schoar, and Severino 2016).

152 See Aaron Ross Sorkin, "JP Morgan Pays $2 a Share for Bear Stearns," *New York Times*, 17 March 2008.

153 See Floyd Norris, "The World's Banks Could Prove Too Big to Fail," *New York Times*, 8 October 2008.

154 Blyth (2013, 51–93) argues that as the euro came onto the scene, European banks lent heavily to the periphery in search of high returns. Sovereign bond spreads between Germany and Ireland or Greece withered to zero.

155 As well as a quantitative sense if we apply the data in figure 1.5.

156 For reference, real per capita growth for the United States was 1 per cent per annum in the nineteenth century and 1.8 per cent between 1900 and 2010 (Maddison 2013).

157 The "veil of ignorance" is a thought experiment in which one imagines what kind of rules free and equal people in a society would choose if they did not know *who* they would be in that society (e.g., if they did not know whether they would be rich or poor).

158 For instance, in terms of purchasing-power parity, the World Bank (2018) considers China's economy to be $3 trillion larger than the American economy.

159 See Ana Swanson, "How China Used More Cement in 3 Years Than the U.S. Did in the Entire 20th Century," *Washington Post*, 24 March 2015.

160 See Keith Bradsher and Chris Buckley, "Market's Dive Could Delay Economic Reforms in China," *New York Times*, 7 July 2015.

161 See Javier C. Hernández, "Wealthy Chinese Scramble for Imperiled Commodity: U.S. 'Golden Visa,'" *New York Times*, 27 April 2017.

162 John Hensarling, quoted in Politico, "House Passes Sweeping Bank Deregulation Bill," 8 June 2017.

163 See Alan Rappeport and Emily Fitter, "Congress Approves First Big Dodd–Frank Rollback," *New York Times*, 22 May 2018.

Works Cited

Acheson, Graeme, Charles Hickson, John Turner, and Qing Ye. 2009. "Rule Britannia! British Stock Market Returns, 1825–1870." *Journal of Economic History* 69 (4): 1107–37. https://doi.org/10.1017/S0022050709001405.

Acheson, Graeme, and John Turner. 2008. "The Death Blow to Unlimited Liability in Victorian Britain: The City of Glasgow Failure." *Explorations in Economic History* 45 (3): 235–53. https://doi.org/10.1016/j.eeh.2007.10.001.

Adelino, Manuel, Antoinette Schoar, and Felipe Severino. 2016. "Loan Originations and Defaults in the Mortgage Crisis: The Role of the Middle Class." *Reviews of Financial Studies* 29 (7): 1635–70. https://doi.org/10.1093/rfs/hhw018.

Admati, Anat, and Martin Hellwig. 2013. *The Bankers' New Clothes: What's Wrong with Banking and What to Do about It.* Princeton, NJ: Princeton University Press.

Ahamed, Liaquat. 2014. *Lords of Finance: The Bankers Who Broke the World.* New York: Penguin Books.

Alborn, Timothy. 1998. *Conceiving Companies: Joint-Stock Politics in Victorian England.* New York: Routledge.

Anceau, Éric. 2012. *Napoléon III: Un Saint-Simon à cheval.* Paris: Tallandier.

Angell, Norman. 1913. *The Great Illusion: A Study of the Relation of Military Power to National Advantage.* New York: Knickerbocker Press.

Armijo, Leslie, Laurissa Mülich, and Daniel Tirone. 2014. "The Systemic Importance of Emerging Powers." *Journal of Policy Modeling* 36 (Supplement 1): S67–S88. https://doi.org/10.1016/j.jpolmod.2013.10.009.

Arrighi, Giovanni. 1994. *The Long Twentieth Century.* New York: Verso.

Atkin, John. 1970. "Official Regulation of British Overseas Investment, 1914–1931." *Economic History Review* 23 (2): 324–34. https://doi.org/10.1111/j.1468-0289.1970.tb01030.x.

Baer, Kenneth. 2000. *Reinventing Democrats: The Politics of Liberalism from Reagan to Clinton.* Lawrence: University Press of Kansas.

Bagehot, Walter. 1873. *Lombard Street: A Description of the Money Market.* New York: Scribner.

Bailin, Alison. 2005. *From Traditional to Group Hegemony: The G7, the Liberal Economic Order and the Core–Periphery Gap.* Aldershot, UK: Ashgate.

Baker, Mae, and Michael Collins. 1999. "Financial Crises and Structural Change in English Commercial Bank Assets." *Explorations in Economic History* 36 (4): 428–44. https://doi.org/10.1006/exeh.1999.0727.

Barber, William. 1988. *From New Era to New Deal: Herbert Hoover, the Economists and American Economic Policy, 1921–1933.* Cambridge: Cambridge University Press.

Barnett, Michael, and Martha Finnemore. 2004. *Rules for the World: International Organizations in World Politics.* Ithaca, NY: Cornell University Press.

Barth, James R., Gerard Caprio, Jr., and Ross Levine. 2006. *Rethinking Bank Regulation: Till Angels Govern.* Cambridge: Cambridge University Press.

Beck, Thorsten, Asli Demirgüç-Kunt, Luc Laeven, and Ross Levine. 2008. "Finance, Firm Size, and Growth." *Journal of Money, Credit and Banking* 40 (7): 1379–405. https://doi.org/10.1111/j.1538-4616.2008.00164.x.

Beck, Thorsten, Asli Demirgüç-Kunt, and Ross Levine. 1999. "A New Database on Financial Development and Structure." World Bank Policy Research Working Paper no. 2146. https://doi.org/10.1596/1813-9450-2146.

Bensel, Richard. 1984. *Sectionalism and American Political Development, 1880–1980.* Madison: University of Wisconsin Press.

Bentson, George. 1994. "Universal Banking." *Journal of Economic Perspectives* 8 (3): 121–44. https://doi.org/10.1257/jep.8.3.121.

Bernanke, Ben. 1983. "Nonmonetary Effects of the Financial Crisis in the Propagation of the Great Depression." *American Economic Review* 73 (3): 257–76. https://doi.org/10.3386/w1054.

– 2005. "The Global Savings Glut and the U.S. Current Account Deficit." Federal Reserve Board. Accessed January 2018. https://www.federalreserve.gov/boarddocs/speeches/2005/200503102/.

Bhagwati, Jagdish. 1998. "The Capital Myth: The Difference between Trade in Goods and Trade in Widgets." *Foreign Affairs* 77 (3): 7–12. https://doi.org/10.2307/20048871.

Bhattacharya, Sudipto, and Anjan V. Thakor. 1993. "Contemporary Banking Theory." *Journal of Financial Intermediation* 3 (1): 2–50. https://doi.org/10.1006/jfin.1993.1001.

Bhidé, Amar. 2009. "An Accident Waiting to Happen." *Critical Review: A Journal of Politics and Society* 21 (2–3): 211–47. https://doi.org/10.1080/08913810902974956.

Biglaiser, Glen, and Karl DeRouen. 2007. "Following the Flag: Troop Deployment and U.S. Foreign Direct Investment." *International Studies Quarterly* 51 (4): 835–54. https://doi.org/10.1111/j.1468-2478.2007.00479.x.

Blake, William. (1804) 2008. "And did those feed in ancient time." *The Complete Poetry and Prose of William Blake*, edited by David Erdman. Reprint, Berkeley: University of California Press.

Blyth, Mark. 2002. *Great Transformations: Economic Ideas and Institutional Change in the Twentieth Century*. Cambridge: Cambridge University Press.

– 2013. *Austerity: The History of a Dangerous Idea*. New York: Oxford University Press.

Bonaparte, Louis-Napoléon. 1839. *Des idées Napoléoniennes*. Brussels: Jules Géruzet Libraire-Éditeur.

Bordo, Michael, Barry Eichengreen, Daniela Klingbiel, Maria Martinez-Peria, and Andrew Ross. 2001. "Is the Crisis Problem Growing More Severe?" *Economic Policy* 16 (32): 53–82. https://doi.org/10.1111/1468-0327.00070.

Bordo, Michael, and Ronald MacDonald. 2003. "The Inter-war Gold Exchange Standard: Credibility and Monetary Independence." *Journal of International Money and Finance* 22 (1): 1–32. https://doi.org/10.1016/S0261-5606(02)00074-8.

Bordo, Michael, Hugh Rockoff, and Angela Redish. 1994. "The U.S. Banking System from a Northern Exposure: Stability versus Efficiency." *Journal of Economic History* 54 (2): 325–41. https://doi.org/10.1017/S0022050700014509.

Britain. Census Office. 1906. *Report on the Census of the British Empire 1901*. London.

Britain. Parliament. 1850, 1854, 1855, 1856, 1879. *Hansard Parliamentary Debates, 3rd series*.

Britain. Parliament. House of Commons. 1837. *Report on the Law of Partnership*.

– 1854. *Royal Commission*. London: Her Majesty's Stationery Office.

– 1918. "Committee on Currency and Foreign Exchanges: First Interim Report." in *Papers by Command*, vol. 7. London: Her Majesty's Stationery Office.

– 1984. *Parliamentary Debates, 5th series*.

Brooks, Stephen. 2013. "Economic Actors' Lobbying Influence on the Prospects for War and Peace." *International Studies Quarterly* 67 (4): 863–88. https://doi.org/10.1017/S0020818313000283.

Brown, David. 2002. *Palmerston and the Politics of Foreign Policy, 1846–1855*. New York: Manchester University Press.

– 2006. "Palmerston and Anglo-French Relations, 1846–1865." *Diplomacy and Statecraft* 17 (4): 675–92. https://doi.org/10.1080/09592290600942918.

Broz, J. Lawrence. 1997a. "The Domestic Politics of International Monetary Order: The Gold Standard." In *Contested Social Orders and International Politics*, edited by David Skidmore, 53–91. Nashville, TN: Vanderbilt University Press.

– 1997b. *The International Origins of the Federal Reserve System*. Ithaca, NY: Cornell University Press.

– 1999. "Origins of the Federal Reserve System: International Incentives and the Domestic Free-Rider Problem." *International Organization* 53 (1): 39–70. https://doi.org/10.1162/002081899550805.

Bruner, Robert, and Sean Carr. 2007. *The Panic of 1907: Lessons Learned from the Market's Perfect Storm*. Hoboken, NJ: John Wiley & Sons.

Bryan, William Jennings. 1896. "Cross of Gold." Speech delivered at Democratic National Convention, 9 July.

Bryer, R.A. 1997. "The Mercantile Laws Commission and the Political Economy of Limited Liability." *Economic History Review* 50 (1): 37–56. https://doi.org /10.1111/1468-0289.00044.

Bytheway, Simon, and Mark Meltzer. 2016. *Central Banks and Gold: How Tokyo, London and New York Shaped the Modern World*. Ithaca, NY: Cornell University Press.

Cain, Philip, and Anthony Hopkins. 1993. *British Imperialism: Crisis and Deconstruction 1914–1990*. New York: Longman.

– 2001. *British Imperialism, 1688–2000*. New York: Longman.

Calder, Kent. 2017. *Circles of Compensation: Economic Growth and the Globalization of Japan*. Stanford, CA: Stanford University Press.

Calomiris, Charles. 2000. *US Bank Deregulation in Historical Perspective*. New York: Cambridge University Press.

Calomiris, Charles, and Stephen Haber. 2014. *Fragile by Design: The Political Origins of Banking Crises and Scarce Credit*. Princeton, NJ: Princeton University Press.

Cameron, Rondo. 1953. "The *Crédit Mobilier* and the Economic Development of Europe." *Journal of Political Economy* 61 (6): 461–88. https://doi.org /10.1086/257433.

Capie, Forrest. 1995. "Commercial Banking in Britain between the Wars." In *Banking, Currency and Finance in Europe between the Wars*, edited by Charles Feinstein, 395–413. Oxford: Oxford University Press.

Capie, Forrest, and Alan Webber. 1985. *A Monetary History of the United Kingdom, 1870–1982*. London: Allen & Unwin.

Cassis, Youssef. 1991. "Financial Elites in Three European Centres: London, Paris, Berlin, 1880s–1930s." In *Banks and Money: International and Comparative Finance in History*, edited by Geoffrey Jones, 53–71. London: Frank Cass.

– 2006. *Capitals of Capital: A History of International Financial Centres, 1780–2005*. Cambridge: Cambridge University Press.

Center for Responsive Politics. 2019a. "Finance Insurance & Real Estate Sector." OpenSecrets.org. Accessed June 2019. https://www.opensecrets.org/pacs /sector.php?cycle=2000&txt=F.

– 2019b. "Sen. Phil Gramm." OpenSecrets.org. Accessed June 2019. https:// www.opensecrets.org/politicians/summary.php?cid=N00005709.

Cerny, Philip G. 2014. "Rethinking Financial Regulation: Risk, Club Goods, and Regulatory Fatigue." In *Handbook of the International Political Economy of Monetary Relations*, edited by Thomas Oatley and W. Kindred Winecoff, 343–63. Cheltenham, UK: Edward Elgar Press.

Chamberlain, Joseph. 1897. "A True Conception of Empire." Speech delivered to the Royal Colonial Institute, 31 March. Bartleby.com. Accessed January 2018. http://www.bartleby.com/268/5/14.html.

Chancellor, Edward. 1999. *Devil Take the Hindmost: A History of Financial Speculation*. New York: Farrar, Strauss, Giroux.

Chandler, Lester. 1958. *Benjamin Strong, Central Banker*. Washington, DC: Brookings Institution.

Chapman, S. 1979. "Financial Restraints on the Growth of Firms in the Cotton Industry, 1790–1850." *Economic History Review* 32 (1): 50–69. https://doi.org/10.1111/j.1468-0289.1979.tb01813.x.

Checkland, S. 1975. *Scottish Banking: A History*. Glasgow: Collins.

Chernow, Ron. 2016. *The Warburgs: The Twentieth-Century Odyssey of a Remarkable Jewish Family*. New York: Vintage Books.

Chevalier, Michel. 1844. *Cours d'économie politique fait au Collège de France*. Vol. 2. Paris: Capelle.

Chinn, Menzie, and Jeffrey Frankel. 2008. "Why the Euro Will Rival the Dollar." *International Finance* 11 (1): 49–73. https://doi.org/10.1111/j.1468-2362.2008.00215.x.

Chinn, Menzie, and Jeffry Frieden. 2011. *Lost Decades: The Making of America's Debt Crisis and the Long Recovery*. New York: W.W. Norton.

Chwieroth, Jeffrey. 2010. *Capital Ideas: The IMF and the Rise of Financial Liberalization*. Princeton, NJ: Princeton University Press.

Cleveland, Harold van B., and Frank Costigliola. 1977. "Anglo-American Financial Rivalry in the 1920s." *Journal of Economic History* 37 (4): 911–34. https://doi.org/10.1017/S0022050700094742.

Cleveland, Harold van B., and Thomas Huertas. 1985. *Citibank: 1812–1970*. Cambridge, MA: Harvard University Press.

Cohen, Benjamin. 2004. *The Future of Money*. Princeton, NJ: Princeton University Press.

– 2010. *The Future of Global Currency: The Euro versus the Dollar*. New York: Routledge.

– 2012. *The Future of Global Currency: The Euro versus the Dollar*. London: Routledge.

– 2015. *Currency Power: Understanding Monetary Rivalry*. Princeton, NJ: Princeton University Press.

Collins, Michael. 1989. "The Banking Crisis of 1878." *Economic History Review* 42 (4): 504–27. https://doi.org/10.2307/2597098.

Conacher, J.B. 1968. *The Aberdeen Coalition, 1852–1855*. Cambridge: Cambridge University Press.

Congressional Quarterly. 1984. "Standoff Blocks Bank Deregulation Bill." *CQ Almanac 1984*. Washington, DC: Congressional Quarterly.

– 1987. "Major Banking Legislation Stalls in Last Hours." *CQ Almanac 1986*. Washington, DC: Congressional Quarterly.

Copeland, Dale. 2000. *The Origins of Major War.* Ithaca, NY: Cornell University Press.

Copelovitch, Mark. 2010. "Master or Servant? Common Agency and the Political Economy of IMF Lending." *International Studies Quarterly* 54 (1): 49–77. https://doi.org/10.1111/j.1468-2478.2009.00577.x.

Corrigan, E. Gerald. 1983. "Statement before the Subcommittee on Telecommunications, Consumer Protection, and Finance of the Committee on Energy and Commerce of the United States House of Representatives." 28 June. Fraser (website). Accessed January 2018. https://fraser.stlouisfed.org/scribd/?item_id=807&filepath=/files/docs/historical/frbminn/presidents/corrigan/corrigan_19830628.pdf.

– 1987. *Financial Market Structure: A Longer View.* New York: Federal Reserve Bank of New York.

Costigliola, Frank. 1988. *Awkward Dominion: American Political, Economic and Cultural Relations with Europe, 1919–1933.* Ithaca, NY: Cornell University Press.

Cottrell, P.L., and L. Newton. 1999. "Banking Liberalization in England and Wales, 1826–1844." In *The State, the Financial System and Economic Modernization*, edited by E. Sylla, R. Tilly, and G. Casares, 75–117. Cambridge: Cambridge University Press.

Craig, R. Bruce. 2004. *Treasonable Doubt: The Harry Dexter White Spy Case.* Lawrence: University Press of Kansas.

Cunningham, Michele. 2001. *Mexico and the Foreign Policy of Napoleon III.* Basingstoke, UK: Palgrave Macmillan.

Dahl, Robert. 1957. "The Concept of Power." *Systems Research and Behavioral Science* 2 (3): 201–15. https://doi.org/10.1002/bs.3830020303.

Davies, Helen. 2016. *Emile and Isaac Pereire: Bankers, Socialists and Sephardic Jews in Nineteenth-Century France.* Manchester, UK: University of Manchester Press.

Dewatripont, Mathias, Jean-Charles Rochet, and Jean Tirole. 2010. *Balancing the Banks: Global Lessons from the Financial Crisis.* Princeton, NJ: Princeton University Press.

Dewatripont, Mathias, and Jean Tirole. 1994. *The Prudential Regulation of Banks.* Cambridge, MA: MIT Press.

Djelic, Marie-Laure. 2013. "When Limited Liability Was (Still) an Issue: Mobilization and Politics of Signification in 19th-Century England." *Organization Studies* 34 (5–6): 683–703. https://doi.org/10.1177/0170840613479223.

Dougui, Noureddine. 1981. "Les origines de la libération des sociétés de capitaux à responsabilité limitée, 1856–1863." *Revue d'Histoire Moderne et Contemporaine* 28 (2): 268–92. https://doi.org/10.3406/rhmc.1981.1142.

Drolet, Michael. 2015. "A Nineteenth-Century Mediterranean Union: Michel Chevalier's *Système de la Méditerranée*." *Mediterranean Historical Review* 30 (2): 147–68. https://doi.org/10.1080/09518967.2015.1117204.

Economist. 2007. "Back from the Grave." 11 October.

Edelstein, Michael. 1982. *Overseas Investment in the Age of High Imperialism: The United Kingdom, 1850–1914.* New York: Columbia University Press.

Eichengreen, Barry. 1995. *Golden Fetters: The Gold Standard and the Great Depression, 1919–1939.* New York: Oxford University Press.

– 1999. "The Baring Crisis in a Mexican Mirror." *International Political Science Review* 20 (3): 249–70. https://doi.org/10.1177/0192512199203002.

– 2012. *Exorbitant Privilege: The Rise and Fall of the Dollar and the Future of the International Monetary System.* New York: Oxford University Press.

Eichengreen, Barry, and Marc Flandreau. 2011. "The Federal Reserve, the Bank of England, and the Rise of the Dollar as an International Currency, 1914–1939." *Open Economies Review* 23 (1): 57–87. https://doi.org/10.1007/s11079-011-9217-1.

Einaudi, Luca. 2001. *Money and Politics: European Monetary Unification and the International Gold Standard (1865–1873).* New York: Oxford University Press.

Encarnation, Dennis J., and Mark Mason. 1990. "Neither MITI nor America: The Political Economy of Capital Liberalization in Japan." *International Organization* 44 (1): 25–54. https://doi.org/10.1017/S002081830000463X.

Endvall, H.D.P. 2015. *Japanese Diplomacy: The Role of Leadership.* Albany, NY: SUNY Press.

Feinstein, C.H., Peter Temin, and Gianni Toniolo. 1997. *The European Economy between the Wars.* New York: Oxford University Press.

Feis, Herbert. 1930. *Europe: The World's Banker.* New Haven, CT: Yale University Press.

Fenton, Laurence. 2013. *Palmerston and the Times: Foreign Policy, the Press and Public Opinion in Mid-Victorian Britain.* New York: I.B. Tauris.

Ferderer, J. Peter. 2003. "Institutional Innovation and the Creation of Liquid Financial Markets: The Case of Bankers' Acceptances, 1914–1934." *Journal of Economic History* 63 (3): 666–94. https://doi.org/10.1017/S002205070354195X.

Ferguson, Niall. 2000. *The House of Rothschild: The World's Banker, 1849–1999.* New York: Penguin Books.

Flandreau, Marc. 2000. "The Economics and Politics of Monetary Unions: A Reassessment of the Latin Monetary Union, 1865–1871." *Financial History Review* 7 (1): 25–44. https://doi.org/10.1017/S0968565000000020.

Flandreau, Marc, and Clemens Jobst. 2009. "The Empirics of International Currencies: Network Externalities, History and Persistence." *Economic Journal* 119 (2): 643–64. https://doi.org/10.1111/j.1468-0297.2009.02219.x.

Fohlin, Caroline. 2007. *Finance Capitalism and Germany's Rise to Industrial Power.* New York: Cambridge University Press.

Fox, Kate. 2014. *Watching the English: The Hidden Rules of English Behaviour.* London: Hodder & Stoughton.

Frank, Andre Gunder. 1998. *ReOrient: Global Economy in the Asian Age.* Berkeley: University of California Press.

Freedeman, Charles. 1965. "Joint-Stock Business Organization in France, 1807–1865." *Business History Review* 39 (2): 184–204. https://doi.org/10.2307/3112696.

Freeman, Christopher, and Luc Soete. 1996. *The Economics of Industrial Innovation.* Cambridge, MA: MIT Press.

– 1997. *The Economics of Industrial Innovation.* 3rd. ed. Cambridge, MA: MIT Press.

Frehen, Rik, William Goetzmann, and K. Geert Rouwenhorst. 2013. "New Evidence on the First Financial Bubble." *Journal of Financial Economics* 108 (3): 585–607. https://doi.org/10.1016/j.jfineco.2012.12.008.

French, Kenneth, and James Poterba. 1991. "Investor Diversification and International Equity Markets." *American Economic Review* 81 (2): 222–6. https://doi.org/10.3386/w3609.

Frieden, Jeffry. 1990. "Sectoral Conflict and Foreign Economic Policy." *International Organization* 42 (1): 59–90. https://doi.org/10.1017/S002081830000713X.

– 1991. "Invested Interests: The Politics of National Economics in a World of Global Finance." *International Organization* 45 (4): 425–51. https://doi.org/10.1017/S0020818300033178.

– 1992. *Debt, Development and Democracy: Modern Political Economy and Latin America, 1965–1982.* Princeton, NJ: Princeton University Press.

– 2015. *Currency Politics: The Political Economy of Exchange Rate Policy.* Princeton, NJ: Princeton University Press.

Friedman, Milton. 1977. "Nobel Lecture: Inflation and Unemployment." *Journal of Political Economy* 85 (3): 451–72. https://doi.org/10.1086/260579.

Friedman, Milton, and Anna Jacobson Schwartz. 1963. *A Monetary History of the United States, 1867–1960.* Princeton, NJ: Princeton University Press.

Frost, Raymond. 1954. "The Macmillan Gap, 1931–1953." *Oxford Economic Papers* 6 (2): 181–201. https://doi.org/10.1093/oxfordjournals.oep.a042241.

Funabashi, Yoichi. 1989. *Managing the Dollar: From the Plaza to the Louvre.* 2nd ed. Washington, DC: Institute for International Economics.

Galbraith, John Kenneth. (1954) 1997. *The Great Crash, 1929.* Boston: Houghton-Mifflin.

Gallarotti, Giulio. 1995. *The Anatomy of an International Monetary Regime: The Classical Gold Standard 1880–1914.* New York: Oxford University Press.

Gallup. 2018. "Presidential Job Approval Center." Accessed January 2018. http://www.gallup.com/interactives/185273/presidential-job-approval-center.aspx.

Gerschenkron, Alexander. 1962. *Economic Backwardness in Historical Perspective: A Book of Essays.* Cambridge, MA: Belknap Press of Harvard University Press.

Gilpin, Robert. 1981. *War and Change in World Politics.* Princeton, NJ: Princeton University Press.

– 1987. *The Political Economy of International Relations.* Princeton, NJ: Princeton University Press.

Global Financial Data. 2018. "Global Financial Data." Accessed January 2018. https://www.globalfinancialdata.com.

Goetzmann, William. 2013. *The Great Mirror of Folly: Finance, Culture, and the Crash of 1720*. New Haven, CT: Yale University Press.

– 2016. *Money Changes Everything: How Finance Made Civilization Possible.* Princeton, NJ: Princeton University Press.

Goldsmith, Raymond. 1969. *Financial Structure and Development.* New Haven, CT: Yale University Press.

Goldstein, Joshua. 1985. "Kondratieff Waves as War Cycles." *International Studies Quarterly* 29 (4): 411–44. https://doi.org/10.2307/2600380.

Goodman, John, and Louis Pauly. 1993. "The Obsolescence of Capital Controls? Economic Management in an Age of Global Markets." *World Politics* 46 (1): 50–82. https://doi.org/10.2307/2950666.

Gordon, Barry. 1979. *Economic Doctrine and Tory Liberalism, 1824–1830.* London: Macmillan Press.

Gorton, Gary. 2010. *Slapped by the Invisible Hand.* New York: Oxford University Press.

Gould, Erica. 2006. *Money Talks: The International Monetary Fund, Conditionality and Supplementary Financiers.* Stanford, CA: Stanford University Press.

Gourinchas, Pierre-Olivier, and Hélène Rey. 2007. "From World Banker to World Venture Capitalist: U.S. External Adjustment and the Exorbitant Privilege." In *G-7 Current Account Imbalances: Sustainability and Adjustment,* edited by R. Clarida, 11–55. Chicago: University of Chicago Press.

Gowa, Janine. 1983. *Closing the Gold Window: Domestic Politics and the End of Bretton Woods.* Ithaca NY: Cornell University Press.

Gower, L.C.B. 1985. *Review of Investor Protection: Report.* London: Her Majesty's Stationery Office.

Green, Fletcher M. 1959. "Origins of the Credit Mobilier of America." *Mississippi Valley Historical Review* 46 (2): 238–51. https://doi.org/10.2307/1891526.

Green, Michael. 2001. *Japan's Reluctant Realism: Foreign Policy Challenges in an Era of Uncertain Power.* New York: Palgrave Macmillan.

Greenspan, Alan. 1996. "Remarks at the New Orleans Forum." New Orleans Forum, New Orleans, LA, 18 March.

– 2008. *The Age of Turbulence: Adventures in a New World.* New York: Penguin Books.

Grossman, Richard. 2010. *Unsettled Account: The Evolution of Banking in the Industrialized World since 1800.* Princeton, NJ: Princeton University Press.

Grossman, Richard, and Masami Imai. 2013. "Contingent Capital and Bank Risk-Taking among British Banks before the First World War." *Economic History Review* 66 (1): 132–55. https://doi.org/10.1111/j.1468-0289.2011.00638.x.

Haggard, Stephan. 2000. *The Political Economy of the Asian Financial Crisis.* Washington, DC: Peterson Institute for International Economics.

Haggard, Stephan, and Sylvia Maxfield. 1996. "The Political Economy of Financial Internationalization in the Developing World." *International Organization* 50 (1): 35–68. https://doi.org/10.1017/S0020818300001661.

Hall, Peter. 1989. *The Political Power of Economic Ideas: Keynesianism across Nations*. Princeton, NJ: Princeton University Press.

Halle, Kay. 1985. *The Irrepressible Churchill: Stories, Sayings and Impressions of Sir Winston Churchill*. London: Robson.

Hammond, Thomas, and Jack Knott. 1988. "The Deregulatory Snowball: Explaining Deregulation in the Financial Industry." *Journal of Politics* 50 (1): 3–30. https://doi.org/10.2307/2131038.

Harris, Ron. 1997. "Political Economy, Interest Groups, Legal Institutions, and the Repeal of the Bubble Act in 1825." *Economic History Review* 50 (4): 675–96. https://doi.org/10.1111/1468-0289.00074.

– 2000. *Industrializing English Law: Entrepreneurship and Business Organization*. Cambridge: Cambridge University Press.

Hart, Jeffrey. 1992. *Rival Capitalists: International Competitiveness in the United States, Japan and Western Europe*. Ithaca, NY: Cornell University Press.

Hawkins, Angus. 1998. *British Party Politics, 1852–1886*. New York: St. Martin's Press.

Helleiner, E. 1996. *States and the Reemergence of Global Finance: From Bretton Woods to the 1990s*. Ithaca, NY: Cornell University Press.

Hendrickson, Jill. 2001. "The Long and Bumpy Road to Glass–Steagall Reform: A Historical and Evolutionary Analysis of Banking Legislation." *American Journal of Economics and Sociology* 60 (4): 849–79. https://doi.org/10.1111/1536-7150.00126.

Henisz, Witold, Bennet Zelner, and Mauro Guillén. 2005. "The Worldwide Diffusion of Market-Oriented Infrastructure Reform." *American Sociological Review* 70 (4): 871–97. https://doi.org/10.1177/000312240507000601.

Hills, Sally, Ryland Thomas, and Nicholas Dimsdale. 2010. "The UK Recession in Context: What Do Three Centuries of Data Tell Us?" *Bank of England Quarterly Bulletin* 50 (4): 277–91. https://www.bankofengland.co.uk/quarterly-bulletin/2010/q4/the-uk-recession-in-context-what-do-three-centuries-of-data-tell-us.

Hilton, Boyd. 1988. *The Age of Atonement: The Influence of Evangelicalism on Social and Economic Thought*. Oxford: Clarendon Press.

Hoover, Herbert. 1952. *The Memoirs of Herbert Hoover: The Cabinet and the Presidency, 1920–1933*. New York: Macmillan.

Horiuchi, Akiyoshi. 2012. "The Big Bang: Idea and Reality." In *Crisis and Change in the Japanese Financial System*, edited by Takeo Hoshi and Hugh Patrick, 233–52. New York: Springer.

Horn, Martin. 2002. *Britain, France and the Financing of the First World War*. Montreal and Kingston: McGill-Queen's University Press.

Horne, James. 1985. *Japan's Financial Markets: Conflict and Consensus in Policymaking*. Boston, MA: George Allen & Unwin.

House, Jonathan. 1976. "The Decisive Attack: A New Look at French Infantry Tactics on the Eve of World War I." *Journal of Military History* 40 (4): 164–9. https://doi.org/10.2307/1986698.

Hugill, Peter. 1999. *Global Communications since 1844: Geopolitics and Technology*. Baltimore, MD: Johns Hopkins University Press.

Hunt, Bishop. 1936. *The Development of the Business Corporation in England, 1800–1867*. Cambridge, MA: Harvard University Press.

Ibbotson, Roger, Richard Carr, and Anthony Robinson. 1982. "International Equity and Bond Returns." *Financial Analyst Journal* 38 (4): 61–83. https://doi.org/10.2469/faj.v38.n4.61.

Ikemoto, Daisuke. 2016. "Re-examining the Removal of Exchange Controls by the Thatcher Government in 1979." Presentation to the Political Studies Association Conference, Brighton, 21 March 2016.

Ikenberry, John. 2001. *After Victory*. Princeton, NJ: Princeton University Press.

Imlah, A.H. 1958. *Economic Elements in the "Pax Britannica."* Studies in British Foreign Trade in the Nineteenth Century. Cambridge, MA: Harvard University Press.

Irwin, Douglas. 1989. "Political Economy and Peel's Repeal of the Corn Laws." *Economics and Politics* 1 (1): 41–59. https://doi.org/10.1111/j.1468-0343.1989.tb00004.x.

– 1994. "The Political Economy of Free Trade: Voting in the British General Election of 1906." *Journal of Law and Economics* 37 (1): 75–108. https://doi.org/10.1086/467307.

Jacobs, Lawrence, and Desmond King. 2016. *Fed Power: How Finance Wins*. New York: Oxford University Press.

Jefferys, James. 1938. "Trends in Business Organization in Great Britain since 1856." PhD diss., University of London.

Jenkins, T.A. 1994. *The Liberal Ascendancy, 1830–1886*. New York: St. Martin's Press.

Johnson, Chalmers. 1982. *MITI and the Japanese Miracle*. Stanford, CA: Stanford University Press.

– 1986. "Tanaka Kakuei, Structural Corruption, and the Advent of Machine Politics in Japan." *Journal of Japanese Studies* 12 (1): 1–28. https://doi.org/10.2307/132445.

Johnson, Simon, and James Kwak. 2010. *13 Bankers: The Wall Street Takeover and the Next Financial Meltdown*. New York: Pantheon Books.

Jordà, Òscar, Moritz Schularick, and Alan M. Taylor. 2013. "When Credit Bites Back." *Journal of Money, Credit, and Banking* 45 (2): 3–28. https://doi.org/10.1111/jmcb.12069.

Jorgensen, Dale. 1988. "Productivity and Economic Growth in Japan and the U.S." *American Economic Review* 78 (2): 217–22.

Kadlec, Charles. 1999. *Dow 100,000: Fact or Fiction*. New York: Prentice Hall.

Kaminsky, Graciela, and Carmen Reinhart. 1999. "The Twin Crises: The Causes of Banking and Balance-of-Payment Problems." *American Economic Review* 89 (3): 473–500. https://doi.org/10.1257/aer.89.3.473.

Kaminsky, Graciela, and Sergio Schmukler. 2008. "Short-Run Pain, Long-Run Gain: Financial Liberalization and Stock Market Cycles." *Review of Finance* 12 (2): 252–92. https://doi.org/10.1093/rof/rfn002.

Katada, Saori. 2008. "From a Supporter to a Challenger? Japan's Currency Leadership in Dollar-Denominated East Asia." *Review of International Political Economy* 15 (3): 399–417. https://doi.org/10.1080/09692290801928756.

Kelemen, R. Daniel, and Eric Sibbit. 2004. "The Globalization of American Law." *International Organization* 58 (1): 103–36. https://doi.org/10.1017/S0020818304581043.

Kennedy, Warren. 1987. *Industrial Structure, Capital Markets, and the Origins of British Economic Decline*. Cambridge: Cambridge University Press.

Keynes, John Maynard. 1920. *The Economic Consequences of the Peace*. New York: Harcourt Brace and Howe.

– 1923. *A Tract on Monetary Reform*. London: Macmillan.

– 1935. *A General Theory of Employment, Interest and Money*. New York: Harcourt, Brace.

Kindleberger, Charles. 1973. *World in Depression, 1929–1939*. Berkeley: University of California Press.

– 1975. "The Rise of Free Trade in Western Europe, 1820–1875." *Journal of Economic History* 35 (1): 20–55. https://doi.org/10.1017/S0022050700094298.

– 1978. *Manias, Panics and Crashes*. New York: Basic Books.

– 1990. *Historical Economics: Art or Science?* Berkeley: University of California Press.

King, Robert, and Ross Levine. 1993. "Finance and Growth: Schumpeter Might Be Right." *Quarterly Journal of Economics* 108 (3): 717–37. https://doi.org/10.2307/2118406.

Kirschner, Jonathan. 1997. *Currency and Coercion: The Political Economy of International Monetary Power*. Princeton, NJ: Princeton University Press.

Knight, Frank. 1921. *Risk, Uncertainty, and Profit*. Boston: Houghton-Mifflin.

Kondratieff, Nikolai. 1979. "The Long Waves in Economic Life." *Review: A Journal of the Fernand Braudel Center* 2 (4): 519–62.

Koughan, Martin, David Ewing, and Robert Krulwich. 1991. "Losing the War with Japan." *Frontline*, 19 November. Alexandria, VA: WHBC Educational Foundation.

Kraemer, Kenneth, Greg Linden, and Jason Dedrick. 2011. "Capturing Value in Global Networks: Apple's iPad and iPhone." Working paper. Irvine: Personal Computing Industry Center, University of California.

Krasner, Stephen. 1976. "State Power and the Structure of International Trade." *World Politics* 28 (3): 317–47. https://doi.org/10.2307/2009974.

Kroszner, Randall S., and Raghuram Rajan. 1994. "Is the Glass–Steagall Act Justified? A Study of the U.S. Experience with Universal Banking before 1933." *American Economic Review* 84 (4): 810–32.

Kroszner, Randall S., and Philip Strahan. 1998. "What Drives Deregulation? Economics and Politics of the Relaxation of Bank Branching Restrictions." *Quarterly Journal of Economics* 114 (4): 1437–67. https://doi.org/10.1162/003355399556223.

Kunz, Diane. 1991. *The Economic Diplomacy of the Suez Crisis*. Chapel Hill: University of North Carolina Press.

LaFeber, Walter. 1989. *The American Age: United States Policy at Home and Abroad since 1750*. New York: Norton.

Lambert, Andrew. 2011. *The Crimean War: British Grand Strategy against Russia, 1853–1856*. London: Ashgate.

Lambert, Emily. 2010. *The Futures: Rise of the Speculator and the Origins of the World's Biggest Markets*. New York: Basic Books.

Landes, David S. 1956. "Vielle banque et banque nouvelle: La révolution financière du dix-neuvième siècle." *Revue d'Histoire Moderne et Contemporaine* 3 (3): 204–22. https://doi.org/10.3406/rhmc.1956.3093.

Lee, Michael. 2016. "How Many Lightbulbs Does It Take to Change the Financial System? Economic Ideas and Financial Regulation, 1846–2007." *British Journal of Politics and International Relations* 18 (4): 866–88. https://doi.org/10.1177/1369148116668078.

Lee, Michael, Adrian Florea, and Nicolas Blarel. 2019. "Opening the Black Box of Finance: North–South Investment, Political Risk, and US Military Intervention." *Political Studies* (forthcoming). https://doi.org/10.1177/0032321718813570.

Lee, Michael, and William Thompson. 2017. "Major Powers vs. Global Powers: A New Measure of Global Reach and Power Projection Capacity." In *Oxford Research Encyclopedia of Politics*, edited by William Thompson. New York: Oxford University Press. Accessed March 2020. https://oxfordre.com/politics/view/10.1093/acrefore/9780190228637.001.0001/acrefore-9780190228637-e-610.

Leeds, Brett. 2003. "Alliance Reliability in Times of War: Explaining State Decisions to Violate Treaties." *International Organization* 57 (4): 801–27. https://doi.org/10.1017/S0020818303574057.

Levine, Ross. 1997. "Financial Development and Economic Growth: Views and Agenda." *Journal of Economic Literature* 35 (2): 688–726.

– 1999. "Law, Finance and Economic Growth." *Journal of Financial Intermediation* 8 (1): 8–35. https://doi.org/10.1006/jfin.1998.0255.

Lévy-Leboyer, Maurice. 1976. *La position internationale de la France*. Paris: Presse de L'Ecole des hautes études en sciences sociales.

Litan, Robert, William Isaac, and William Taylor. 1994. "Financial Regulation." In *American Economic Policy in the 1980s*, edited by Martin Feldstein. Chicago: University of Chicago Press 519–73.

Loayza, Norman, and Romain Ranciere. 2006. "Financial Development, Financial Fragility and Growth." *Journal of Money, Credit and Banking* 38 (4): 1051–76. https://doi.org/10.1353/mcb.2006.0060.

Loftus, Donna. 2002. "Capital and Community: Limited Liability and Attempts to Democratize the Market in Mid-nineteenth Century England." *Victorian Studies* 45 (1): 93–120. https://doi.org/10.2979/VIC.2002.45.1.93.

London Stock Exchange. n.d. "UK: Number of Companies and Market Capitalisation." Market Information and Analysis. Accessed March 2020. http://www.londonstockexchange.com/statistics/historic/stats-summary-pre-2005/pre-2005.pdf.

Lowenstein, Roger. 2000. *When Genius Failed: The Rise and Fall of Long Term Capital Management*. New York: Random House.

– 2015. *America's Bank: The Epic Struggle to Create the Federal Reserve*. New York: Penguin Press.

Lucas, Robert E. 1990. "Why Doesn't Capital Flow from Rich Countries to Poor Countries?" *American Economic Review* 80 (2): 92–6.

Maddison, Angus. 2009. "Statistics on World Population, GDP and Per Capita GDP, 1–2008 AD." Groningen, The Netherlands: Groningen Growth and Development Centre, Faculty of Economics and Business, University of Groningen. Accessed March 2020. http://www.ggdc.net/maddison/oriindex.htm.

– 2013. Maddison Historical Statistics. The Maddison Project. Groningen, The Netherlands: Groningen Growth and Development Centre, Faculty of Economics and Business, University of Groningen. Accessed February 2019. http://www.ggdc.net/maddison/maddison-project/home.htm.

Magaziner, Ira C., and Robert B. Reich. 1983. *Minding America's Business: The Decline and Rise of the American Economy*. New York: Vintage Books.

Major, Aaron. 2012. "Neoliberalism and the New International Financial Architecture." *Review of International Political Economy* 19 (4): 536–61. https://doi.org/10.1080/09692290.2011.603663.

Malhotra, Neil, and Yotam Margalit. 2009. "State of the Nation: Anti-Semitism and the Financial Crisis." *Boston Review*, May/June.

Maurer, Noel. 2013. *The Empire Trap: The Rise and Fall of US Intervention to Protect American Property Overseas, 1893–2013*. Princeton, NJ: Princeton University Press.

McCarty, Nolan, Keith Poole, and Howard Rosenthal. 2013. *Political Bubbles: Financial Crises and the Failure of American Democracy*. Princeton, NJ: Princeton University Press.

McGillivray, Fiona. 2004. *Privileging Industry: The Comparative Politics of Trade and Industrial Policy*. Princeton, NJ: Princeton University Press.

McKeown, Adam. 2008. *Melancholy Order: Asian Migration and the Globalization of Borders*. New York: Columbia University Press.

McNally, Christopher. 2011. "China's Changing *Guanxi* Capitalism: Private Entrepreneurs between Leninist Control and Relentless Accumulation." *Business and Politics* 13 (2): 1–29. https://doi.org/10.2202/1469-3569.1339.

McNamara, Kathleen. 2008. "A Rivalry in the Making? The Euro and International Monetary Power." *Review of International Political Economy* 15 (3): 439–59. https://doi.org/10.1080/09692290801931347.

Meacham, Jon. 2015. *Destiny and Power: The American Odyssey of George Herbert Walker Bush*. New York: Random House.

Mehmood, JahanZaib. 2017. "The World's 100 Largest Banks." S&P Global: Market Intelligence, 11 April. Accessed May 2018. http://www.snl.com /web/client?auth=inherit#news/article?id=40223698&cdid=A-40223698-11568.

Meltzer, Allan. 2003. *A History of the Federal Reserve*. Chicago: University of Chicago Press.

Mendoza, Enrique, and Marco Terrones. 2008. "An Anatomy of Credit Booms: Evidence from Macro Aggregates and Micro Data." NBER Working Paper 14049. Cambridge, MA: National Bureau of Economic Research.

Michie, Ronald. 2001. *The London Stock Exchange: A History*. Oxford: Oxford University Press.

Mikuni, Akio, and R. Taggart Murphy. 2002. *Japan's Policy Trap: Dollars, Deflation, and the Crisis of Japanese Finance*. Washington, DC: Brookings Institution Press.

Minsky, Hyman. 1992. "The Financial Instability Hypothesis." Jerome Levy Economics Institute Working Paper no. 74.

Mishkin, Frederic. 1999. "Financial Consolidation: Dangers and Opportunities." *Journal of Banking & Finance* 23 (2): 675–91. https://doi.org/10.1016/S0378 -4266(98)00084-3.

Mitchell, B.R. 2013. *International Historical Statistics: Africa, Oceania and Asia, 1750–2010*. Basingstoke, UK: Palgrave-Macmillan.

Modelski, George. 1978. "The Long Cycle of Global Politics and the Nation-State." *Comparative Studies in Society and History* 20 (2): 214–35. https://doi .org/10.1017/S0010417500008914.

Modelski, George, and William Thompson. 1988. *Seapower in Global Politics, 1494–1993*. Seattle: University of Washington Press.

– 1996. *Leading Sectors and World Powers: The Co-evolution of Global Economics and Politics*. Columbia: University of South Carolina Press.

Moe, Espen. 2007. *Governance, Growth and Global Leadership: The Role of the State in Technological Progress, 1750–2000*. Burlington, VT: Ashgate.

Moggridge, Donald. 1972. *British Monetary Policy, 1924–1931: The Norman Conquest of $4.86*. Cambridge: Cambridge University Press.

Moran, Michael. 1991. *The Politics of the Financial Services Revolution: The USA, UK and Japan*. New York: Palgrave Macmillan.

Mouré, Kenneth. 2002. *The Gold Standard Illusion: France, the Bank of France and the International Gold Standard 1914–1939*. New York: Oxford University Press.

Mundell, R.A. 1961. "A Theory of Optimum Currency Areas." *American Economic Review* 51: 657–64.
– 1963. "Capital Mobility and Stabilization Policy under Fixed and Flexible Exchange Rates." *Canadian Journal of Economics and Political Science* 29 (4): 475–85. https://doi.org/10.2307/139336.
– 1993. "EMU and the International Monetary System: A Transatlantic Perspective." Working paper. Vienna: Austrian National Bank.
Murakami, Yasusuke. 1992. *An Anti-classical Political–Economic Analysis: A Vision for the New Century.* Stanford, CA: Stanford University Press.
Murmann, Johann. 2003. *Knowledge and Competitive Advantage: The Coevolution of Firms, Technology and National Institutions.* New York: Cambridge University Press.
Napier, Susan. 2006. "Matter out of Place: Carnival, Containment, and Cultural Recovery in Miyazaki's 'Spirited Away.'" *Journal of Japanese Studies* 32 (2): 287–310. https://doi.org/10.1353/jjs.2006.0057.
Neal, Larry. 1993. *The Rise of Financial Capitalism: International Capital in the Age of Reason.* Cambridge: Cambridge University Press.
– 1998. "The Financial Crisis of 1825 and the Restructuring of the British Financial System." *Federal Reserve Bank of Saint Louis Review* 80 (3): 53–76. https://doi.org/10.20955/r.80.53-76.
Nelson, Stephen, and Peter Katzenstein. 2014. "Uncertainty, Risk and the Financial Crisis of 2008." *International Organization* 68 (2): 361–92. https://doi.org/10.1017/S0020818313000416.
Niskanen, William A. 1988. *Reaganomics: An Insider's Account of the Policies and the People.* Oxford: Oxford University Press.
Norloff, Carla. 2010. *America's Advantage: US Hegemony and International Cooperation.* Cambridge, MA: Cambridge University Press.
North, Douglass. 1990. "A Transaction Cost Theory of Politics." *Journal of Theoretical Politics* 2 (4): 355–67. https://doi.org/10.1177/0951692890002004001.
North, Douglass, and Barry Weingast. 1989. "Constitutions and Commitment: The Evolution of Institutions Governing Public Choice in Seventeenth-Century England." *Journal of Economic History* 49 (4): 803–32. https://doi.org/10.1017/S0022050700009451.
Oatley, Thomas. 2011. "The Reductionist Gamble: Open Economy Politics in the Global Economy." *International Organization* 65 (2): 311–41. https://doi.org/10.1017/S002081831100004X.
– 2015. *A Political Economy of American Hegemony: Buildups, Booms and Busts.* Cambridge: Cambridge University Press.
– 2016. *A Political Economy of American Hegemony: Buildups, Booms and Busts.* Oxford: Oxford University Press.
Oatley, Thomas, and Robert Nabors. 1998. "Redistributive Cooperation: Market Failure, Wealth Transfers, and the Basle Accord." *International Organization* 52 (1): 35–54. https://doi.org/10.1162/002081898550545.

Oatley, Thomas, and Bilyana Petrova. 2016. "Banker to the World: Global Capital and America's Financialization." Under review.

Oatley, Thomas, William Winecoff, Andrew Pennock, and Sarah Danzman. 2013. "The Political Economy of Global Finance: A Network Model." *Perspectives in Politics* 11 (1): 133–53. https://doi.org/10.1017/S1537592712003593.

O'Brien, Patrick. 1988. "The Political Economy of British Taxation, 1660–1815." *Economic History Review* 41 (1): 1–32. https://doi.org/10.2307/2597330.

Obstfeld, Maurice, and Alan Taylor. 2004. *Global Capital Markets: Integration, Crisis and Growth*. Cambridge: Cambridge University Press.

Odlyzko, Andrew. 2010. "Collective Hallucinations and Inefficient Markets: The British Railway Mania of the 1840s." Under review.

Officer, Lawrence, and Samuel Williamson. 2020. "Defining Measures of Worth." MeasuringWorth. Accessed March 2020. https://www.measuringworth.com/defining_measures_of_worth.php.

Olson, Mancur. (1965) 1993. *The Logic of Collective Action: Public Goods and the Theory of Groups*. Cambridge, MA: Harvard University Press.

O'Reilly, John E. 1991. *American Public Opinion and U.S. Foreign Policy 1991*. Chicago: Chicago Council on Foreign Relations.

– 1995. *American Public Opinion and U.S. Foreign Policy 1995*. Chicago: Chicago Council on Foreign Relations.

Ostrom, Elinor. 1990. *Governing the Commons: The Evolution of Institutions for Collective Action*. Cambridge, MA: Cambridge University Press.

– 2005. *Understanding Institutional Diversity*. Princeton, NJ: Princeton University Press.

Pak, Susie. 2013. *Gentlemen Bankers*. Cambridge, MA: Harvard University Press.

Paul, Helen. 2011. *The South Sea Bubble*. New York: Routledge.

Paulson, Henry. 2010. *On the Brink: Inside the Race to Stop the Collapse of the Global Financial System*. New York: Hachette Book Group.

Perez, Carlota. 2002. *Technological Revolutions and Financial Capital*. Northampton, MA: Edward Elgar Press.

Peteri, Gyorgy. 1992. "Central Bank Diplomacy: Montagu Norman and Central Europe's Monetary Reconstruction after World War I." *Contemporary European History* 1 (3): 233–58. https://doi.org/10.1017/S0960777300000163.

Phillips, A.W. 1958. "The Relations between Unemployment and the Rate of Change of Money Wages in the United Kingdom, 1861–1957." *Economica* 25 (100): 283–99. https://doi.org/10.2307/2550759.

Plessis, Alain. 1985. *The Rise and Fall of the Second Empire, 1852–1871*. Cambridge, MA: Cambridge University Press.

– 1994. "The History of Banks in France." In *Handbook on the History of European Banks*, edited by Manfred Pohl, 185–296. Brookfield, VT: Edward Elgar Press.

Polanyi, Karl. 1944. *The Great Transformation: The Political and Economic Origins of Our Time*. New York: Rinehart.

Posen, Barry. 2003. "Command of the Commons: The Military Foundation of U.S. Hegemony." *International Security* 28 (1): 5–46. https://doi.org/10.1162/016228803322427965.

Price, Roger. 2001. *The French Second Empire: An Anatomy of Political Power.* Cambridge: Cambridge University Press.

Pyle, Kenneth. 1987. "In Pursuit of a Grand Design: Nakasone betwixt the Past and the Future." *Journal of Japanese Studies* 13 (2): 243–70. https://doi.org/10.2307/132470.

– 1996. *The Japanese Question: Power and Purpose in a New Era.* 2nd ed. Washington, DC: American Enterprise Institute Press.

Quillin, Bryce. 2008. *International Financial Cooperation: Political Economics of Compliance with the 1988 Basel Accord.* New York: Routledge.

Rajan, Raghuram. 2006. "Has Finance Made the World Riskier?" *European Financial Management* 12 (4): 499–533. https://doi.org/10.1111/j.1468-036X.2006.00330.x.

– 2010. *Faultlines: How Hidden Fractures Still Threaten the Global Economy.* Princeton, NJ: Princeton University Press.

Rajan, Raghuram, and Luigi Zingales. 2004. *Saving Capitalism from the Capitalists: Unleashing the Power of Capital Markets to Create Wealth and Spread Opportunity.* Princeton, NJ: Princeton University Press.

Ramey, Garey, and Valerie Ramey. 1995. "Cross-Country Evidence on the Link between Volatility and Growth." *American Economic Review* 85 (5): 1138–51. https://doi.org/10.3386/w4959.

Rapoza, Kenneth. 2016. "U.S. Sanctions, Weak Ruble, Forced Collapse of Russian Bank Earnings." *Forbes,* 16 January.

Rasler, Karen, and William Thompson. 1989. *War and State Making: The Shaping of Global Powers.* Boston, MA: Unwin Hyman.

– 1994. *The Great Powers and Global Struggle, 1490–1990.* Lexington: University Press of Kentucky.

Rawls, John. 1971. *A Theory of Justice.* Cambridge, MA: Harvard University Press.

Regan, Donald. 1988. *For the Record: From Wall Street to Washington.* San Diego, CA: Harcourt Brace Jovanovich.

Reich, Robert. 1997. *Locked in the Cabinet.* New York: Vintage Books.

Reinhart, Carmen, and Kenneth Rogoff. 2009. *This Time Is Different: Eight Centuries of Financial Folly.* Princeton, NJ: Princeton University Press.

Reinicke, Wolfgang. 1995. *Banking, Politics and Global Finance: American Commercial Banks and Regulatory Change.* New York: Edward Elgar Press.

Reuveny, Rafael, and William Thompson. 2004. *Growth, Trade and Systemic Leadership.* Ann Arbor: University of Michigan Press.

Rey, Hélène. 2015. "Dilemma, not Trilemma: The Global Financial Cycle and Monetary Policy." NBER Working Paper 21162. Cambridge, MA: National Bureau of Economic Research.

Robb, George. 1992. *White Collar Crime in Modern England: Financial Fraud and Business Morality, 1845–1929*. New York: Cambridge University Press.

Roberts, Cynthia, Leslie Elliott Armijo, and Saori Katada. 2017. *The BRICS and Collective Statecraft*. New York: Oxford University Press.

Rockoff, Hugh. 1990. "The 'Wizard of Oz' as a Monetary Allegory." *Journal of Political Economy* 94 (4): 739–60. https://doi.org/10.1086/261704.

Rodrik, Dani. 1998. "Who Needs Capital-Account Convertibility?" *Essays in International Finance*. Princeton, NJ: International Finance Section, Economics Department, Princeton University.

Romer, Paul. 1987. "Crazy Explanations for the Productivity Slowdown." *NBER Macroeconomics Annual*: 163–210.

Rosas, Guillermo. 2009. *Curbing Bailouts: Bank Crises and Democratic Accountability in Comparative Perspective*. Ann Arbor: University of Michigan Press.

Rosenbluth, Frances. 1989a. *Financial Politics in Contemporary Japan*. Ithaca, NY: Cornell University Press.

– 1989b. "The Political Economy of Financial Reform in Japan: The Bank Act of 1982." *Pacific Basin Law Journal* 6 (1–2): 62–102.

Rothbard, Murray N. 1972. *America's Great Depression*. Auburn, AL: Ludwig von Mises Institute.

Royama, Shoichi. 2012. "The Big Bang in Japanese Securities Markets." In *Crisis and Change in the Japanese Financial System*, edited by Takeo Hoshi and Hugh Patrick, 253–76. New York: Springer.

Ruggie, John. 1982. "International Regimes, Transactions and Change: Embedded Liberalism in the Postwar Economic Order." *International Organizations* 36 (2): 379–415. https://doi.org/10.1017/S0020818300018993.

Sanders, Elizabeth. 1999. *Roots of Reform: Farmers, Workers and the American State, 1877–1917*. Chicago: University of Chicago Press.

Sayers, R.S. 1976. *The Bank of England, 1891–1944*. Cambridge: Cambridge University Press.

Scherer, Paul. 1999. *Lord John Russell: A Biography*. Selinsgrove, PA: Susquehanna University Press.

Schlesinger, Jacob. 1999. *Shadow Shoguns: The Rise and Fall of Japan's Political Machine*. Stanford, CA: Stanford University Press.

Schonhardt-Bailey, C. 2006. *From the Corn Laws to Free Trade: Interests, Ideas and Institutions in Historical Perspective*. Cambridge, MA: MIT Press.

Schularick, Moritz, and Alan Taylor. 2012. "Credit Booms Gone Bust: Monetary Policy, Leverage Cycles and Financial Crises, 1870–2008." *American Economic Review* 102 (2): 1029–61. https://doi.org/10.1257/aer.102.2.1029.

Schwartz, Herman M. 2009. *Subprime Nation: American Power, Global Capital and the Housing Bubble*. Ithaca, NY: Cornell University Press.

Séguin, Philippe. 1990. *Louis Napoléon le Grand*. Paris: Grasset & Fasquelle.

Selmier, W. Travis. 2017. "An Institutional Perspective on Governance, Power, and the Politics of Risk." *Business and Politics* 19 (2): 215–240. https://doi.org/10.1017/bap.2017.8.

Selsdon Group. 1973. "The Selsdon Manifesto." Margaret Thatcher Foundation. Accessed January 2018. http://www.margaretthatcher.org/document/110860.

Sheng, Andrew. 2009. *From Asian to Global Crisis: An Asian Regulator's View of Unfettered Finance in the 1990s and 2000s*. Cambridge: Cambridge University Press.

Sherman, Dennis. 1974. "Governmental Policy toward Joint-Stock Business Organizations in Mid-nineteenth Century France." *Journal of European Economic History* 3 (1): 149–68.

Sherman, Matthew. 2009. "A Short History of Financial Deregulation in the United States." Center for Economic and Policy Research. Accessed January 2018. http://cepr.net/documents/publications/dereg-timeline-2009-07.pdf.

Shih, Victor. 2008. *Factions and Finance in China: Elite Conflict and Inflation*. Cambridge, MA: Cambridge University Press.

Shiller, Robert. 2000. "U.S. Stock Markets 1871–Present and CAPE Ratio." *Robert Shiller* (website). Accessed March 2020. http://www.econ.yale.edu/~shiller/data.htm.

– 2005. *Irrational Exuberance*. Princeton, NJ: Princeton University Press.

Sibler, William. 2008. *When Washington Shut Down Wall Street: The Great Financial Crisis of 1914 and the Origins of America's Monetary Supremacy*. Princeton, NJ: Princeton University Press.

Simmons, Beth, and Zachary Elkins. 2004. "The Globalization of Liberalization: Policy Diffusion in the International Political Economy." *American Political Science Review* 98 (1): 171–89. https://doi.org/10.1017/S0003055404001078.

Singer, David Andrew. 2007. *Regulating Capital: Setting Standards for the International Financial System*. Ithaca, NY: Cornell University Press.

Skidelsky, Robert. 2010. *Keynes: The Return of the Master*. London: Penguin Books.

Snidal, Duncan. 1985. "The Limits of Hegemonic Stability Theory." *International Organization* 39 (4): 579–614. https://doi.org/10.1017/S002081830002703X.

Sobel, Andrew. 2012. *Birth of Hegemony: Crisis, Financial Revolution, and Emerging Global Networks*. Chicago: University of Chicago Press.

Solis, Mireya. 2004. *Banking on Multinationals: Public Credit and the Export of Japanese Sunset Industries*. Stanford, CA: Stanford University Press.

Solow, Robert. 1956. "A Contribution to the Theory of Economic Growth." *Quarterly Journal of Economics* 70 (1): 65–94. https://doi.org/10.2307/1884513.

Sorkin, Aaron Ross. 2010. Too Big to Fail: The Inside Story of How Wall Street and Washington Fought to Save the Financial System – and Themselves. E-reader format. New York: Penguin Books.

Spiro, David. 1999. *The Hidden Hand of American Hegemony: Petrodollar Recycling and International Markets*. Ithaca, NY: Cornell University Press.

Stein, Ernesto, and Jorge Streb. 2004. "Elections and the Timing of Devaluations." *Journal of International Economics* 63 (1): 119–45. https://doi.org/10.1016/S0022-1996(03)00040-0.

Stein, Judith. 2010. *Pivotal Decade: How the United States Traded Factories for Finance in the Seventies*. New Haven, CT: Yale University Press.

Stockman, David. 1986. *Triumph of Politics: Why the Reagan Revolution Failed*. New York: Harper & Row.

Strange, Susan. 1971. "The Politics of International Currencies." *World Politics* 23 (2): 215–31. https://doi.org/10.2307/2009676.

– 1986. *Casino Capitalism*. New York: Blackwell.

– 1988. *States and Markets: An Introduction to International Political Economy*. London: Pinter Publishers.

Stuenkel, Oliver. 2013. "The Financial Crisis, Contested Legitimacy, and the Genesis of Intra-BRICS Cooperation." *Global Governance* 19 (4): 611–30. https://doi.org/10.1163/19426720-01904008.

Suarez, Sandra, and Robin Kolodny. 2011. "Paving the Road to 'Too Big to Fail': Business Interests and the Politics of Financial Deregulation in the United States." *Politics and Society* 39 (1): 74–102. https://doi.org/10.1177/0032329210394999.

Summers, Lawrence H., Alan Greenspan, Arthur Levitt, and William J. Rainer. 1999. "Over-the-Counter Derivatives Markets and the Commodity Exchange Act." Report of the President's Working Group on Financial Markets. Washington, DC: Department of the Treasury.

Suter, Christian. 1992. *Debt Cycles in the World Economy*. Boulder, CO: Westview Press.

Tallman, Ellis W., and Jon R. Moen. 1990. "Lessons from the Panic of 1907." *Economic Review* (Federal Reserve Bank of Atlanta) May/June: 2–13.

Taniguchi, Tomohiko. 1999. "Japan's Banks and the 'Bubble Economy' of the Late 1980s." In *Banking in Japan*. Vol. 3, *Japanese Banking since 1973: Deregulation, Internationalization and Adjustment*, edited by William M. Tsutsui, 181–209. London: Routledge.

Taylor, James. 2006. *Creating Capitalism: Joint-Stock Enterprise in British Politics and Culture, 1800–1870*. London: Royal Historical Society.

Taylor, Mark. 2016. *The Politics of Innovation: Why Some Countries Are Better Than Others at Science and Technology*. New York: Oxford University Press.

Temin, Peter. 1989. *Lessons from the Great Depression*. Cambridge, MA: MIT Press.

Terrell, Henry. 1990. "The Activities of Japanese Banks in the United Kingdom and the United States, 1980–1988." *Federal Reserve Bulletin* 76 (2): 39–50.

Thurow, Lester. 1992. *Head to Head: The Economic Battle between Japan, Europe and America*. New York: HarperCollins.

Tilly, Charles. 1990. *Coercion, Capital, and European States, AD 990–1990*, Cambridge, MA: Blackwell Publishers.

Tilly, Richard. 1989. "Banking Institutions in Historical and Comparative Perspective: Germany, Great Britain and the United States in the Nineteenth and Early Twentieth Century." *Journal of Institutional and Theoretical Economics* 145 (1): 189–209.

Tomz, Michael. 2007. *Reputation and International Cooperation: Sovereign Debt across Three Centuries*. Princeton, NJ: Princeton University Press.

Treaster, Joseph. 2004. *Paul Volcker: The Making of a Financial Legend*. New York: John Wiley.

Triffin, Robert. 1960. *Gold and the Dollar Crisis*. New Haven, CT: Yale University Press.

Trollope, Anthony. 1858. *The Three Clerks: A Novel*. London: Richard Bentley.
– 1875. *The Way We Live Now*. London: Chapman and Hall.

Tsebelis, George. 2002. *Veto Players: How Institutions Work*. Princeton, NJ: Princeton University Press.

Turner, John. 2014. *Banking in Crisis: The Rise and Fall of British Banking Stability, 1800 to the Present*. Cambridge: Cambridge University Press.

Twomey, Michael. 2000. *A Century of Foreign Investment in the Third World*. New York: Routledge.

Tyson, Laura. 1993. *Who's Bashing Whom: Trade Conflict in High-Technology Industries*. Washington, DC: Institute for International Economics.

United States. Bureau of Labor Statistics. 2020. "Labor Force Statistics from the Current Population Study." U.S. Bureau of Labor Statistics (website). Accessed March 2020. http://www.bls.gov/cps.

United States. Bureau of the Census. 1975. *Historical Statistics of the United States: Colonial Times to 1970; Bicentennial Edition*. Washington, DC: Government Printing Office.

United States. Bureau of Economic Analysis. 2018. "Personal Saving Rate." Accessed January 2018. https://fred.stlouisfed.org/series/PSAVERT.

United States. Congress. House of Representatives. 1999. Congressional Record, 106th Congress, 1st sess., vol. 145, H11542. Accessed March 2020. https://www.congress.gov/crec/1999/11/04/CREC-1999-11-04.pdf.
– 2017a. "H.R.10 – Financial Services Act of 1998." 105th Congress. Accessed January 2018. https://www.congress.gov/bill/105th-congress/house-bill/10/all-actions?overview=closed&q=%7B%22roll-call-vote%22%3A%22all%22%7D.
– 2017b. "H.R.10 – Financial Services Act of 1999." 106th Congress. Accessed January 2018. https://www.congress.gov/bill/106th-congress/house-bill/10/related-bills.
– 2017c. "H.R.5660 – Commodity Futures Modernization Act of 2000." 105th Congress. Accessed January 2018. https://www.congress.gov/bill/106th-congress/house-bill/5660.

United States. Congress. Senate. Committee on Finance. 1985. *Review of Findings of the President's Commission on Industrial Competitiveness: Hearing before the Committee on Finance, United States Senate, Ninety-Ninth Congress, First Session, 29 March.* Washington, DC: U.S. Printing Office.

United States. Department of the Treasury. 1998. "Joint Statement by Robert E. Rubin, Federal Reserve Board Chairman Alan Greenspan and Securities and Exchange Commission Chairman Arthur Levitt." https://www.treasury .gov/press-center/press-releases/Pages/rr2426.aspx.

United States. Department of the Treasury. OCC (Office of the Comptroller of the Currency). 1998. "Quarterly Derivatives Fact Sheet – First Quarter 1998." https://www.occ.gov/publications-and-resources/publications /quarterly-report-on-bank-trading-and-derivatives-activities/files/q1-1998 -derivatives-quarterly.html.

– 2007. "OCC's Quarterly Report on Bank Derivatives Activities First Quarter 2007." https://www.occ.gov/publications-and-resources/publications /quarterly-report-on-bank-trading-and-derivatives-activities/files/q1-2007 -derivatives-quarterly.html.

United States. FDIC (Federal Deposit Insurance Corporation). 2018. "Commercial Banks – Historical Statistics on Banking." Accessed January 2018. https://www5.fdic.gov/hsob/SelectRpt.asp?EntryTyp=10&Header=1.

United States. Financial Crisis Inquiry Commission. 2011. *The Financial Crisis Inquiry Report.* Accessed January 2018. http://www.fcic.gov/.

United States. National Science Foundation. 2016. "Foreign-Born Workers in S&E Occupations, by Education Level: 1993, 2003, and 2013." National Science Board Science and Engineering Indicators. Accessed January 2018. https://www.nsf.gov/statistics/2016/nsb20161/uploads/1/6/tt03-25.pdf.

United States. SEC (Securities and Exchange Commission). 1988. "Internationalization of the Securities Markets: Report of the Staff of the U.S. Securities and Exchange Commission to the Senate Committee on Banking, Housing and Urban Affairs and the House Committee on Energy and Commerce." Washington, DC: SEC.

van Dormael, Armand. 1978. *Bretton Woods: Birth of a Monetary System.* New York: Macmillan.

Van Duijn, Jacob. 1983. *The Long Wave in Economic Life.* Boston, MA: Unwin.

Van Horne, James. 1984. "Of Financial Innovations and Excesses." *Journal of Finance* 40 (3): 620–31. https://doi.org/10.1111/j.1540-6261.1985. tb04984.x.

Vitu, Auguste. 1864. *Guide financier: Répertoire générale des valeurs financières et industrielles.* Paris: Hachette.

Vogel, Steven. 1996. *Free Markets, More Rules: Regulatory Reform in Advanced Industrial Countries.* Ithaca, NY: Cornell University Press.

Wallerstein, Immanuel. 1974. *The Modern World-System: Capitalist Agriculture and the Origins of the European World-Economy in the Sixteenth Century.* San Francisco, CA: Academic Press.

– 1984. *The Politics of the World-Economy: The States, the Movements, and the Civilizations*. New York: Cambridge University Press.

Walter, Stefanie. 2013. *Financial Crises and the Politics of Macroeconomic Adjustments*. Cambridge: Cambridge University Press.

Warburg, Paul, ed. 1910. "The Discount System in Europe." In *The Federal Reserve System: Its Origin and Growth; Reflections and Recollections*, vol. 1, 183–219. New York: Macmillan.

– 1930. *The Federal Reserve System: Its Origin and Growth; Reflections and Recollections*. Vol. 2. New York: Macmillan.

White, Harry Dexter. 1933. *The French International Accounts, 1880–1913*. Cambridge, MA: Harvard University Press.

White, Eugene. 1983. *Regulation and Reform of the American Banking System*. Princeton, NJ: Princeton University Press.

– 1986. "Before the Glass–Steagall Act: An Analysis of Investment Banking Activities of National Banks." *Explorations in Economic History* 23 (1): 33–55. https://doi.org/10.1016/0014-4983(86)90018-5.

Wicker, Elmus. 2000. *Banking Panics of the Gilded Age*. New York: Cambridge University Press.

– 2005. *The Great Debate on Banking Reform: Nelson Aldrich and the Origins of the Fed*. Columbus: Ohio State University Press.

Widmaier, Wesley W. 2016. *Economic Ideas in Political Time: The Rise and Fall of Economic Orders from the Progressive Era to the Global Financial Crisis*. Cambridge: Cambridge University Press.

Widmaier, Wesley W., Mark Blyth, and Leonard Seabrooke. 2007. "Endogenous Shocks or Exogenous Constructions? The Meanings of Wars and Crises." International Studies Quarterly 51 (4): 747–59. https://doi.org/10.1111/j.1468-2478.2007.00474.x.

Williamson, Samuel. 2018. "Annualized Growth Rates and Graphs of the DJIA, S&P500 and NASDAQ in the United States between Any Two Dates." *MeasuringWorth* http://www.measuringworth.com/DJIA_SP_NASDAQ/.

– 2020. "Daily Closing Values of the DJA in the United States, 1885–Present." *MeasuringWorth* http://www.measuringworth.com/DJIA_SP_NASDAQ/.

Willis, Henry Parker. 1901. *A History of the Latin Monetary Union: A Study of International Monetary Action*. Chicago: University of Chicago Press.

Winecoff, William. 2017. "Global Finance as a Politicized Habitat." *Business and Politics* 19 (2): 267–97. https://doi.org/10.1017/bap.2017.7.

Witko, Christopher. 2016. "The Politics of Financialization in the United States, 1949–2005." *British Journal of Political Science* 46 (2): 349–70. https://doi.org/10.1017/S0007123414000325.

Woodruff, William. 1966. *Impact of Western Man: A Study of Europe's Role in the World Economy 1750–1960*. New York: St. Martin's Press.

World Bank. 2017. "Military Spending (% of GDP)," Accessed January 2018. https://data.worldbank.org/indicator/MS.MIL.XPND.GD.ZS.

– 2018. "GDP, PPP (Current International $)." Accessed May 2018. https://data.worldbank.org/indicator/NY.GDP.MKTP.PP.CD.

– 2020. "Market Capitalization of Listed Domestic Companies (current US$)." Accessed March 2020. http://data.worldbank.org/indicator/CM.MKT.LCAP.CD.

Wueschner, Silvano. 1999. *Charting Twentieth-Century Monetary Policy: Herbert Hoover and Benjamin Strong, 1917–1927*. Westport, CT: Greenwood Press.

Yale School of Management. n.d. *London Stock Exchange: Investor's Monthly Manual Project, 1869–1929*. Accessed March 2020. https://som.yale.edu/faculty-research/our-centers-initiatives/international-center-finance/data/historical-financial-research-data/london-stock-exchange.

Yasutomo, Dennis. 1989. "Why Aid? Japan as an 'Aid Great Power.'" *Pacific Affairs* 62 (4): 490–503. https://doi.org/10.2307/2759672.

Young, Kevin. 2012. "Transnational Regulatory Capture? An Empirical Examination of the Transnational Lobbying of the Basel Committee on Banking Supervision." *Review of International Political Economy* 19 (4): 663–8. https://doi.org/10.1080/09692290.2011.624976.

Young, Kevin, Tim Marple, and James Heilman. 2017. "Beyond the Revolving Door: Advocacy Behavior and Social Distance to Financial Regulators." *Business and Politics* 19 (2): 327–64. https://doi.org/10.1017/bap.2017.10.

Ziegler, P. 1988. *The Sixth Great Power: A History of One of the Greatest of All Banking Families, the House of Barings 1762–1929*. London: Collins.

Zysman, John. 1983. *Governments, Markets and Growth: Financial Systems and the Politics of Industrial Change*. Ithaca, NY: Cornell University Press.

Index

www.ingramcontent.com/pod-product-compliance
Ingram Content Group UK Ltd.
Pitfield, Milton Keynes, MK11 3LW, UK
UKHW040847190325
456432UK00012B/47/J